The Prehistory of Home

The Prehistory of Home

Jerry D. Moore

UNIVERSITY OF CALIFORNIA PRESS
Berkeley · Los Angeles · London

University of California Press, one of the most distinguished
university presses in the United States, enriches lives around
the world by advancing scholarship in the humanities, social
sciences, and natural sciences. Its activities are supported by
the UC Press Foundation and by philanthropic contributions
from individuals and institutions. For more information, visit
www.ucpress.edu.

University of California Press
Berkeley and Lòs Angeles, California

University of California Press, Ltd.
London, England

Library of Congress Cataloging-in-Publication Data

Moore, Jerry D.
    The prehistory of home / Jerry D. Moore.
        p.   cm.
    Includes bibliographical references and index.
    ISBN 978-0-520-27221-7 (cloth : alk. paper)
    1. Dwellings, Prehistoric.   2. Architecture, Prehistoric.
3. Home.   4. Social archaeology.   I. Title.
    GN799.B8M66   2012
    392.3'60901—dc23   2011035704

Manufactured in the United States of America

 21   20   19   18   17   16   15   14   13   12
 10   9   8   7   6   5   4   3   2   1

In keeping with a commitment to support environmentally
responsible and sustainable printing practices, UC Press
has printed this book on Rolland Enviro100, a 100%
post-consumer fiber paper that is FSC certified, deinked,
processed chlorine-free, and manufactured with renewable
biogas energy. It is acid-free and EcoLogo certified.

Contents

Illustrations

Acknowledgments

"Digressions, incontestably, are the sunshine;—they are the life, the soul of reading!"
—Laurence Sterne, *Tristram Shandy*

It is customary to thank one's family at the end of the acknowledgements, but in this case it would be utterly inappropriate. My wife and colleague, Janine L. Gasco, and our son, Nathan Moore, read various versions of this manuscript, pointed out weakness in its organization and my explication, and through it all remained steadfastly supportive. More importantly, Jan and Nate are my home, and thus shaped this entire project and my scholarly interest in home in profound and subtle ways. This book is dedicated to Jan and Nate, who bring me home.

I am also privileged to have a group of friends and colleagues who read and commented on this project, when it was just a loose set of ideas that were progressively transformed into a book. I am particularly indebted to Brenda Bowser, Andrew Stewart, and Leah Weed for their careful insights on previous drafts. I also want to thank Bill Fox for his support of this project from its inception, his insights into place-making, and for his companionship on archaeological journeys in Baja California and Chile. I also appreciate the constant support provided by other friends and colleagues including Joanne Pillsbury, Helaine Silverman, and Charles Stanish.

For scholars who answered specific questions about their respective fields of research, I thank Patricia J. O'Brien, Professor Emerita, Department of Sociology, Anthropology, and Social Work, Kansas State University; and Esther Jacobson-Tepfer, Maude I. Kerns Professor Emeritus, Department of Art History, University of Oregon. For permissions to reproduce original artwork I want to thank Meredith Chasson and Eric Carlson, Notre Dame University; Janine Gasco, California State University–Dominguez Hills; Stephanie Hawkins, New Mexico State University; John Middendorf; Christopher Rodning, Tulane University; and Santiago Uceda, Universidad Nacional de Trujillo, Peru. A full list of illustration credits is found on page 261.

I would like to acknowledge the granting agencies who have supported my archaeological projects over the last three decades, investigations that are discussed at various points in this book: National Science Foundation/Archaeology Program (1981–1982, Manchan; 1998–1999, Baja California; 2006–2007, Tumbes); the Wenner-Gren Foundation for Anthropological Research (1995, Baja California; 2010, Perú and Ecuador); National Geographic Society/Waitt Grants Program (2010–2011, Baja California); the H. John Heinz Foundation (1996, Tumbes); the University Research Expeditions Program, University of California (1986, Quebrada Santa Cristina); the Curtis and Mary T. Brennan Foundation (2003, Tumbes); and the CSUDH Research and Scholarly and Creative Activities Program (1991, 1994, 1995, Baja California; 2000, 2003, Tumbes).

At the University of California Press, I want to thank Blake Edgar, for his support and guidance of this project. Although inundated by book "pitches" at an annual archaeology meeting, Blake expressed interest in this book, stimulating me to actually complete a long-considered project. I also thank Hannah Love at the University of California Press, for her cheery assistance. I particularly appreciate the calm guidance of Lynn Meinhardt, editorial coordinator, Science Publishing Group, at the University of California Press, who shepherded this book into existence, and to Marilyn Schwartz, managing editor at the University of California Press, for seeing the project through to conclusion. I also grateful for the careful copy-editing provided by Jennifer Eastman. I am deeply indebted to all these individuals for all their contributions.

I am grateful to Wendy Ashmore, Professor of Anthropology, University of California–Riverside, and two anonymous readers for reviewing the manuscript for University of California Press; it was gratifying that these three scholars understood the objective and audience of this book.

The final manuscript was prepared with modest support from the California State University–Dominguez Hills grant, providing a course off from a normal heavy teaching load. I want to thank my colleagues in the Department of Anthropology, California State University–Dominguez Hills—Jan Gasco, Susan Needham, and Ana Pitchon—for creating such a supportive academic environment in which to work. Also at CSUDH, I want to thank Dr. Sandra Parham, Dean of the Library, and Ms. Faye Phinsee-Clack, Inter-Library Loans, for their support of my research and writing projects.

Finally, I must acknowledge the efforts and insights of the scores of archaeologists whose investigations are summarized in this book. As I researched this book, reading the sometimes dry and technical reports of archaeological data—a genre as spare as haiku—I was so impressed by the scope and detail of research by my fellow archaeologists. As an archaeologist, I understand the difficulties involved in fieldwork, the painstaking and meticulous lab work that understatedly summarized in a simple data table or figure. In their independent but ultimately collective efforts, the archaeologists discussed in the following pages and referenced in the footnotes have recovered the fragments of the past, preserved it for future generations, and illuminated the contours and specifics of the human experience. I and any person interested in the question "What does it mean to be human?" all stand in their debt.

CHAPTER I

The Prehistory of Home

Our trowels scrape through time. A dozen of us—archaeologists, students, and workmen—are excavating in far northern Peru. Digging through hard layers of ash-black clay and past thick jumbles of ancient oyster shells, we carefully scoop up the loosened midden and sieve it through dry shaker screens, trapping durable potsherds and glinting flakes of obsidian. We watch for traces of archaic structures: postholes from long-gone timbers, subtle variations in soil color and texture, a slightly more compacted surface. We speak in low voices as we dig, afraid that any distraction will cause us to miss the ancient traces of home.

Various animals build shelters, but only humans build homes. Humans build dwellings in different environments, constructed with diverse materials and in distinct forms, and associated with nuanced meanings. We have done this for millennia.

No other species lives in such a variety of shelters. Despite the diversity of the constructions that other animals create—the pendulous baskets of oriole nests, the intricate dens of prairie dogs, or the decorated nests of bowerbirds—humans construct the broadest array of dwellings on Earth.

Our words for "dwelling" point to this diversity:

Palace, hovel, hogan, ranch house, croft.

Tipi, chalet, duplex, kraal.

Igloo, bungalow, billet, cabin.

Cottage, crannog, adobe, manor.

Wickiup, villa, lean-to, abbey.

Hacienda, barrack, lodge, shanty.

Pithouse, penthouse, pueblo, condo.

In the Kalahari Desert, !Kung San women construct veldt-brush wind-breaks for their families in less than an hour, a dwelling abandoned in a few days when the foraging band moves on.

Among the Toraja of Sulawesi, the saddleback roof and sweeping facades of noble "origin houses" *(tongkonan)* link generations of kin-folk and spatially anchor rituals shared by members of "house societies."

And in Beverly Hills, the home of the late television producer Aaron Spelling was put up for sale in March 2009 and finally sold in July 2011 for a discounted price of $85 million to the 22-year-old British heiress, Petra Ecclestone. Generally considered the largest home in Los Angeles County, the 56,500-square-foot, 123-room mansion on six acres includes such amenities as four wet-bars, a screening room, a bowling alley, a gift-wrapping room, parking for one hundred cars, and a 17,000-square-foot attic containing a beauty salon and a barbershop. Built in a "French cha-teau style," the Spelling house is nonetheless only one-fourth the size of the Palace of Versailles.

All these places are homes.

The social anthropologist Timothy Ingold has written about the dif-ference between "animal architecture" and our buildings. Comparing, as an example, beaver lodges to human dwellings, Ingold notes that "wher-ever they are, beavers construct the same kinds of lodges. . . . Human beings, by contrast, build houses of very diverse kinds, and although certain house forms have persisted for long periods, there is unequivo-cal evidence that these forms have also undergone significant historical change." As the instinctual expression of the beaver's evolutionary leg-acy, "the beaver is no more the designer of the lodge than is the mollusk the designer of its shell. . . . Human beings, on the other hand, are the authors of their own designs, constructed through a self-conscious deci-sion process—an intentional selection of ideas."[1]

The human creation of home—as dwelling, as social unit, as meta-phor—is extraordinarily varied; every home is a constructed compromise. As the architectural historian Joseph Rykwert has written, "Unlike even the most elaborate animal construction, human building involves deci-sion and choice, always and inevitably; it therefore involves a project."[2]

Such projects counterpoise decisions about different issues—cost, material constraints, environmental stresses, functions, style, social statuses, and symbolic contents, among others—and then express a specific resolution of those issues in architectural form. This is true of all buildings, whenever and wherever humans have constructed them.

And this is particularly true of homes. In addition to their basic and fundamental function of providing shelter from natural elements, dwellings are powerful and complex concentrates of human existence. More than passive backdrops to human actions, our dwellings reflect and shape our lives. Dwellings are powerful condensers of meanings, second only to the human body as a model for thinking about the world. The anthropologist Clifford Geertz wrote that "man is an animal suspended in webs of significance he himself has spun," and those webs thickly drape our homes.[3]

This is all relatively obvious: humans build and occupy a diversity of dwellings, those constructions require assessing multiple factors, and dwellings are a pivotal place around which humans construct cultural meanings. Yet, two facts make these relatively noncontentious propositions challenging.

First, the specific constellations of dimensions and meanings encoded by dwellings are extraordinarily variable and complex. And this truth was made abundantly clear to me during a long and confused conversation with a campesino in far northern Peru.

Since 1996 I have conducted archaeological investigations in the Department of Tumbes, on Peru's tropical northern frontier. A distinctive type of vernacular architecture is built in Tumbes known as *tabique*. The building technique uses natural materials from the dry scrub forest, a thicket of thorn-covered shrubs, vines, and cacti interspersed with kapok and algarobbo trees. Although the vegetation is dense, few trees grow sufficiently tall or straight to be sawn into boards.

Tabique buildings accommodate these material constraints. The dwellings are rectangular in plan, framed by upright posts planted in the corners and at 1- to 2-meter intervals along the wall. Horizontal paired lengths of split bamboo are tied or nailed onto the inside and outside of the uprights posts, leaving a 5- to 10-centimeter gap into which sticks are jammed. The wedged sticks form the fabric of the wall, which may be left as a ragged comb of sticks or—if the residents can afford it—a plasterer is hired to slather the tabique wall with daub mixed from clay and steer manure.

In 2003 we were excavating a small site, and I was walking near the

FIGURE 1. A *tabique* house, Tumbes, Peru, 2003.

site when I saw a man making adobe bricks. The man recognized me as the gringo archaeologist, and we began to chat.

The man already had a house made from tabique, so I was curious why he was preparing to build another house of adobes. In the tropics, wooden structures are usually felled by rot and termites, so I assumed that the tabique house was approaching the end of its use-life. This simple assumption was profoundly wrong.

The man and I exchanged "buenos días" and then I said the obvious:

"I see you're making adobes."

"Yes, señor."

"Is your tabique house very old?"

"No, señor, it is only a few years old. It's a good, solid house."

"So, why are you making adobe bricks?"

"Because there is no work around here."

I paused to digest this information. "Are you going to sell the bricks?"

"No, I am going to build a new house. My wife left me."

Another pause.

"Do you think she will come back if you build a new house for her?"

"No, señor. She ran off with that son-of-a-bitch, Guillermo Flores.[4] She's never coming back." He shook his head in disgust.

"So, why are you building a new house?"

"Because there is no work around here."

At this point I was completely confused: "I'm sorry—I don't understand. *Why* are you building a new house?"

The man gave me a look reserved for the mentally challenged: "There is no work around here. I have to go to town to find work. My wife left me, so there will be no one here to watch over my belongings. Anyone can break into a tabique house. So I have to build a stronger house of adobe bricks."

It was an ethnographic encounter reminiscent of the story of the Three Little Pigs.

In a marvelously pragmatic but complex way, this man's decision to build a house of adobes was based on his own technical expertise, his access to raw materials, regional socioeconomic factors, security concerns, and his matrimonial tumults. Far from being a straightforward matter of imposing a mental construct onto passive raw materials, this house reflected multiple decision domains.

And every house always does.

Thus, the first factor that makes understanding human dwellings so interesting and challenging is that they are the material expressions of intersecting considerations. Our homes provide shelter and they express our identities. Dwellings enclose social groups of various sizes, from single individuals to entire religious communities. Houses vary in size, permanence, symbolic valence, functions, and so on, reflecting the varieties of the domestic experience.

And the second challenge to understanding home is this: We have been building homes longer than we have been *Homo sapiens*.

. . .

For the last thirty years, I have been digging into people's homes. Working in the dry desert coast of Peru, I have excavated ancient houses built from river canes in A.D. 1400–1500 and uncovered a large work camp built circa A.D. 1350. I studied a small eighteenth-century native

Chumash hut in Southern California built during the cultural penumbra between initial contact with Europeans and the full onslaught of Spanish colonialism. As a member of my wife's archaeological project in southern Mexico, I excavated the remnants of pole and thatch houses from the Colonial period and studied architecturally similar modern pole and thatch houses to understand the dynamics of construction and decay in the hot tropics. In Baja California, I have mapped open-air encampments and rock shelters of hunters and gatherers who occupied the peninsula from 4500 B.C. to A.D. 1800. In my recent expeditions in far northern Peru, I have excavated small elliptical pole and thatch houses that date to 4700–4300 B.C., large structures that probably housed extended families at 3500–3100 B.C., rectangular houses built from wattle and daub after 900–500 B.C., and the remnants of tabique houses occupied when the Inca Empire expanded into the region after A.D. 1470.

Although all my archaeological fieldwork has been in the Americas—Southern California, Baja California, southern Mexico, and Peru—these projects explored various prehistoric and historic cultures, occupying distinct environments, organized as diverse societies, and pursuing different livelihoods. The common element among them is that home was central to all these divergent lives.

I am endlessly intrigued by the prehistory of home. The creativity invested in dwellings is astounding. But beyond this, I must confess to a somewhat personal and what some might see as a less-than-scholarly interest in the prehistory of home: I deeply love my home.

My family and I live in a modest house in Long Beach, California. Long Beach is notable among Southern California beach communities for its lack of pretension. It is known as "Iowa by the Sea," in part because of the large number of Midwesterners who settled here in the decades flanking World War II, but also because of its lack of flash. It is a comfortable but unprepossessing community.

The main part of our house was built in 1913; we are the fourth family to live in it. The wall studs are century-old redwood, the window glass has settled with age, and the oak floors have the patina of good sherry. This original part of the house was small, only 900 square feet, and after five years of living in very close quarters, my wife, my son, and I added a new wing to the house in 1999, but one that maintained the architectural lines and building materials used in 1913. While we wanted to be a little more comfortable, we wanted to do so in an unobtrusive way—much like the city where we live.

Beyond this, though, our house anchors our lives. It is where our son has grown from toddler to man. It is where we have hosted a score of Thanksgiving dinners and dozens of parties. It is where we write books, prepare lectures, read, and think. It is where we have been at our best and at our worst. It is our home.

I am acutely aware that my experience of home differs from that of ancient people living in different cultures in other dwellings, but a line of empathy threads through my archaeological inquiries into the prehistory of home. I look at a curve of cobblestones that mark the edge of a five thousand year old house in Tumbes, and I want to know about the families who lived under its thatched roof. If I come across an ancient campsite in Baja California, I strain to hear its occupants' voices, now muted by time. If I am excavating the faint traces of an ancient hut, I am acutely aware that for someone at sometime this too was home.

. . .

Multiple meanings reside in "home." In modern English usage, the term may refer to the place where one lives, the house or dwelling one lives in, the family or residence group living in a dwelling or place, one's country or birthplace, a person's or animal's typical range or habitat, the place where something was invented or created ("Atlanta, Georgia—the home of Coca-Cola"), a place of ease distinct from one's normal dwelling ("a home away from home,") a sense of familiarity ("at home with"), a sense of recognition or responsibility (as in "this brought home the consequences") or finally an orphanage, asylum, or retirement community that takes the place of "home."[5]

The etymology of the English "home" untangles some of its strands of meaning.[6] *Home,* from the Old English *hām,* has cognates in other Germanic languages: the Old Saxon *hēm,* Old High German *heima,* and the Old Scandinavian *heimr.* In turn these words are probably derived from the proto-Germanic **χaim-* which comes from the Lithuanian *kiēmas* and *káima.* These older versions of home imply distinct meanings and concepts. The Old English *hām* refers to a collection of dwellings or village (a "homestead"), while the Old High German and Old Scandinavian words couple the notion of a residence with the idea of "the world." The earlier Lithuanian terms connote a village or farm as opposed to a town, and link back to the Sanskrit *ksêmas,* which denotes a safe or secure dwelling, abode, or refuge.

These Gothic notions of home are rooted in the expansion of Neolithic societies into temperate Europe beginning at circa 5500–5300 B.C. Reliant on crops (wheat, barley, peas, and flax) and livestock (predominantly cattle, but also sheep and pigs) first domesticated in the Near East, these agriculturalists had colonized mainland Europe and the British Isles by 3800 B.C. The initial farming communities of temperate Europe were small clusters of households, not towns or cities. As late as A.D. 98 the Roman urbanite and historian Tacitus wrote:

> That none of the several people in Germany live together in cities, is abundantly known; nay, that amongst them none of their dwellings are suffered to be contiguous. They inhabit apart and distinct, just as a fountain, or a field, or a wood happened to invite them to settle. They raise their villages in opposite rows, but not in our manner with the houses joined one to another. Every man has a vacant space quite round his own, whether for security against accidents from fire, or that they want the art of building.[7]

The original English "home" refers not only to a house—and explicitly not to an urban existence—but to a small cluster of buildings hacked from a temperate forest, a constructed oasis that defined one's world. Due to this prehistoric agrarian legacy, the meanings embedded in the English word and its Germanic cognates are distinct from those in other Indo-European languages.

As Joseph Rykwert has noted, ancient Romans distinguished between overlapping concepts of constructed domesticity.[8] *Domus* referred to the house as household, a sense combining architectural and social units. In contrast, Romans used *aedus* to refer to the constructed building and *mansio* for a place of rest and comfort. A humble rural hut—as different from a country estate or villa—was a *casa* and was applied to the Gauls of Iberia, which led to the Spanish word for house and was transformed into the rustic informality implied by the French *chez moi*.

The Greek *domos* (δόμος), although apparently similar to the Latin *domus*, refers explicitly to the constructed house or building, and is derived from the verb *demō* (δέμω) to build or construct. Distinct from the *domos*, the household was the *oikos*, a meaning retained in "economy" (the study of the law, *nomos*, of the household, *oikos*). The process of building a home for a household was *oikodomein*, a term that united those distinct meanings into a single process.

One could pursue such etymological strands further, but there would come a point for which we have no written records that hint at domestic variations. Beyond the border of literacy, only archaeology illuminates the deep human experience of home.

. . .

In general, the public receives a distorted vision of what archaeology is and what archaeologists do. Television documentaries breathlessly describe the hidden riches of long-lost tombs, the moldering glories of ancient temples. With astounding luck, major discoveries are made during the three days the film crew is on site—and this happens week after week! An archaeologist directs a major excavation in the humid tropics of Guatemala, yet appears on camera in a clean shirt free of sweat stains. Archaeological research projects are presented as yet another spin-off of *Survivor.*

An admission is in order: I am profoundly susceptible to the romance of archaeology. I fell in love with archaeology as an eighteen-year-old, and I am still passionate about it decades later. I own copies of every Indiana Jones movie. I married an archaeologist, my best friends are archaeologists, and when I go on vacation I tend to visit archaeological sites. And I watch the documentaries just like everybody else.

But the "treasure and temple" emphasis does not really reflect what archaeologists generally do. For all the dazzle and excitement of gilded discoveries, most archaeologists actually engage in an intellectual project that is substantially more profound: "What does it mean to be human?"

Mentally traversing a path of inferential steps that would surprise Sherlock Holmes, archaeologists connect the material traces of the past to reconstruct the nature of the human experience. In his classic book, *In Small Things Forgotten: An Archaeology of Early American Life,* the historical archaeologist James Deetz argued that even in literate societies with written histories, archaeology uncovers aspects of human life that are so fundamental and quotidian that no one bothered to record them.

As the adage "history is written by the victors" implies, the historical record often overlooks the lives and voices of the powerless, the subjugated, or the ignored—in short, the majority of human beings. Written history unevenly illuminates human experience. The earliest written records from Mesopotamia are cuneiform tablets dating to 2800 B.C. that principally record economic transactions and administrative matters. The oldest Egyptian hieroglyphs date to 2920–2680 B.C., texts that proclaimed the pharaohs' authority and implemented his will. The written record from Asia dates to circa 1300–1000 B.C. and comes from Shang China; it is a historical record that, not surprisingly, highlights Shang accomplishments over those of rival kingdoms.

Contemporary with the developments in Mesopotamia and Egypt, the Harrapan civilization employed the Indus script by circa 2800–2600 B.C., although scholars cannot read it nor are they certain what language family it relates to (Indo-European vs. Dravidian).

In the Aegean, hieroglyphic writing was used by circa 2000 B.C.; it remains undeciphered. The equally unreadable Linear A script was employed around 1700 B.C., while Linear B was used by Mycenaean Greeks at 1450–1000 B.C., at which point the Aegean devolved into a nonliterate Dark Age that lasted until 750 B.C.

Turning to the Americas, the recently discovered Cascajal Block is associated with the Olmec culture of Veracruz and dates to 900 B.C., thus making it the earliest known Mesoamerican writing system, followed by Zapotec (ca. 600 B.C.), the phonic system associated with Mixteca-Puebla, and Teotihuacan, Mayan, and Aztec writing systems.[9]

These are the regions in the world with the longest literary traditions, yet the written record covers a small fraction of these areas' histories. A few temporal reference points illustrate this.

Detailed historical materials for Ancient Greece exist for the Archaic and Classical Eras of circa 750–400 B.C., yet archaeological sites containing stone choppers and scrapers that date to 400,000 to 200,000 years ago have been found in gravel deposits in the Thessaly region, Lower Paleolithic artifacts probably associated with Neanderthals. Subsequent sites associated with modern humans in the region date to 60,000 to 30,000 years ago. In the prefecture of Argolis, southwest of Athens, Franchthi Cave has a remarkable occupation that spans from at least 20,000 to 3000 B.C., the longest archaeological sequence currently known from Greece.[10] This means that approximately 98% of Greek history falls outside of the written record.

The archaeological record from China extends back to *Homo erectus,* and the famous site of Zhoukodian (the place where "Peking Man" was discovered) has archaeological layers dating from 670,000–400,000 years ago.[11] Between 99.1% and 99.5% of Chinese history occurred before the first Shang scribe picked up a paintbrush.

And so it goes. Australia has been occupied for at least 50,000 years; its written history begins in the late seventeenth century A.D. Humans occupied South America by some 14,000 to 12,000 years ago; the written record covers less than the last 600 years. New Guinea was occupied 40,000 years ago; its written history begins in the 1930s.

Most of human experience has slipped through the lines of texts. Archaeology is the only way those ancient lives can be recovered and added to the consultable record of what it means to be human.

The human past is a vast and fascinating domain. Archaeology is more than the pursuit of temples and tombs.

Archaeology is a way to learn who we are.

. . .

Home is central to the human experience, and the following chapters explore the antiquity and diversity of human domestic life. In this, the range of *The Prehistory of Home* is broader than Witold Rybczynski's wonderful 1985 book, *Home: A Short History of an Idea,* with its emphasis on comfort and dwelling in the Western European tradition, or the engaging sprawl of Bill Bryson's 2010 *At Home: A Short History of Private Life,* which focuses on the United Kingdom and the United States. Neither is this a complete compendium of prehistoric structures, which would require an encyclopedic coverage similar to the magnificent, three-volume 1997 *Encyclopedia of Vernacular Architecture* edited by Paul Oliver.

My objective is simultaneously broader and more circumscribed. The goal of this book is to survey the ways that small, forgotten things from the past illuminate the varieties of the domestic experience. *The Prehistory of Home* explores how the broad archaeological goal of understanding the past intersects with the continuing human domestic project.[12]

Although integral to human experience, our hominid ancestors did not always make dwellings, and the archaeological evidence for the earliest domesticities is the subject of chapter 2, "Starter Homes." Since the times of ancient Greece, architects and philosophers have proposed what Rykwert calls "fabulized prehistories," imaginary reconstructions about the evolution of homes like those put forth by the Roman architect Vitruvius or centuries later by Enlightenment philosophers. The archaeological evidence suggests a developmental path that was more complex and divergent, as two of our ancestral species—*Homo ergaster* and *Homo erectus*—emerged from Africa to explore and settle Europe and Asia. These early hominid pioneers were replaced by us, *Homo sapiens,* who left Africa in a second great wave of migration approximately 100,000 to 50,000 years ago, colonizing the areas occupied by earlier hominids, but also moving into previously unoccupied regions of Australia, the Americas, and the islands of the Pacific Ocean.

The peripatetic nature of *Homo sapiens* is reflected in the archaeology of impermanent dwellings, the topic of chapter 3, "Mobile Homes." Humans occupied a diverse array of environments, in part because dwellings were elements of their cultural toolkit. The dwellings of hunters and gatherers reflect their nomadism, whether it occurred 20,000 years on the periglacial steppes of Palaeolithic Ukraine or over the last 6,000 years in Baja California in the desert between the seas.

The development of more sedentary life is discussed in chapter 4,

"Durable Goods." While today most people live in relatively permanent houses, the process towards sedentism occurred rather late in human prehistory. In the Near East, archaeological sites dating between 18,000 and 8,000 B.C. mark waypoints on the path to settled life, when dwellings became more substantial and rooted as humans relied more on intensively collected foods and ultimately made the transition towards agriculture. Parallel trajectories are discernible in archaeological sites around the world. In Japan, for example, the abundant resources of forest and sea allowed Jomon cultures to build substantial dwellings 8000 years before wet-rice agriculture became the basis of economy, but after gathered foods had to be stored and large objects were necessary to process them. The connection between sedentism and our possessions is not new, although the problems of having "too much stuff" are faced by modern human societies around the globe, particularly in the United States. And finally, the connections between dwellings and identity are transformed when our possessions include the reliquiae of our dead kin.

Our homes are more than simple shelters or storage sheds. We imbue our dwellings with complex meanings, and our houses serve as metaphoric templates of the cosmos, a broad set of topics discussed in chapter 5, "Model Homes." Houses become architectonic models for diverse and fundamental meanings about cosmic order and social distinctions. Whether we think about the creation of male vs. female spaces in a Navaho hogan or the implications of the term "master bedroom" in an American suburban house, humans use their dwellings as models. The symbolic analogies between house and cosmos are derived from earlier human efforts to give symbolic concepts material form, a process that began at least 70,000 years ago. However, the domestic expressions of cosmologies only occurred after the dwelling became a recurrent experience for social groups—either when nomads erected the same tents in different places or when sedentary households lived in the same dwelling for extended periods. At that point the symbolic associations of home become breathtakingly complex.

Bees live in hives, prairie dogs in colonies, and humans in apartment buildings. The origins and implications of densely settled group life are explored in chapter 6, "Apartment Living." In eastern Anatolia, the Neolithic site of Çatalhöyük was a dense warren of tightly packed buildings holding residences and shrines between ca 7300–6000 B.C. Examples of multifamily dwellings consist of Banderkeramik long houses of temperate Europe (5300–4900 B.C.), Native American plank houses in the Pacific Northwest (A.D. 200/500–1950), and Iroquois longhouses (A.D.

1350–1800). In the American Southwest, similarly dense constructions include the "Great Houses" at Chaco Canyon (A.D. 900–1150), the cliff houses of the Colorado Plateau (A.D. 1150–1300), the Classic Period Hohokam complex at Casa Grande (A.D. 1150–1350), or Zuni Pueblo (A.D. 1500–present). In each of these cases, apartment life posed problems of density and dissent.

At various times and for a variety of reasons, humans have lived behind walls, the topic explored in chapter 7, "Gated Communities." Although walled cities first emerged in ancient Mesopotamia amidst a landscape of conflict, humans build walls for different reasons: to defend, to define, to hide, or to separate. Though the medieval walled city and the Benedictine monastery were both walled communities, those similar architectural constructions referenced different social realities. In ancient Persia and on the North Coast of Peru, kings lived behind the tall walls of royal compounds to hide their humanity from their subjects. Walls are built to separate genders, and the archaeology of Christian convents and the architecture of Swahili houses are similarly designed to ensure the chaste purity of women. Not only a common domestic practice in the ancient world, today gated communities are the fastest growing human settlement form, a global phenomenon known as the "New Enclavism."

The domestic and the political realms can intersect in our dwellings, a topic explored in chapter 8, "Noble Houses." Noble houses frequently combine multiple functions—they are seats of authority, warehouses and treasuries, arenas for political display and religious rituals—such as at the House of Tiles (2500–2000 B.C.), located on the Greek mainland, or in elaborate palace complexes of Knossos and other Minoan palace polities (2200–1450 B.C.) of Crete. This intersection of roles occurs among small-scale societies living in the Ecuadorian Amazon, among Nootka living in British Columbia in large plank houses in the late eighteenth and nineteenth centuries, and in the fifteenth-century Palace of Chilimassa on the far north coast of Peru. In all of these cases, politics, hospitality, and ritual intersected at home.

Just as dwellings may encode cosmological symbols, the structures may themselves be transformed into "Sacred Houses" (chapter 9). The Tabernacle was the "House of the Lord," a tented dwelling built for Yahweh by a migratory pastoral society. In many cultures, past and present, domestic altars are one terminus of an axis between house and temple, functioning "variously as satellite, extension and miniaturization of the local temple."[13] In other cultures, the sacred may literally be incorporated into the walls of a dwelling as rituals surround the collection of construction materials, building, and completion of a house. Alternatively, supernatural beings may be invited into the home (at least to visit), transforming the house by their presence.

It may seem an ironic contradiction, but one way to preserve a home is to burn it. In chapter 10, I discuss the different manners and cultural logics reflected in "Home Fires." The houses of Pompeii and of Cerén, El Salvador, were preserved in ashes. Across a broad swath of southeastern Europe, houses were consistently burned during the Neolithic, apparently not by raiders or accidents but by their own inhabitants, even though this required stacking kindling and firewood within the structure. This did not mean the end of the house, but its regeneration, and new dwellings were built on or nearby the house's charred remains. Analogous practices in distant archaeological sites—including historic Cherokee villages in the southeastern United States—demonstrate that preservation and remembrance do not require permanent constructions.

Our homes encompass and demarcate our lives, and dwellings may provide analogous shelters for souls in the afterlife. Chapter 11, "Going Home," examines the cultural creation of parallel domesticities in lives after death. The astounding mortuary complexes constructed in the Old Kingdom of ancient Egypt were predicated on earlier funerary architecture in which a subterranean home was created and equipped for life after death. In Neolithic Europe, long houses metamorphosed into long barrows, becoming commemorative constructions that anchored identity. In a broad array of human societies, the ancestors dwell in villages of the dead. Similarly diverse conceptions of the relationship between death and home characterize American society in different points in our history, as our ideas have changed about the corpse and the soul, the graveyard and the home

A final note: each of these chapters contains a brief description from my own archaeological investigations into the prehistory of home. Whether excavating an Archaic house in far northern Peru, investigating an impermanent campsite in Baja California, or documenting the labyrinthine patterns of royal Chimú palaces, I am fascinated by the archaeology of home. Thus, my specific investigations intersect with the broader themes that run through this book, and those broader themes recursively inform the way I approach my specific investigations. As the following chapters traverse different centuries and distant places, I am acutely aware of my task as an archaeologist: to recover the past and to make it part of the consultable record of the human experience.

And much of that experience occurred at home.

CHAPTER 2

Starter Homes

Mid pleasures and palaces though we may roam,
Be it ever so humble, there's no place like home!
—John Howard Payne, *Home, Sweet Home*

With its thin melody that sounds saccharine to the modern ear, it is worth remembering that "Home, Sweet Home" is one of the most popular songs in all of American history. The song was born on the London stage in 1823, in a popular opera "Clari, or the Maid of Milan," written by John Howard Payne with music by Sir Henry Bishop (the first composer to be knighted, allegedly because Queen Victoria loved "Home, Sweet Home" so much).[1] A native of New York, Payne had gone to London as an actor and gained modest standing as a playwright and librettist. His fortunes oscillated between outstanding success and crushing debts. Payne wrote the lyrics to "Home, Sweet Home" in a dull autumn in Paris, when "the depressing influences of the sky and air were in harmony with the feelings of solitude and sadness which oppressed his soul."[2]

The opera was a modest success, but the song was a phenomenon. In the year of its debut, some one hundred thousand copies of sheet music for "Home, Sweet Home" sold, and it was tremendously popular throughout the nineteenth century, especially in the United States and particularly during the American Civil War.

"Home, Sweet Home" was one of Abraham Lincoln's favorite songs, and it was cherished by both Union and Confederate soldiers. The images of home tugged at the hearts of even war-hardened troops, including those engaged in the December 1862 Battle of Stones River, a bloody clash in the vicinity of Murfreesboro, Tennessee.

The 44,000 Federalist soldiers of the Army of the Cumberland faced the 34,000 men in the Confederate Army of Tennessee. In miserable weather on the cold night of December 30, 1862, the two armies were within earshot of each other, stretched along the battlefront of stony outcrops and cedar brakes. As the short winter day ended, military bands on both sides began to play. A soldier in the First Tennessee Infantry later remembered that "the still winter night carried their strains to great distance. At every pause on our side, far away could be heard the military bands of the other."

One of the bands began "Home, Sweet Home," and as the well-known chorus echoed in the night air, Federal and Confederate bands on both sides of the battle line united in the refrain "one after another until all the bands of each army were playing 'Home Sweet Home.' And after our bands had ceased playing, we could hear the sweet refrain as it died away on the cool frosty air."[3]

Over the next three days, the two armies suffered more than 23,515 casualties, with over 3,000 dead, one of the bloodiest engagements in the western campaigns of the Civil War.

John Howard Payne died further from home than any of the fallen at the Battle of Stones River. Approaching his fifties and after decades of travail to little effect—first as a composer and then as a low-level diplomat—Payne lobbied for the sinecure of a consulship. In and out of office with changing presidential administrations, in 1851 Payne was reappointed consul of Tunis and set sail that spring. Less than a year later, he died and was laid to rest in the Protestant cemetery of St. George in Tunis.

But because of the popularity of "Home, Sweet Home," Payne was not forgotten. The U.S. government placed a marble marker on his Tunisian grave, and twenty years later a bronze bust was erected in Prospect Park, Brooklyn, New York, in a ceremony attended by thirty thousand onlookers.[4] Ten years later, a group of Payne's friends and former backers organized the return of the author's remains from distant lands. In March 1883 Payne's time-blackened bones arrived in New York, thirty years after his death. His remains were carried on a special train to Washington, D.C., where an elaborate funeral celebration, attended by President Chester Arthur and other dignitaries, was held in Oak Hill Cemetery on the occasion of what would have been Payne's ninety-fifth birthday.[5]

Finally, John Howard Payne was home.

. . .

Exile and longing, wandering and return—for humans there is no place like home. These complex attachments originated among our distant hominid ancestors, millions of years in the past. "Foxes have holes, and birds of the air have nests," Jesus observed before contrasting animal domesticity with his own wanderings. Astoundingly varied constructions are built by animals, and it is tempting to trace a connecting line from nests and dens to condos and tipis.

For all animals, including humans, constructions extend the bodily limits of existence. As the Nobel Laureate Karl von Frisch observed, "The most usual purpose of building activities in animals is to make a home that will give protection,"[6] but animal constructions also serve as traps, pantries, stages for mating and display, climate control systems, nurseries, roadways, and so on. Animal constructions protect offspring, regulate moisture and humidity, ventilate gasses, communicate information, and camouflage occupants.[7]

Such constructions are sometimes considered examples of what Richard Dawkins has called "the extended phenotype," the external manifestations of natural selection at the genetic level that extend beyond the organism. In Dawkins's view, the creation of nests and dens, burrows and webs is driven by the essential genetic objectives: survival and reproduction.[8]

Such fundamental evolutionary drives have produced some astounding constructions. Termites can build towering nests 20 feet tall and excavate wells 150 feet deep, yet the animals are only one-tenth of an inch long; at a human scale these would be constructions 2½ miles tall and excavations 20 miles deep. Termite nests house several million inhabitants and are built by small individual insects laboring in the dark.[9]

Similarly, it is worth recalling that the largest construction on earth that is visible from outer space is not the Great Wall of China, as usually claimed (see chapter 7), but Australia's Great Barrier Reef, a 1,600-mile-long structure made by organisms no longer than your fingernail.

Despite such awe-inspiring features of the natural world, not all animals build. As the biologist Mike Hansell has written, "The occurrence of building behaviors is neither confined to a narrow range of taxa nor scattered evenly through the animal kingdom. Instead, it has a few outbursts of virtuosity with talented displays of skill occurring sporadically across the animal spectrum."[10]

The most stunning architects in the nonhuman world are spiders, mites, insects, and birds. Our closest animal relations—chimpanzees, bonobos, and gorillas—are uninspired builders. Nest-building by chimpanzees and bonobos is a fairly impromptu construction process.[11] Both species settle nightly in trees, building nests of branches, sometimes with rough thatchings of leaves. As night falls, the apes groom each other, rest, and mate in their arboreal love-nests—behaviors in common with many modern humans. Unlike most of us, however, chimps do not eat in bed.

In field studies of chimpanzee and bonobo nesting behavior, one of the few patterns common to all the study-groups is that they avoid nesting in trees with ripe fruit. The height of nests varies based on environment: constructed 15–80 feet above the ground, nests tended to be higher in wetter environments or during the rainy season. Nests tend to be regularly spaced, but this may differ based on the threat of predators. Most nests are only occupied once, although in some study groups as many as one-third of the nests were reoccupied, but only when the a particular food source attracted the nomadic troop to linger in a particular locale.

Regardless of these variations, all chimpanzees build nests each night. The primatologist W. C. McGrew writes, "There is nothing more predictable in chimpanzee daily life than this universal behavioral sequence and its artifactual outcome. It is the cornerstone of chimpanzee nature."[12]

Since they are imposing animals, gorillas worry less about predators—except for human poachers—and their homes reflect this nonchalance.[13] Given their large bulk, gorillas tend to nest on the ground, although occasionally they nest in trees. The primatologist Dian Fossey described their nests as "sturdy, compact structures, sometimes resembling oval, leafy bathtubs."[14] The mountain gorilla, as the biologist George Schaller documented, "stands or sits, and pulls, breaks, or bends in vegetation which it places around and under its body." Regardless of their basic construction technique, "the precise method employed varies with the particular circumstance—whether the nest is in a tree or on the ground, whether it is on a steep slope or a flat area."[15] Similar to the chimpanzees, gorillas apparently reoccupy nests only when abundant fruits or other foods tempt them to stay in an area.[16]

In less than five minutes, a gorilla can make a treetop nest, bending down the branches in a tree's crown or weaving limbs into a platform bed. Ground-level nests take even less time, built from a few handfuls of foliage roughly arranged in less than thirty seconds.[17]

But what are the functions of the nests built by chimpanzees, bonobos, and gorillas?

There are several possible answers.[18] Arboreal nests may protect sleeping primates from predators, although various monkeys sleep in trees without building nests. Sleeping in treetops may protect primates from mosquitoes and other biting insects that transmit diseases. One of the strongest explanations links nest building and body heat, the "thermoregulation hypothesis," because the differences appear linked to local environment and weather. Unlike other animals—whose constructions are uniform, presumably because those behaviors are genetically hardwired—higher apes appear to have a basic drive to nest, but vary their constructions based on local circumstances. As the authors of one study of gorillas living in the Congo put it, the variations in nests "appear to be in response to wet and cool conditions, clearly suggesting that the gorillas call on innate nest-building tendencies with a quite flexible, adaptive specificity."[19]

These findings suggest that the nests built by African apes differ from other examples of animal architecture in one fundamental regard: the constructions vary in response to local conditions. While we recognize that modern apes are not our hominid ancestors, it is interesting to realize that, like these primate relatives, all humans make shelters but do so in different ways. It may be that this common adaptive propensity is the essential connection. Despite the variations and differences between ape nests and human dwellings, there exists this broad connection, leading one primatologist to ask, "Was there no place like home?"[20]

. . .

As of this writing, the oldest home I have excavated is merely 6,000 years old. In June and July of 2006, I directed excavations in far northern Peru at a small prehistoric site called El Porvenir. I had first seen the site in 1996 during an archaeological reconnaissance near the border between Peru and Ecuador; it had taken ten years to raise the funds to return and excavate the site (not an uncommon occurrence in archaeology).

El Porvenir caught my attention and drew me back a decade later because I thought it would contain evidence of ancient homes. The site consisted of a group of six earthen mounds around an open space, which I assumed was a cluster of house mounds around a central plaza. El Porvenir covered an area a bit larger than a football field, 120 × 90 meters. The mounds were simple ovals, 10 to 30 meters at their bases, and the tallest mound was only 1.6 meters tall. The mounds were noticeable, but not impressive. What these surface details suggested was this: these were not monumental constructions or carefully built public architecture, but rather simple mounds probably containing archaeological

evidence of ancient dwellings and households. And that is why I excavated El Porvenir.

On the surface of the site, we found a few stray burnished brick-red
potsherds decorated with lines and dots of a creamy white. Based on
what we knew in 2006, we thought this pottery style dated sometime
between 500 B.C. and A.D. 500 (the vagueness of the date simply reflecting how little we understood of the region's prehistory). Since the El
Porvenir mounds were relatively small (these were not massive accumulations like Near Eastern tells) I expected that even the oldest layers of
El Porvenir would date sometime within the 500 B.C. to A.D. 500 range
or perhaps a few centuries older—but not by much.

I was very wrong.

We began excavating the mounds of El Porvenir. We laid out 2 × 2
meter test pits arranged in a row to transect the mound, their edges lined
by taut staked strings. We scraped through the hard dun clay, and within
inches of the surface encountered the first traces of ancient dwellings.

There was not much to see. A few irregular lumps of adobe bricks,
fire-reddened and ashy—the remains of a cooking hearth. A harder surface was a floor compacted by footsteps. A right-angled line of postholes penetrated the floor, small divots darkened by the rotted wooden
poles that once supported the walls. A cluster of sun-dried clay chunks
bore grooved imprints of river canes. From such prosaic traces, we discovered a portion of a roughly rectangular structure built from wattle
and daub, and the cooking hearth indicated that we had uncovered an
ancient home.

Below this floor was a jumbled stratum of fill, a craze of rubble and
shells. The shells were principally of oysters and other mollusks that lived
in mangrove swamps now located 6–10 kilometers west of El Porvenir.
The clutter of shells, cocked at every angle, was a garbage dump, or midden, rather than the floor of a prehistoric home.

Under the midden layer were the fragments of another earlier house.
Later occupants of El Porvenir had dug into and destroyed the lower
levels, yet enough remained of the earlier structure to partially reconstruct it. In one corner there was a basin-shaped hearth molded from
mud and holding grey ash and charcoal flecks. We found sections of
compact floor made from intentionally poured layers of grayish river
mud; the grey mud floor was ripped away in places by later trenching,
but clearly defined an earlier dwelling. More post-molds were visible
in the preserved patches of flooring, arching in a broad curve that indicated an elliptical structure. There were no traces of mud daub, indicat-

ing that this earlier house differed in plan and construction from the rectangular wattle and daub house perched above it.

We troweled into even earlier layers. As each stratum was uncovered, all the features were mapped and photographed. The soil was screened to recover the smallest fragments of the past.

We dug through another thick stratum of oyster, removing over 500 kilograms of bone-grey shells. In the same layers we found hundreds of fragile fish bones from catfish, mullet, tuna, sea bass, and other delectable fish. Some species had been netted and hooked in the quiet mangrove estuaries, others taken from boats on the open sea. Small pottery shards and stone flakes sprinkled the shell midden as we dug down in the mound.

And finally we came upon the very oldest house at El Porvenir.

The traces of the house were simply a curved wall marked by small post-molds. The posts had been set in pairs, presumably on both sides of an elliptical wall. Additional posts were set in the middle of the floor, apparently supporting narrow roof-beams that intersected like the spokes of a wheel. We estimated that the structure would have been about five meters in diameter. The floor consisted of a compact layer of dense midden.

When we excavated this floor we thought it was old, but only six months later—after we were able to export samples for radiocarbon dating and obtained the laboratory results—did we know just how old. The samples from the oyster shell layer dated to 4700–4340 B.C. and the floor was older than that—the house was more than 6,000 years old. The prehistoric house at El Porvenir is one of the oldest houses known from northern South America.

The dwellings at El Porvenir exemplify the archaeological evidence of home. First, the evidence we found in our excavations bore the imprints of human intention. The post-molds were evenly spaced and aligned, well-made pits; they were neither root bores nor animal burrows. In the upper layers the floors were made from thick caps of grey river clays and the lower floors were compacted midden; both were human made. These were cultural features, not natural products, and they reflected a plan. They were, to recall Tim Ingold's observation, a human project.

Second, people carried things to these dwellings, a point so obvious that it is easily overlooked. People transported shellfish and fish, pottery and stone tools to these places—moving these materials kilometers, bringing these things home.

Finally, each of the dwellings contained the traces of a suite of human activities—cooking meals and making tools, in addition to building huts—all pointing to simple domesticities six millennia ago.

And while there is a great deal about the early villagers of El Porvenir that remains unknown, we do know this: like humans elsewhere in the past, they built homes.

. . .

So *why* is there home? *Why* did the human home evolve?

One prominent hypothesis argues that the human home originates from two biological imperatives: reproductive success and the extended dependency of human offspring.[21]

Obviously, all species either reproduce or become extinct, but not all species demand the high levels of parental investment in offspring as humans do. The California mussel gives birth to 60,000–70,000 spawn in the crashing waters of the Pacific coast without giving her offspring another thought.

In contrast, human infants cannot walk until nine to twelve months after birth and they do not have all their teeth until sometime after two years old, leading one wag to suggest that instead of a mere nine months of pregnancy, humans have a 32-month gestation period: 9 *in utero* plus 24 *ex utero*.

Further, since humans rarely bear more than a single offspring at a time, both parents' genetic heredity is dependent on one child's survival to reproductive age (although the more offspring the better the odds). Thus, the argument goes, both parents have a vested genetic interest in the survival of their young.

But the mother's and father's investments differ. In traditional societies, mothers typically breastfeed their infants for two to three years or more.[22] While the mother-child interactions are sustained and intimate, how does the father contribute? He brings home food, particularly meat. Similarly, male hominids ensured the survival of their offspring by provisioning their families, wandering out to forage (and becoming increasingly bipedal in the process), and returning with food. Rather than risk their parental investment, it is to the reproductive advantage of both parents to have their offspring in a relatively safe location to which resources are transported.

Such are the evolutionary advantages of home.

When this eminently plausible "home-base hypothesis" was first articulated, it seemed to account for a broad range of anthropological facts that relatively quickly became matters of dispute.[23] For example, the hypothesis explained the idea of "Man the Hunter" in which males venture out in quest of game, returning with highly prized meat.

But when more detailed ethnographic research was conducted, a different picture emerged. Women in foraging societies often contributed more calories to the diet than men did. Men were not the only hunters, but women, children, and the elderly also hunted small game, fished, or collected shellfish. More surprisingly, detailed studies of meat-sharing indicated that relatively little of a hunter's catch actually went to his own offspring because of strong social requirements to share meat with other kin or band members.

Finally, critics argued, the classic ethnographies of hunter-and-gatherer societies overlooked the transformations that many of these societies had endured due to contacts with other agrarian or industrial societies and empires. Driven into marginal environments, decimated by introduced diseases, or ensnared through commercial and/or political ties, these ethnographic cases were not frozen representatives of a Lower Paleolithic past.

Ultimately, resolving the questions of the earliest hominid social group was stymied by a simple but daunting fact: it is extremely difficult to find archaeological sites more than one million years old.

First, to find one-million-year-old sites, you have to search one-million-year-old landforms, which are often deeply buried deposits. For example, the Great Rift Valley system of eastern Africa has proven so rich in hominid and other fossils precisely because ancient and deeply buried strata are laid bare in its eroded exposures.

Second, if the artifacts and features created by chimpanzees, bonobos, and gorillas are a guide, the sites created by hominids probably were ephemeral and incompletely preserved. It is unlikely that one-million-year-old termite-hunting twigs or improvised leafy nests will ever be discovered by archaeologists.

Finally, even if durable artifacts are found on ancient land surfaces, there is a good chance that such materials will have been moved about by erosion or other natural processes and the archaeological materials are no longer in their original in situ associations.

These challenges only made the sites excavated by Mary Leakey all the more exciting. In meticulous excavations conducted throughout the 1960s, Mary Leakey and her colleagues focused on a number of sites located in the oldest sediments in the main gorge at Olduvai, sediments deposited by a now-dry lake between 1.87 and 1.71 million years old. Leakey excavated in two main areas exposed by streams that cut down through Olduvai's strata over the last 200,000 years, the DK Locality and the FLK Complex.[24]

The sites contained a variety of animal bones and stone artifacts: crude choppers, hammer stones, and stone flakes with utilized edges. The faunal remains were surprisingly diverse, including big game (such as ancient relatives of giraffes, elephants, rhinos, zebras, and wildebeests) as well as two species of turtles and one species of tortoise. Twenty-three different taxa of mammals were found, including a large number of crocodile teeth.

In one portion of the DK Locality, Leakey's team discovered an amazing feature: a circular array of stones. Leakey wrote, "At DK there is a stone circle which is the earliest man-made structure known. It is built of loosely pile blocks of lava and measures three and a half to four metres in diameter. It bears a striking similarity to crude stone circles constructed for temporary shelter by present-day nomadic peoples such as the Turkana in Kenya."[25]

Confessing to her own suspicions, Leaky admitted, "The Olduvai structure was a most surprising discovery in view of its age and for a while I was reluctant to believe that the blocks of lava had been artificially arranged into a circle. However, the geologists and prehistorians who have since seen the circle are almost unanimous in considering that it is likely to be the work of the early hominids and not a natural feature."

Mary Leakey had found the oldest known house on earth.

Other archaeological projects expanded on the Olduvai discoveries, particularly at the FXJj 50 site in northern Kenya, where excavations in the 1970s and early 1980s were directed by Richard Leakey and Glynn Isaac.[26] At FXJj 50 a litter of chipped stone tools and animal bones (representing mammals, birds, and fish) suggested the existence of a home base about 1.6–1.5 million years ago. Further, it was possible to fit together the chipped stone flakes and cores at the site—like pieces of a lithic jigsaw puzzle—indicating that the artifacts at FXJj 50 were largely in their original places, undisturbed by time.

Thus, the archaeological evidence indicated that by 1.5 million years ago our very ancient ancestors had developed home bases where they made tools, butchered game, shared food, and even (possibly) built simple shelters.

Or did they?

Various scholars pointed out flaws in the data from the DK Locality.[27] For example, nearly half the identifiable animal bones came from croco-

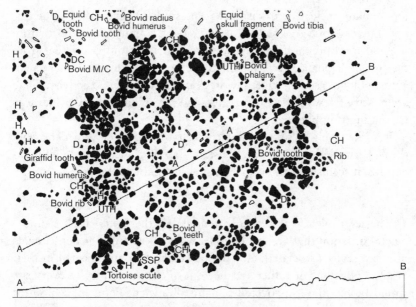

Equid tooth, Bovid tooth, Bovid radius, Bovid humerus, Equid skull fragment, Bovid tibia, CH, D, H, DC, Bovid M/C, B, UTH Bovid phalanx, H, H, A, H, D, D, A, CH, Giraffid tooth, A, Bovid tooth, Rib, Bovid humerus, CH, H, Bovid rib, UTH, D, CH, Bovid teeth, CH, A, H, SSP, CH, B, Tortoise scute, A, B

FIGURE 2. Site DK I, Olduvai Gorge. Redrawn from Leakey 1979.

diles—an unlikely game animal for a small hominid armed with crude stone tools. Eighty-six percent of the crocodile bones were teeth, which crocodiles lose naturally. Other animal bones incised with cut marks from stone tools also showed evidence of being gnawed by hyenas or other carnivores. While stone flake tools and choppers showed evidence of hominid intent, it was far from certain that hominids had actually hunted game: they could have used stone tools to scavenge and scrape meat from dead game killed by other, more effective, nonhuman predators.

And finally, the circular stone feature that Mary Leakey reluctantly concluded was an ancient shelter in fact consisted of chunks of the underlying bedrock jutting into the layers containing bone and stone tools. The circular pattern of bedrock blocks probably resulted from a combination of weathering and stones moved by tree roots. These were not shelter walls built by the ancient occupants of Olduvai Gorge. Mary Leakey had not found the oldest house on earth.

The archaeology of African sites dating between 2.6 and 1.6 million years ago provides a fragmentary and partial vista into the behavior of early hominids.[28] While these ancestors made simple stone tools, ate meat, and carried raw materials and some food to sites, other behaviors remain unclear or in dispute. Some studies suggest that while certain Lower Stone Age sites in Africa might contain evidence for tool use and food preparation, the sites are not significantly different from the archaeological patterns potentially left by chimpanzees. Other paleoanthropologists see the same sites as evidence for hominid activity. There are relatively few of these older sites, and the archaeological evidence is frustratingly ambiguous.

It is like trying to see complex constellations on a cloudy night from the flickering light of a handful of stars. Based on such uncertain illuminations, it seems that these ancient sites were not yet homes.

. . .

The basic problem is this: there are no Paleolithic Pompeiis.[29] A fundamental question that archaeologists always ask is "Are the constituents of a site really associated? Are the objects in situ and located in their original positions or rather are they out of context?" Ideally, every site would be like the ash-covered remains of ancient Pompeii: a moment frozen in time in the autumn of A.D. 79. In fact, only rarely are archaeological sites sealed deposits, intact and stilled.

A wide array of natural processes can modify or disturb an archaeological site. Bacteria and scavenging animals consume organic materials, leaving behind only indigestible stone, pottery, and bone. Flowing water—varying in volume from raindrops to flash floods—can move artifacts, cut through strata, or erode objects. Badgers, gophers, lizards, worms, and other burrowing animals change the soil matrix and move archaeological materials. As clay soils expand when wet and shrink when dry, archaeological objects are moved through the profile along with rocks and gravels.

While all archaeological sites are affected by these vagaries of preservation, the problem is most pronounced for sites from the dawn of humanity. Obviously, the oldest sites have the greatest opportunities for disturbance and decay. Further, such early sites usually have a relatively light material footprint. The sites are rarely the result of a permanent occupation because humans were highly mobile and nomadic; the archaeological record is correspondingly slight. And it may be ambiguous whether the objects and features in these early sites are the result of human actions. For example, charred wood may be from an ancient campfire or a lighting-struck tree. Cut marks on apparently butchered bones may prove to be tooth marks from nonhuman predators.

Consider the controversial site of Terra Amata, located in Nice on the French Riviera. The site was excavated over six months in 1966 after construction crews trenched into the archaeological deposit. Construction was suspended and a salvage excavation was begun, directed by Henry de Lumley.[30]

Terra Amata may have evidence of one of the earliest human dwellings, 350,000–450,000 years old. De Lumley and his team uncovered thousands of stone tools and flakes, an array of bones from fauna large and small, levels that contained a few postholes, small hearths, and blocks of stone and oval clusters of archaeological materials that de Lumley interpreted as the remains of ancient huts 7–15 × 4–6 meters in size. Further, de Lumley interpreted the archaeological strata as forming thin, discrete layers that represented annual reoccupations of Terra Amata by mobile hunters and gatherers camped during successive springtimes on the shore of the Mediterranean Sea. De Lumley identified eleven of these layers and interpreted them as separate "living floors."

But de Lumley's interpretation was challenged by the analysis of the stone tools and flakes, research conducted by Paola Villa, then a doctoral student at the University of California at Berkeley. One aspect of Villa's project involved conjoining stone tools and flakes, literally fitting back together the stone pieces that fly off as a core is struck with a hammer stone. Through careful analysis, Villa reconstructed the way tools were made, and in the process she made an awkward discovery.

Some conjoinable flakes came from Terra Amata's different living floors. The discrete layers de Lumley had proposed were cross-cut by stone fragments from the same original core.

This led some scholars to dismiss Terra Amata as the fanciful reconstruction of archaeological imagination, an impression made somewhat worse by incomplete reporting on the excavation.[31] Other archaeologists simply erased Terra Amata from the list of ancient European sites.

That seems too dismissive. Although the evidence for vertical movements of flakes undermines the idea that Terra Amata contained eleven seasonal encampments, it does not mean that Terra Amata is archaeologically irrelevant. For example, even the cautious and critical Villa concluded that Terra Amata "is a site with material diffused through deposits 1.5–2.0 meters thick. Features such as hearths, post-holes, and alignments of [limestone] blocks were preserved, but site formation processes have resulted in partial mixing of the residues of probably separate occupation episodes."[32]

So here is what we may infer: Terra Amata was a home base dating to between 450,000 and 350,000 years ago, a place that members of the genus *Homo* (but not *Homo sapiens*) modified by building fires and simple structures—probably windbreaks—and where they made stone tools and prepared food. In this narrow and spartan sense, Terra Amata was a home.

Other sites present similarly ambiguous evidence of home. For example, at the site of Bilzingsleben, in eastern Germany, excavations uncovered a small lakeside site that may contain evidence of three elliptical shelters dating to 418,000–280,000 years ago.[33] Travertine blocks and large animal bones were placed to anchor windbreaks. Small features of burned earth and charcoal are associated with each dwelling, as are activity areas consisting of elephant bones and anvils formed from blocks of travertine. Stone tools from Bilzingsleben are clearly artifacts: pebble tools, hammer-stones, knives, scrapers, points, and other flake tools. Fauna remains include rhino, beaver, red deer, elephant, and bear; none of the bones show gnaw marks, yet some of the elephant foot bones have geometric cut marks incised with a stone tool. An intriguing circular pavement of stones pressed into the softer underlying sediments was partially excavated on the edge of the site; measuring nine meters in diameter, it is clearly an archaeological feature.[34]

Given this archaeological assemblage, one would think that Bilzingsleben would handily pass every conceivable objection to its authenticity. And yet one archaeologist has argued that Bilzingsleben was a place where hominids met but did not dwell, and that the circular "shelters" are mere natural features around which hominids camped, ate, and made tools—but did not build.

Even the patient reader may wonder, "Is there nothing about archaeology that is certain? What type of intellectual discipline (if that is even the right word!) can be whipsawed by alternative explanations?"

And that, itself, requires a confession and an explanation.

. . .

Archaeology is not, by and large, an experimental science. With few exceptions, it is impossible to replicate the conditions and observations that led to an inference or discovery. It is usually impossible to recreate conditions or recombine elements to reproduce results—the way a high school chemistry teacher can use electrolysis to separate water into hydrogen and oxygen every single semester, year after year.

Archaeological excavations are particularly irrevocable. Once an artifact has been removed from the soil, it cannot be re-excavated. Which is why archaeologists spend so much time laying out grids, measuring the depths of strata, recording, photographing, drawing and so on—all the painstaking efforts to document an irreproducible set of scientific data. You cannot "un-excavate" a site.

This, of course, also allows for doubts. Were the patterns in the excavated data really there, or are they the figments of hyperactive archaeological interpretation? If the patterns are real, are they the product of natural processes, cultural manipulations, or some combination of different factors? Are the objects really associated, is the site accurately dated, was the excavation competent? And on, and on, and on.

At times, archaeologists appear to be an apostleship of Doubting Thomases.

Take what, at first glance, would seem to be a fairly uncomplicated event: building a campfire. If bipedalism separates hominids from our ape cousins, then the use of fire separates humans from all other animals. As Richard Wrangham has argued, fire and the ability to cook food is the transcendent technological breakthrough in human history.[35]

Anthropogenic fire should be relatively easy to discover in the archaeological record. Fires leave behind charcoal and ash, burn soils brick-red, and reorder the magnetic fields of clays. All these are regularly found by archaeologists. Natural fires are caused by lightening strikes, sparks from falling rocks, volcanic eruptions, and spontaneous combustion of rotting organic materials. In principle we would expect naturally occurring fires to be widespread and unconstrained and human campfires to be relatively small and contained (although obviously humans regularly cause enormous, uncontrollable "wild" fires).[36]

So it a shock to learn of the uncertainties of the evidence for early human fire. A broad and hypercritical review dismissed most claims of hominid fire use before 200,000–100,000 years ago.[37] For example, in China the famous site of Zhou-k'ou-tien—where "Peking Man," an Asian example of *Homo erectus,* was found in the 1930s—was long thought to contain traces of campfires kindled by hominids 500,000–200,000 years ago. More recent analyses suggest that the yellowish-red lenses interpreted as hearths are actually reddish brown sediments that collected in small, still pools of drip water, leaving traces that looked like hearths but were not.[38]

And yet, three sites—two in Africa, the other in Israel—indicate much earlier hominid use of fire. In Kenya, at the 1.5-million-year-oldsite of FXJj 20 East at Koobi Fora, excavations exposed four small features, 30–40 cm in diameter and 10–15 cm thick, on the same flat layer of pale yellowish brown silt.[39] Three of the patches were slightly reddened earth, and the fourth was a dark-grey hue. The surrounding soils had not been burned, indicating that these fires were discrete events. Geophysical analyses showed that two of the baked soil features had been burned at 200°C–400°C, about the temperature of an open campfire, and although brushfires combust at similar temperatures, they do not burn the soils as deeply. Further, some stone artifacts had been altered by heat, but other tools had not—again pointing to a controlled burn instead of a broad conflagration.

Five hundred kilometers to the south, another site with evidence of early fire was found at Chesowanja, where a cluster of baked clay lumps appears to have been an ancient hearth. Stone tools surround the cluster, and a fragment of skull apparently came from the robust form of *Australopithecus*. The site is dated to about 1.42 million years old.

Gesher Benot Ya'aqov is located in northern Israel on the banks of the Jordan River.[40] Acheulian hand-axes were found at the site in the 1930s, but excavations over the last twenty years have led to a remarkable picture of Middle Paleolithic life. The site is partially water logged, and plant remains have been found from wild grapes, water chestnuts, wild olive, wild pistachio, acorns, and jujube. Small pitted stones were used to crack nuts. The bones of small game like hares and hyrax were found. Stone tools were abundant: basalt bifacial hand-axes and cleavers, limestone choppers, flint cores, and flake tools. The flint had been carried from sources at least ten kilometers away. And there is solid evidence for fire. Not only were burned seeds and wood recovered from Gesher Benot Ya'aqov, but there were two clusters of burned flints. Flints were burned only in these two clusters, and not in other areas of the site—suggesting that fires were contained and intentional. And this occurred 790,000 years ago.

. . .

So with all the caveats in place and in mind, the archaeological pursuit of the elusive traces of ancient home seems to lead us to this conclusion. Long before the first *Homo sapiens* left Africa, more distant relatives journeyed into Europe and Asia. Between about 1.4 and 0.7 million years ago, hominids created the sites that we can recognize as temporary encampments. More anchored than chimp or gorilla nests, these sites were places of arrival and return, locations where our ancestors made stone tools and cooked over ancient fires. Little suggests that these encampments were imbued with deep meanings or emotional attachments that are so common in later human homes. Rather, these earliest camps are

probably yet another example of cultural practices as extended phenotype, to recall Richard Dawkins's phrase. In its simplest forms, home was
a place where fires, tools, and basic shelters co-occurred, but—and this
is extremely important—those forms of home varied. Unlike oriole nests
or beaver dens, the earliest hominid residences were not identical "constructions," but differed based on the resources used, the duration of stay,
and the local environment. These earliest sites—consisting of little more
than hearths and stone scatters—contain evidence of the origins of that
fundamental human project, the creation of home.

CHAPTER 3

Mobile Homes

Let us never lose sight of our little rustic hut.
—Marc-Antoine Laugier, *An Essay on Architecture*

The portaledge is a collapsible platform of tubing and rip-stop nylon that big-wall rock climbers use when a prolonged ascent requires spending nights out on a sheer rock face. First designed in the 1980s, the portaledge allows climbers to make multi-day ascents of big walls in regions with severe weather. It extends the climbers' reach.[1]

The platform is just large enough for two climbers to sleep in. A web of nylon lines binds the portaledge to a central anchor point, such as a pair of expansion bolts drilled into solid rock. A separate protection point is placed away from the portaledge; other gear is snapped into this anchor especially metal carabineers, chock nuts, or ice axes that might attract lightening bolts. A small bucket dangles from a tent pole, supporting a tiny stove for heat and cooking. Covered with a durable tent designed to both shed moisture and allow air circulation, the portaledge is a secure, though improbable, refuge in a storm.

Few humans occupy such perilous environments as the vertical granite massif of El Capitan in the Yosemite Valley or the sheer red cliffs of Zion National Park. But just as the portaledge allows climbers a sheltered night's rest as they dangle hundreds of feet in the air, humans use dwellings to extend their reach even for just a night or a few days. And we have done so for more than seven hundred thousand years.

. . .

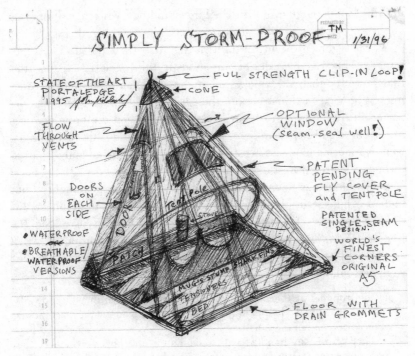

FIGURE 3. J. Middendorf, *The Portaledge,* circa 1990. Drawing courtesy of John Middendorf.

The most influential American archaeologist of his generation, Lewis Binford (1931–2011) spent decades carefully examining ethnographic accounts of traditional cultures and searching for patterns in human behavior that would be discernible in the archaeological record. Explicitly committed to the scientific search for law-like generalizations, Binford compiled massive data sets based on literally hundreds of case studies about historic and modern hunting and gathering societies. While those hunting and gathering societies are not static representatives of earlier Paleolithic people, the case studies suggested some basic patterns relevant to thinking about the past. Although Binford's studies ranged over different aspects of the lives of hunters and gatherers, one analysis explored the question: Why do hunters and gatherers build such different kinds of homes?[2]

One of the first conclusions from Binford's study is simultaneously surprising and obvious: *All* hunters and gatherers build shelters, even at camps they occupy for a single night. This would be an uninteresting conclusion, were it not for the long-standing, Western assumptions about the rootless, *au naturel* existence of hunters and gatherers.

As the eighteenth-century thinker Giambattista Vico succinctly observed, "This was the order of human institutions: first the forests, after that the huts, then the villages, next the cities, and finally the academies."[3] In Vico's reconstruction, the earliest wild and sylvan stage occurred in the aftermath of the Great Flood, "when the impious races of the three children of Noah, having lapsed into a state of bestiality, went wandering like wild beasts until they were scattered and dispersed through the great forest of the earth."[4]

Similar musings form a recurrent theme in Western thought about human origins. During the first century B.C., the Roman architect Vitruvius considered the origins of the earliest buildings in his classic *Ten Books of Architecture*. Humans came together, Vitruvius proposed, when attracted by the unusual warmth of lightening-struck trees. Since they were bipedal,

> having from nature this boon beyond other animals, that they should walk, not with the head down, but upright, and should look upon the magnificence of the world and of the stars.
> They also easily handled with their hands and fingers whatever they wished. Hence after thus meeting together, they began, some to make shelters of leaves, some to dig caves under the hills, some to make of mud and wattles places for shelter, imitating the nests of swallows and their methods of building. Then observing the houses of others and adding to their ideas new things from day to day, they produced better kinds of huts.[5]

The homelessness of savage nations is a theme touched on by different writers, not surprisingly by Enlightenment authors discussing the origins of architecture. In his 1791 "A Treatise on the Decorative Part of Civil Architecture," the British Neoclassical architect Sir William Chambers imagined a Paleolithic idyll, in which "every grove afforded shade from the rays of the sun, and shelter from the dews of the night" and our ancient forebears "fed upon the spontaneous productions of the soil, and lived without care, as without labor."[6]

Chambers's model of human origins combined an Enlightenment version of selective pressures with a Stone Age precursor of Hedonism II. The seductive tropical climate inevitably led to procreation, and as population increased, competition intensified for scarce resources. Consequently, Chambers opined, "separation became necessary; and colonies dispersed to different regions: where frequent rain, storms and piercing cold, forced the inhabitants to seek for better shelter than trees." The

FIGURE 4. "The First Building." After Viollet-le-Druc.

tropical emigrants "at first . . . most likely retired to caverns . . . but soon disgusted with the damp and darkness of these habitations, they began to search after more wholesome and comfortable dwellings."

Binford's analysis is a relief after these florid musings. He argued that the shelters hunters and gatherers build—and remember, they *all* build shelters—reflect, in part, their broader adaptations to physical environments, whether they live in the equatorial tropics or arctic tundra. First, hunters and gatherers vary in their mobility. Fully nomadic groups move camps throughout the year, while seminomadic hunters often construct a substantial dwelling each winter, but spread out to seasonal camps when the weather is less severe. Semisedentary hunters and gatherers construct residences that they regularly reoccupy, although venturing out from those hubs and constructing temporary shelters before returning home. Sedentary hunters occupy dwellings year-round, although hunting par-

TABLE I   MOBILITY AND HOUSE PLAN IN HUNTING AND GATHERING SOCIETIES

| | Ground Plan | | | | | | | | | | |
| | Circular | | Semi-Circular | | Elliptical | | Rectangular | | Complex | | Total | |
Mobility	n	%	n	%	n	%	n	%	n	%	n	%
Fully nomadic	4	12.9	22	71.0	0	0	5	16.1	0	0	31	100
Semi-nomadic	0	0	65	69.8	10	10.7	18	19.4	0	0	93	100
Semi-sedentary	0	0	12	38.7	1	3.2	18	58.1	0	0	31	100
Fully sedentary	0	0	3	14.3	0	0	17	80.9	1	4.8	21	100
Totals	4		102		11		58		1		176	

SOURCE: Binford 1990

ties or foraging groups may journey out to find key resources and bring them back home.

Second, mobility shapes the form and construction of hunter-gatherer houses. More nomadic groups build circular or semicircular dwellings. More sedentary groups build rectangular houses. More nomadic groups either transport the building materials—for example, the canvas and poles of a tent—or they build their homes from immediately available materials. More sedentary hunters and gatherers will transport construction materials to the house site, often building the roof and walls of different materials, which more mobile hunters and gatherers do not. Seminomadic and semisedentary groups often have different types of dwellings lived in during different seasons or by different groups of people, while the most mobile and the most sedentary groups tend to occupy only one kind of dwelling, whether impermanent or enduring.

Third, such variations are shaped by the specific demands of subsistence. When a people's diet is based on hunted game, they tend to move more frequently, occupying circular or semicircular dwellings built from locally available or transported materials—especially if they have dogs, horses, or caribou that can carry tents and poles. When a people's diet is based on fish, mollusks, or marine mammals, they tend to be less mobile, living in more permanent and substantial dwellings.

Binford's insights imply that the earliest forms of mobile homes reflect the calculations of survival. We have to consider the dwelling within a complex framework of other decisions—about food-getting and movement—that hunter-gatherers make in order to survive. Rather than the blind clawings away from beastliness as the Enlightenment thinkers had suggested, such little rustic huts reflect a rationality that those savants would have prized.

. . .

On the Pacific Coast of Baja California, powerful waves chisel away at the coastal terrace. The coastal terrace consists of uplifted marine sediments, ancient shorelines raised as the Earth's tectonic plates groaned and buckled. The soils are an unconsolidated jumble of wave-rolled cobbles, clays, and silts. In deep, ancient times when glaciers melted and sea levels rose, the Pacific Ocean cut a long escarpment that runs for 150 kilometers, still visible 130,000 years later. A handful of brief rivers and numerous small arroyos cut through the coastal terrace in search of the sea.

Arroyo Hondo forms a large and (as the name suggests) deep drainage that slices a convoluted landscape whose names portray the difficulties of travel by Catholic missionaries and Mexican soldiers. Almost two hundred years after sea voyagers claimed the Californias for Spain, the colonization of Baja California was a slow and painful process in a landscape of agony. Even when translated into English, the place-names reflect this. Viper Pass. Arroyo of the Martyrs. The Sacrifice.

The Native American experience of this same place was profoundly different. Traveling over the cactus-spiked mesas between the warm waters of the Gulf of California and the cold waves of the Pacific Ocean, small bands of Kiliwa and Cochimi sought food, raised children, and told legends of the making of the land. The legends recounted how Menchipa, the gigantic original deity, created freshwater springs with the tip of his walking staff as he strode across the world. Each night the three Mountain Sheep stars, known to Europeans as the stellar trio in Orion's belt, galloped across the peninsula in the luminous night sky.

Few Europeans perceived this order, the way landscape and movement could result in the creation of home. One Jesuit missionary, the German priest John Jakob Baegert, described the natives as *Naturvoelklein* who "by no means represented communities of rational beings, . . . but resembled nothing less than a herd of swine, each of which runs around grunting as it likes, together today and scattered tomorrow till they meet again by accident at some future time."[7] Another Jesuit, the usually informative observer Miguel del Barco, said of the generally naked natives, "The house and dwelling of the Californians are no better nor comfortable than their costumes and dresses."[8] A Mexican Jesuit who spent the late eighteenth century in northern Baja California lamented the general disorder of indigenous society: "They have no government nor do they recognize a king . . . but only some captain and as they possess no titles to land, no houses, no real estate, nor have any sort of towns, . . . the need to find food prevents them from establishing themselves in fixed places."[9] What these Europeans failed to see was the stability of movement, a durably flexible response that is evident in the archaeology of Baja California.

Since the early 1990s, I have conducted archaeological research in the San Quintín–El Rosario region, on the Pacific coast about two hundred miles south of the U.S.-Mexico border. My students and I have recorded hundreds of sites.[10] The oldest known site dates to 5890–5660 B.C., and a handful of other sites are from the first half of the sixth millennium B.C. Since older sites have been discovered to the north and south, I assume that people moved through the region even earlier. Presumably, these older sites were eroded away or flooded as glacial sheets melted and sea levels rose to modern heights after the Pleistocene.

But after about 5500 B.C., we have dated enough archaeological sites to suggest how people made this landscape into home. First, just as the Jesuits had observed, there were no towns or cities: sites are relatively small open-air camps, most probably inhabited for a single season. There are no traces of permanent houses or other structures, and dwellings were probably brush windbreaks. Second, people seem to have followed the same basic pursuits: they made stone tools, collected shellfish from sandy beaches and rocky coastlines, hunted deer with spear-throwers and darts, and gathered agaves, trimming away the barbed leaves and roasting the agave hearts. Third, the prehistoric foragers lived in the region only part of the year. Most of their sites are kilometers away from permanent springs and rivers, suggesting that people camped in the area when temporary water sources were available during the wet winter months. And this basic pattern of seasonal, short-term encampments along the coast seems to have been followed for nearly seven thousand years.

In 1996 my students and I mapped a small site on the north bank of Arroyo Hondo. Stretching over three hundred meters, the site consisted of several discrete clusters of the debris of prehistoric daily life. The clusters formed two groups, probably reflecting two or more encampments by different bands of hunters and gatherers. Bright white shells of mussels, clams, and abalones glinted among the chaparral, but they too formed clusters of species: mussels and abalones from rocky coasts, Pismo clams from open sandy beaches, and Pacific littleneck clams from quieter, protected waters. Each cluster of mollusks represented a separate collecting trip to the seashore, a distance of three kilometers or more, and then the return to the sheltered campsite at Arroyo Hondo.

Other features and objects were evidence of ancient lives. A circular platform of fire-cracked rock was the base of a hearth where agave had been roasted. Two concentrations of dark grey basalt cores, hammerstones, and flakes were temporary workshops where stone tools were made. And sprinkled across the site were eighteen *metates*, flat-topped cobble grinding slabs, and a half dozen *manos*, fist-sized cobblestone tools rubbed back and forth to pulverize and mill hard seeds or dried meat on the metates. Because the metates are heavy stone slabs, they were not carried from place to place but simply cached under a bush until the band returned. And this was the case at Arroyo Hondo: there were two piles of cached metates, stored under sagebrush in anticipation of return.

In contrast to the Jesuits' biases, the native occupants of Arroyo Hondo were anything but a disorganized horde, desperately roaming the landscape in search of something to eat. The site at Arroyo Hondo clearly demonstrated planning, forethought, and order. The anthropologist Michael Jackson, who lived with mobile Aboriginal peoples in Australia, has written of "the Eurocentric bias to see all human experience from the perspective of the sedentary cultivator or householder. . . . In the West we have a habit of thinking of home as a house. Walls make us feel secure. Individual rooms give us a sense of privacy. We tend to believe that living in a house is synonymous with being civilized."[11]

But, in fact, even when hunters and gatherers make brief encampments, they clear brush, build windbreaks, light fires, and cook food. They make home.

. . .

One of the defining qualities of modern human behavior is the way we organize the places where we live. In early hominid sites, there is a jumble of activities; flakes, cut bones, and hearths are intermixed. However, with the emergence of Homo sapiens there is a greater tendency to spatial order.

For example, in Kebara Cave, located in Israel on the western escarpment of Mt. Carmel and overlooking the eastern Mediterranean Sea, excavations in the 1980s uncovered a complex record of place-making by Neanderthals.[12] Archaeologists had excavated different portions of Kebara Cave since the 1930s, and by the late 1950s the Middle Paleolithic antiquity of the site was recognized (see chapter 4). The excavations in the 1980s brought together a team of different specialists to examine Kebara Cave from multiple perspectives. In addition to detailed information on tool-making and faunal remains (such as gazelle, boar, horse, and deer among others), the Kebara Cave excavations uncovered evidence for the creation of spatial order. From the back wall of the cave, the archaeological deposits extended out some 33 meters to a small terrace past the cave's drip-line, and Kebara Cave's complex, inter-fingered stratigraphy in places was nearly 9 meters deep. The earliest levels contained numerous shallow oak-fueled hearths, particularly in the central portion of the cave. Elsewhere discrete concentrations of bones and stone flakes were uncovered, while the back wall of the cave was used as a garbage dump.

A Neanderthal burial was in the center of the cave at a depth of nearly 8 meters. A tall man in his late twenties or early thirties, the corpse had been laid in a shallow grave between 64,000 and 59,000 years ago. The skeleton was generally intact; it had not been scavenged by the hyenas that occasionally den in Kebara Cave. But there was a curious feature: the man's skull was missing.

The lower jaw was present and an upper molar indicated that the Neanderthal man was not headless when he was put into the grave. The cranium had been removed after the ligaments connecting spine and skull had rotted away. The skull apparently was retrieved by other Neanderthals.

At later sites in the Levant, skull taking became common. In Late Natufian and Early Neolithic sites, skulls were removed and buried separately from the rest of the body, while in the Late Neolithic (ca. 9,400–7,600 years ago) skulls were sometimes removed from the corpse, covered with plaster, and decorated with cowry shells placed in the eye sockets.

But the headless corpse from Kebara was 50,000 years older than those manipulated skulls.

It is difficult to imagine what motivated the Neanderthal inhabitants of Kebara Cave. Was the head removed in an act of ancestor veneration or to defile the last remains of a hated enemy? It is impossible to know.

But we can know that the Neanderthal residents of Kebara Cave were making place, distinguishing cooking areas and tool-making spaces, differentiating the space of the living from the space of the dead. They exhibited this human propensity to create order at home.

This attention to domestic order even in simple dwellings is evidenced by the amazing discoveries at the site of Ohalo II in Israel. Dating to

23,000 years ago, Ohalo II is an open-air camp site on the edge of the Sea of Galilee. In the late 1980s water levels dropped 2–3 meters during a seven-year drought, and, as the lake waters receded, Ohalo II was exposed.

Because the site had been flooded soon after it was abandoned, the preservation of organic materials was extraordinary: charred seeds and fruits from more than one hundred plant species. Thousands of bone fragments—from gazelles, sixty species of waterfowl, and freshwater fish—indicated a year-round occupation that probably lasted no more than a few generations, a relative permanent settlement only abandoned when rising lake waters flooded the site.

In an area of 35 × 30 meters, archaeologists at Ohalo II uncovered the remains of six ancient huts interspersed with a half-dozen open-air hearth areas. The open-air hearth areas were large patches that had been burned at different times. Food debris and flint flakes clustered around the hearth areas. The huts were oval shelters built from branches of tamarisk, willow, and oak—quickly constructed dwellings, each 5–13 square meters in area. Sometime in antiquity, the huts had burned down, creating a dense layer of carbonized materials that preserved food remains and building materials.

The hut floors dipped slightly below the ground surface, and cross-sectioning excavations in Hut 1 exposed three different floors interspersed with thin layers of clays and sands. The meticulous excavations uncovered fascinating details of ancient life. People chipped flint tools inside the huts. Small clusters of tiny fish bones were from baskets of stored fish. But perhaps the most fascinating discoveries were the beds.

Three huts contained evidence of beds made from the stems of alkali grasses. The most complete bed was found in the lowest floor of Hut 1. Hut 1 had a central hearth surrounded by a layer of grass. Alkali grasses have soft and delicate stems, and the people of Ohalo II had harvested the grasses by cutting them off at the ground (no roots were found), tying them into bundles, and then carefully placing the grass stems on the hut floor, forming an inch-thick cushion.

Ohalo II has the earliest evidence of human bedding yet known, and it illustrates how ancient people constructed space. In the case of Ohalo II, the advantages of the location were obvious: the lake provided fresh water, fish, and waterfowl, wild plants supplied food and building materials, and the shoreline was a nice flat spot for a camp site. But onto that natural landscape, the people of Ohalo II imposed another layer of order: distinguishing areas for cooking and tool making, separating hearth areas and huts, and then taking that extra little step—a soft bed of grass.

Even after 23,000 years, it makes me want to take a nap.

This human propensity towards spatial order is evident in archaeological sites throughout prehistory. Different activities occur in different places. For example, detailed studies of Upper Paleolithic sites in France show how the different stages of butchering reindeer left behind distinctive patterns: the first stages of cutting up the large bloody carcass occurred away from the center of the camp, and leaving behind circular patches empty of bones or artifacts where the carcass had lain, surrounded by bones from less-desirable cuts like vertebrae.[13] In contrast, haunches, ribs, and other meaty chunks were carried back to the cooking hearths. At the site of Pincevent it was possible to refit bone fragments from the same reindeer to show how meat was shared among three households.

Another fascinating study of modern hunters and gatherers documented this same human care in making space, even in highly mobile camps only occupied for a few days at a time.

During the 1970s, archaeologist James F. O'Connell spent twenty months studying mobile groups of modern Alyawara, an aboriginal group living in the sand plains and scrub forests of central Australia.[14] The Alyawara had been in contact with Anglo-Australians since the late nineteenth century, although sustained contact only occurred after livestock ranches were established in the 1920s. By the time of O'Connell's study, the Alyawara were tightly tied to Australia's national economy, working for wages as ranch hands, dependent on government support, and living in large, semipermanent settlements near ranches or on government reserves. Nevertheless, about one-quarter of the Alyawara's food came from hunting and gathering, and the traces of these activities were evident in their modern, residential sites.

The Alyawara are not fossilized representatives of the Upper Paleolithic, as their camps made obvious. Shelters often consisted of windbreaks—roofed for shade in the summer or open to capture the warmth of winter sun—built from corrugated sheet metal, brush, and canvas tarpaulins.

As the Alyawara moved through their days, they left behind different clusters of artifacts and domestic debris, concentrations O'Connell referred to as "activity areas." The larger the household and/or the longer they lived in one place, the larger and more diffuse the activity areas became. With longer occupancies, a distinctive circle of garbage formed around the camp, as the central zone of the camp was swept and trash was redeposited (particularly on the downwind side).

Even when the activities and artifacts were utterly "modern," their distributions had aspects paralleling ancient hunting and gathering sites. Alyawara men own cars and light trucks, vehicles generally in poor condition and requiring frequent repair. O'Connell mapped activity areas he dubbed "auto repair stations." These activity areas were adjacent to, but away from, the owner's household activity area. The auto repair station consisted of an open area 10–20 meters in diameter, surrounded by a dump of parts designed to keep the working area clear of obstacles. Beverage lids and pull tabs clustered under shade trees or sunscreens or in the areas surrounding roasting pits and hearths, while large cans ended up in the peripheral dumps. Households near each other tended to be occupied by closely related women. And, finally, only the very smallest artifacts and debris were found in the places where they were originally used; larger objects were cleaned up and dumped elsewhere in any camp occupied for more than a few days.

But despite other significant differences between the sites, I feel a bemused pleasure in the idea that a group of Alyawara men bent over the chassis of a battered Volvo create an archaeological feature similar to the bloody men butchering reindeer at the Upper Paleolithic site of Pincevent.

• • •

Mobile hunters and gatherers think about landscape in ways that are fundamentally different from those of more sedentary folks, whether fishing or farming communities. The archaeologist Deni Seymour, who has conducted extensive research in the southern American Southwest, highlights the fundamental difference in the way mobile vs. sedentary groups choose places to live. "For mobile groups," she writes, "the arrival at a residential location involves an appraisal of the character of place. . . . Whereas sedentary groups establish a place, modify the space, organize within it, structure it, and build it, many mobile groups find an appropriate location and adjust their activities to the circumstance and setting. Thus, it is a 'selection' of place rather than a 'creation' of place that differentiates mobile groups. This difference is fundamental for understanding the ways mobile groups use space and transform the properties of a place."[15]

The ephemeral traces of short-term dwellings are easily overlooked, even in sites that are not particularly old. For example, Seymour has studied the material traces of dwellings at one of the last camps occu-

FIGURE 5. Geronimo's Camp, 1886. Library of Congress.

pied by Geronimo and his band at Cañon de los Embudos, in northern Sonora, Mexico. Harried by the U.S. cavalry and threatened by the Mexican army, Geronimo's band numbered three dozen men, women, and children. Camped among the rocky ridges, the refugees fashioned circular huts by clearing the stony surface, making a dome of spiny ocotillo stalks—some still rooted and merely bent over and tied—tented with canvas and blankets.

Obviously, this Apache band was under extraordinary stress, and it would be tempting to see these impermanent huts as the scant shelters of desperate peoples. Yet, as Seymour points out, the archaeological traces of the last camp at Cañon de los Embudos are similar to those found at other Apache sites: circular constructions of fieldstones, "sleeping circles" brushed clear of rocks, and similarly slight modifications of landscape. And while the reason for Geronimo's mobility (trying to evade impending attack by two different armies) was different, the response was similar to other hunters and gatherers who must frequently move: find a place that meets your needs, use the area, and move on.

Hunters and gatherers approach landscape in varying ways. Food-collecting societies may become more sedentary for different reasons. Some groups are seasonally tethered by the availability of fresh water, plant foods, or other critical resources. Other societies may be constrained by the presence of competing human societies. But one common pattern, as Binford has observed, is that hunters and gatherers tend to become less mobile the further they live from the Equator.

This seems to result from two central facts: 1) there are greater seasonal changes in ambient temperatures the further one moves from the Equator, and 2) the principal advantage of a dwelling is the regulation of heat loss. For example, a detailed analysis of the temperatures created in simple dwellings—replicas of windbreaks, shade structures, and simple huts—found that the real advantages of buildings are marked in colder climates: a domed hut with a warming fire is a better means for controlling temperatures than a sunshade in a hot environment.[16] While this seems a fairly obvious conclusion, it suggests that one would expect people to build more substantial dwellings as they moved into more rigorous environments.

That is precisely what occurred in the Upper Paleolithic (at about 45,000 to 13,000 years ago) in Europe during the Last Glacial Maximum. As modern humans migrated from Africa into Eurasia and beyond, they adapted to new and often challenging environments using a variety of technologies—including shelters. Sometime between 37,000 and 34,000 years ago, humans had migrated almost to the Arctic Circle.[17] Continental glaciers reached their maximum extents between 33,000 and 26,500 years ago, a period of peak cold.[18] As expanding glaciers in western Europe drove people south to the Iberian Peninsula, the vast plains of eastern Europe remained occupied despite its severe climate.[19] At this time, temperatures of central and eastern Europe were roughly equivalent to northern and central Siberia today, with cool summers (10°C–11°C/50°F–52°F) and achingly frigid winters (−19°C–−27°C/−2.2°F–−17°F). In eastern Europe a vast expanse of tundra and permafrost steppe fronted the glacial sheet, forming a band of cold grasslands 200–300 kilometers wide. With winter temperatures that plunged below −30°C–−40°C, these periglacial steppes were severe landscapes that nonetheless supported dense herds of mammoths, bison, horses, and reindeer—big game that tempted hunters out onto the icy plains.

To survive in this environment, shelters were as essential as spearpoints and flake tools. Huts and tents extended the hunters' range beyond the limits of rock shelters and caves. As early as 30,000 years ago, structures 5–6 meters in diameter with indoor hearths were erected at sites in western Ukraine and Slovakia. By 25,000 years ago, at the Russian site of Gagarino on the Don River, hunters built circular, semi-subterranean winter homes by excavating shallow house pits 4–6 meters across and raising hide-covered tents. The people of Gagarino warmed themselves by hearths that burned bone on a treeless steppe.[20]

Bone was used for more than fuel. At a dozen sites in the Dnepr and

Desna river basins of Ukraine and Russia, people built their homes from mammoth bones.[21]

The mammoth-bone huts generally date to 15,000–14,000 years ago, after the Last Glacial Maximum but still sufficiently frigid to create a cold tundra-steppe environment. The sites were located on promontories and terraces, providing a commanding view of the game herds that moved in the river bottoms and ravines.

At Mezhrich (Mejiriche) four mammoth-bone houses were found. The houses are circular or oval, 3–6 meters in diameter, and enclosing a living area of 12–24 square meters. The curving Vs of mammoth mandibles were stacked along the base of the huts' walls; in one building 95 mammoth mandibles were incorporated into the base of the wall, 40 tusks may have served as roof supports, and a staggering 20,584 kilograms of mammoth bone was used for the dwelling. So much mammoth bone was required, it was necessary to stockpile bone and scavenge natural kill sites. It would have required ten men working four days just to build this house.

Outside, storage pits dug down to the permafrost kept meat cold. Besides mammoth meat, the tundra hunters ate a wide variety of game: ptarmigans and geese, horse, boar, musk ox, and hare. They also hunted for furs, killing ermine, fox, and wolverine.

Deep hearths warmed the inside of the houses and the houses held a wide array of artifacts. Chipped stone blades, scrapers, and burins. Worked bone needles, awls, and shaft straighteners. And there were decorative objects: pieces of amber from sources 100 kilometers away, necklaces and bracelets made from beads of fossilized marine shells from 300 kilometers away.

The massive mammoth-bone houses are amazing dwellings, although not the only places lived in by their occupants. As the archaeologist Olga Soffer points out, the mammoth dwellings represent a single, although essential, element in a larger hunting and gathering strategy. While the mammoth-bone dwelling encampments had evidence for a wide array of activities, other camps reflected a narrower range of pursuits. There were warm-season hunting camps, where dwellings were tents or other lightweight shelters. Sites with storage pits but with no evidence for dwellings were places where game was butchered and cached in the permafrost. Other sites were lithic workshops where stone was quarried and worked, but with little evidence for hunting and no structures. Some of these sites were occupied only once, while the sites with mammoth-bone dwellings were lived in again and again. But all the sites—

whether with solid mammoth-bone houses or hide tents—included shelter as the essential tool of the human adaptation.

• • •

The archaeology of ancient hunters and gatherers illuminates the significance of home. The creation of dwellings was a central innovation that allowed humans to occupy the diverse environments of earth, extending humanity's reach much as the portaledge allows climbers to scale otherwise unattainable peaks. Although our nonhuman primate relatives make nests—and as discussed in chapter 2, chimpanzees actually modify their nests in light of local conditions—only humans create a diverse array of dwellings. Paleolithic dwellings were vital for expansion into higher latitudes, especially during glacial periods. Dwellings allowed humans to range further, exploiting regions and resources inaccessible from rare and stationary rock shelters and caves.

And yet the creation of houses involved more than shelter. Mobile hunters and gatherers used dwellings to map onto landscape, incorporating new regions into the broad spaces that were part of their home ranges. Across that landscape mobile hunters and gatherers made camp. Those encampments varied in duration and placement as people lingered over abundant stocks of food, fled enemies, or buried their dead. For at least 25,000 years, humans have made substantial shelters as elements of a larger cultural strategy. Often, as in the case of Mezhrich, the dwellings became a place of return. When that occurred—and it did so at different places at different times for different reasons—new sets of connections were created between culture and shelter, connections that only intensified and changed as humans became more sedentary.

The archaeology of mobile homes shows how humans organize the spaces where they dwell. Work occurs in certain areas, the dead are buried in others, and—as the excavations at Kebara Cave demonstrate—humans have done this for more than 60,000 years. In open air encampments, people will tend to deal with messy or potentially dangerous tasks on the edge of camp, whether butchering reindeer at Pincevent during the Upper Paleolithic or rebuilding a truck engine in central Australia in the 1970s. This is not, I repeat, because the Alyawara are representatives of the Upper Paleolithic, but because this is what humans do. Whether in a desperate camp in the Sonoran desert or a comfortable encampment on the shores of the Sea of Galilee, we humans order space, we modify our worlds, and in that process we leave archaeological signatures of our passing.

CHAPTER 4

Durable Goods

A house is just a pile of stuff with a cover on it.

—George Carlin, *Braindroppings*

Enlightenment philosophers were fascinated by Savages. In their efforts to devise a natural history of social life, Enlightenment thinkers either imaginatively reconstructed the earliest stages of human life or extrapolated from the miscellany of ethnographic "data" gleaned from explorers' journals, missionaries' accounts, or classical Latin and Greek texts. Originally, these philosophers agreed, savage life was lived without farming, law, or permanent dwellings.

Whether this original state was "rude," as Montesquieu saw it, or an Edenic state of individual liberty, as Rousseau claimed, Enlightenment thinkers connected hunting and gathering, lawlessness, and impermanent dwellings. Central to these reconstructions was the assumption that hunting and gathering always required frequent movements in search of food. As the Scottish jurist John Millar described it: "A Savage who earns his food by hunting and fishing, or by gathering the spontaneous fruits from the earth, is incapable of attaining any considerable refinement in his pleasure. . . . His wants are few, and in proportion to the narrowness of his circumstances. His great object is to be able to satisfy his hunger; and, after the utmost exertion of labour and activity, to enjoy the agreeable relief of idleness and repose."[1]

This constant mobility, Montesquieu asserted, affected the institutions of society, as people wandered in grasslands and forests, mating in brief liaisons, unfettered by home-ownership, and given to "sometimes mix indifferently like brutes."[2]

In yet another passage linking homelessness and casual sex, Rousseau observed that the absence of permanent dwellings also meant social relationships were similarly transient, "whereas, in this primitive state, men had neither houses, nor huts, . . . every one lived where he could, seldom for more than a single night; the sexes united without design; . . . and they parted with the same indifference."[3]

The shift to agriculture and permanent dwellings led to the frictions of property, turning people against each other. Rousseau wrote that when people "ceased to fall asleep under the first tree, or in the first cave that afforded them shelter; they invented several kinds of implements of hard and sharp stones," thus introducing "a kind of property, in itself the source of a thousand quarrels and conflicts."[4]

Sedentism had additional consequences: lust and envy. In language simultaneously prurient and prudish, Rousseau imagined that "permanent neighbourhood could not fail to produce, in time, some connection between different families. Among young people of opposite sexes, living in neighbouring huts, the transient commerce required by nature soon led, through mutual intercourse, to another kind not less agreeable, and more permanent."

Although proximity and young love bound society together, permanence and neighborly scrutiny led to the sin of covetousness. "Men began now to take the difference between objects into account, and to make comparisons; they acquired imperceptibly the ideas of beauty and merit, which soon gave rise to feelings of preference. In consequence of seeing each other often, they could not do without seeing each other constantly. A tender and pleasant feeling insinuated itself into their souls, and the least opposition turned it into an impetuous fury: with love arose jealousy; discord triumphed, and human blood was sacrificed to the gentlest of all passions."[5]

Many of these Enlightenment speculations were simply wrong, and archaeologists have long known this. In 1936 the archaeologist V. Gordon Childe wrote, "The adoption of cultivation must not be confused with the adoption of sedentary life. It has been customary to contrast the settled life of the cultivator with the nomadic existence of the 'homeless hunter.' The contrast is quite fictitious."[6] Childe famously coined the term "Neolithic Revolution," underscoring the seismic transformations that occurred when humans domesticated plants and animals. Childe understood, however, that agriculture and sedentism were two distinct, though often linked, phenomena.[7]

In contrast to the overblown Enlightenment musings, archaeology does point to two fundamental truths: Societies change when they form permanent settlements and where you live depends a lot on your stuff.

. . .

In the waning decades of the twentieth century, my wife and I moved thirteen times in six years. While this was hardly an itinerant lifestyle compared to highly mobile hunters and gatherers like the Ache of Paraguay, who reportedly moved fifty times each year, we had them beat in distance, thanks to the internal combustion engine and jet turbines.

In August 1988 we left Santa Barbara, California, and took separate jobs in Manhattan, Kansas, and Minneapolis, Minnesota, where we each taught as one-year temporary lecturers in anthropology departments. At that point our peregrinations began in earnest: we went from Kansas and Minnesota to southern Mexico (for fieldwork); back to Minneapolis (teaching); and then to Antigua Guatemala (a Fulbright grant); on to Albany, New York ("soft-money" research jobs); to Southern California (finally, a tenure-track job); back to Albany (birth of son); south to Washington, D.C. (fellowship); back to Albany (summer jobs and housesitting); return to Southern California (return to tenure-track job); then to the United Kingdom (fellowship); and finally back to Southern California in August 1994.

It was a six-year *Wanderjahre* that covered 30,862 miles.

About midway through this phase of our lives (I think we were in Guatemala), someone pointed out that all the time I had spent moving was the equivalent of getting up on a Saturday morning, loading up my truck, driving nonstop until Sunday afternoon, parking and unloading the truck . . . and doing this every weekend for three years. It was a very depressing analogy.

We seriously considered renting a self-storage unit near the geographical center of the lower forty-eight states. We calculated this would be around Kansas City, Missouri, where the north-south Interstate 35 and the east-west Interstate 40 intersect. That way, if we needed something in the course of another cross-country journey—"Do you know whatever happened to the espresso maker?"—we could simply swing by and pick it up.

Although our situation seems excessive, it was not far from the average American experience. According to the U.S. Census Bureau, the average American moves 11.7 times in a lifetime, although most people move relatively short distances. Fifty-seven percent of Americans have never lived outside of their home state; 37% have never left their hometown.[8] Since the 1950s, when more than 20% of Americans changed residences each year, Americans' mobility actually has decreased, although 11%–12% of Americans moved in 2008 alone.

A number of factors account for Americans' mobility. The principle reason for moving is employment: people move to find work and support themselves, a rationale understandable to any hunter-gatherer. Interestingly, people who *earn* more *move* more. Only 25% of Americans with household incomes of $100,000 or more live in the community where they were born. Similarly, more educated Americans have moved more, going away to college and then moving on to pursue jobs.

The young move more than the elderly. Westerners move more than Midwesterners. When Americans move, they tend to head south.

These patterns of mobility in the United States are not shared by other industrialized nations. Overall, Europeans move about half as much as Americans.[9] While mobility in the United Kingdom and the Scandinavian countries approaches the American pace, in other nations—such as Italy, Portugal, Greece, and Ireland—less than 5% of the population moves annually.

So despite a decrease in mobility over the last sixty years, Americans still move a lot. Which you would think would mean that we would have less stuff.

But if you have moved recently, you know that isn't true.

. . .

The prehistoric shift to permanent dwellings and settled villages occurred after 18,000–15,000 years ago, but at various times in different places for distinct reasons. In southwestern Japan in southern Kyushu, summer villages and winter villages existed by 13,500 years ago. These were the prehistoric forebears of a durable cultural tradition known as Jomon.[10] The Jomon tradition lasted for approximately 10,000 years, the name ("cord-marked") associated with the distinctive pottery with its twine-stamped exterior, some of the earliest ceramic vessels known in the world. Initially recognized from its pottery, more recent archaeological research has pushed knowledge of Jomon back in time to its preceramic antecedents.

The origins of sedentism in Japan is nuts. Quite literally nuts, because the diet was based on acorns, beechnuts, walnuts, buckeyes, and chestnuts. Previously, Paleolithic foragers had used stone mortars, pestles, and hammer-stones to crack and pulverize nuts to supplement their diets. But as climate warmed and deciduous broadleaf groves replaced conifer forests, nuts became staples in ancient Japanese cuisine.[11]

The earliest Jomon houses were pit-houses or tents associated with other features that suggested a prolonged stay. Special hearths with sloping underground flues may have been used to smoke meat. Heavy grinding stones—some weighing more than 85 pounds—indicate sustained encampments.

Even more substantial and permanent communities developed by 13,000 years ago. For example, the site of Uenohara contains one area—Sector 4—that was the largest known Japanese settlement of its time. Spread over 13,000 square meters, the site has 52 house pits, a dozen of which were occupied at a single time during the four different phases in the hamlet's history. The houses were roughly rectangular, approximately 3 × 5 meters in area, and some of the dwellings had ventilated hearths. In addition to the houses, storage pits and networks of paths indicate that Uenohara was a permanent Jomon village, inhabited until 12,800 years ago when it was covered by ash and cinders from a nearby volcano's eruption.

Despite this volcanic setback at Uenohara, over subsequent millennia sedentary life was fundamental to Jomon culture. Throughout the Japanese archipelago, the number of Jomon sites increased through time with population peaking after 5000 B.C. during the Middle Jomon period. Houses became more substantial, especially in the cooler northern islands.

Given the Jomon tradition's long duration, it is not surprising that settlements would vary in size and composition. But most known Jomon sites are small; most Jomon houses are tiny. In part, these limits were not a mark of failure, but an index of sustainability. Bigger is not always better.

Located in the middle of the bustling port city of Aomori on the northern tip of Honshu, the site of Sannai Marayama is the largest known Jomon site.[12] Discovered in the mid-1990s during a construction project, the site was excavated and then preserved as a major cultural center. More than 600 buildings have been uncovered at Sannai Marayama, dating over 12 phases between 3900 and 2300 B.C. Most of these houses were small pit houses and rectangular raised dwellings less than 5 meters long. A few much larger buildings were constructed, a couple of them 23–32 meters long, but it is unclear what these structures were or exactly how long they were occupied.

FIGURE 6. Reconstructions of Jomon houses at Sannai Maruyama.

In the case of the Jomon, it was not the sheer abundance of food that allowed for larger and more permanent homes and hamlets. Rather, it was the timing and location of foods that selected for those human responses. Acorns, chestnuts, buckeyes, and walnuts were harvested in the fall, stored in pits, and eaten throughout the winter. Fall was also the time for fishing for migrating salmon, hunting fat deer, and—in general—preparing stored foods for winter.[13]

Such a diet tends to select for sedentary life, especially when different habitats are relatively close. Living near the ocean in a delta crossed by rivers and streams and with densely forested hills and mountains only 5–10 kilometers to the south, the people of Sannai Marayama were ideally positioned to take advantage of rich natural resources. Similar factors account for Jomon sedentism through much of the Japanese archipelago.

And that explains the successful growth of the community—until it grew just a little too big.

The excavations uncovered a complex history of ancient Japanese homes. For much of its history, Sannai Marayama was a modest village, larger than Uenohara, but usually with fewer than 50 dwellings, housing 200–300 people. In the middle of the Middle Jomon, however, the settlement experienced a building boom, growing into a large village of

200 houses. But after reaching this peak population, Sannai Marayama withered in size, reverting to a modest village of people living in small huts.

What happened?

Junko Habu, an archaeologist from the University of California, Berkeley, who has excavated at Sannai Marayama, argues that the site's population grew to unsustainable levels. Because of poor preservation, ancient plant and animal remains were unevenly preserved at the site. In order to gain an indirect insight into subsistence at Sannai Marayama, Habu analyzed in great detail the different stone tools used in hunting, gathering, and food preparation (like inferring dietary differences based on the ratios of salad forks to steak knives in a vegan's and a meat-lover's respective kitchens).

Habu's analysis pointed to major shifts in subsistence over time. Beginning with the Early Jomon levels, the relative number of grinding stones increased, until peaking in the early phases of the Middle Jomon, when these tools used for grinding plants comprised 80% of all the stone tools. Then the pattern changed calamitously: the percentage of grinding tools was halved and arrowheads became the most common stone tool. The preponderance of arrowheads marked an increased emphasis on hunted game rather than collected plant foods.

Habu argues that the people of Sannai Marayama were victims of overspecialization. When hunters and gatherers are mobile, they usually collect and hunt a wide array of plants and animals. When hunters and gatherers become more sedentary, they become more specialized. The people of Sannai Maruyama could no longer be sustained by wild plant foods. Adjustments were critical. People first tried to make up for lost calories by hunting more; that was not enough. The community inevitably declined. Ultimately Jomon hunting and gathering—a supremely successful adaptation for more than ten thousand years—gave way to village life based on cultivating rice.

This is one of the fundamental lessons from the past. Human communities may evolve extraordinarily successful ways of life, but they do this by making specific choices with often unforeseen consequences. In the process, the range of possible options inevitably narrows, which presents a problem when circumstances change. The changes need not be dramatic, just enough to tip the balance of stability. When this happens, humans—like all other animals—have a fundamental choice: Adapt or die.

And here is another lesson from the past: transitions are reversible. Like the Enlightenment philosophers, we often think of human history as progressing inevitably from gathering to farming, from wind-breaks to substantial dwellings, from mobile hunters to sedentary town folk and city dwellers. But prehistory demonstrates that these cultural thresholds, once crossed, are not inevitably permanent.

. . .

In the last six decades, we Americans have doubled our rates of consumption and we are paying the price. Measured in constant 1982 dollars, the average American spent $6,600 on consumption in 1947; in 1990 that number had grown to $14,400.[14] Which means that although the average American house size has increased (see chapter 5) and the average American family has decreased, we literally have tons and tons more stuff.

If you move from your comfortable three-bedroom, 2,000-square-foot house, you will need to schlep about 16,000 pounds of stuff (this is after the garage sale and the trip to the dump).[15]

Our most mobile home-owning fellow Americans—people whose only homes are their recreational vehicles—calculate that their RV's must be sufficiently sturdy to accommodate 1,500 pounds of stuff per person (and remember, this doesn't count their already built-in beds, fridge, stoves, and other furnishings).[16]

Correlated with our consumptions is the growth in self-storage facilities, now a $20 billion business.[17] Worldwide there are approximately 60,000 self-storage facilities; 52,000 of them are in the United States. In 1984 there were 6,601 storage facilities with a total volume of 289.7 million square feet. By late 2008 this had increased more that 800% to 2.35 billion square feet. The single largest self-storage facility in the United States is thought to be Alpine Storage, an enormous, sixteen-acre facility located in north Salt Lake City, with easy access from Interstate 15.

The burdens of the American dream are demonstrated by ongoing archaeological research into modern material culture. At the University of California, Los Angeles, the Sloan Center on Everyday Lives of Families includes a research group led by the archaeologist Jeanne Arnold. Arnold is an expert on the evolution of prehistoric Chumash chiefdoms on the coast of Santa Barbara, California, and on late prehistoric and contact period Sto:lo villages in the Fraser River Valley of British Columbia. In these regions, Arnold's research frequently considered how ancient households were reshaped by changing patterns of politics and economy.

Since 2001, Arnold has applied archaeological methods to modern

American households. Beginning with a sample of homes in Los Angeles, Arnold and her team carefully mapped houses with detailed locations of modern artifacts. Residents were video-interviewed about their ideas and uses of domestic spaces. The researchers systematically clocked how people used different parts of their homes and backyards, contrasting what informants *said* they did with what they actually *did*. Digital photos recorded interiors and exteriors, resulting in a 21,000-image archive of the use of domestic space in early twenty-first-century America.

Arnold and her colleagues have documented "archaeologically" the modern American "storage crisis."[18] The crisis has various causes—the increase in American consumerism, the explosion of goods—but also results from some unexpected factors illuminated by the modern archaeology of home.

Collecting data in the Los Angeles area before the recession-driven foreclosures of 2008–2012, Arnold and coauthor Ursula Lang noted that skyrocketing real estate prices had forced middle-class families into less-expensive housing, including older and smaller houses. Unlike homes in the Midwest and East, California houses rarely have basements for heaters, and attics are smaller because ridgelines are lower, since steep roofs are not necessary to shed snow.

So that leaves the garage.

As the garage was transformed from a carriage shed in the backyard or alley to an integrated sector of a house, the garage became, as the late landscape historian J.B. Jackson noted, "thoroughly domesticated, an integral part of home life and the routine of work and play."[19]

And in that process, the garage's function changed. No longer a place for protecting automobiles, especially in the mild weather of Southern California, the garage was transformed into home office, entertainment, and exercise areas, but preeminently a place for stuff.

Only 25% of the households in Arnold and Lang's study actually parked a car in the garage, and nobody used the space exclusively for an auto.

Most families didn't even try.

Some garages had been converted into bedrooms or recreation areas, but the majority of garages were exclusively for storage. "The garages of middle-class America," Arnold and Lang write, "are suffering an identity crisis."

The disorder of the middle-class American life is captured by the qualitative variable used to describe storage in 14 of the 24 houses in the study: "chaotic."[20]

There is no doubt that American consumerism is excessive at a global scale. As the planet's principal consumers of fossil fuels and everything else, one would expect no less. Even so, is ours the only society that has too much stuff?

Obviously, the spreading forces of globalization encourage the "global consumer culture." Studies of global household wealth indicate the shameful inequalities: the wealthiest 10% of the world's adults own approximately 85% of global wealth, while the poorest 50% scrape by with barely 1% of global wealth.[21] So clearly, current consumption in the developed world—and particularly in the United States—is excessive by global standards.

But how does this translate into material possessions? The World Bank's Living Standards Measurement Study provides national summaries for a number of developing countries, but a more visual if less systematic view of global consumption is found in the photography collection, *Material Worlds: A Global Family Portrait*.[22]

The project was designed by the photojournalist Peter Menzel, as "a unique tool for capturing cross-cultural realities." In the early 1990s, Menzel and a team of photographers focused on thirty of the 183 countries that belonged to the United Nations. In each sample country, Menzel and colleagues chose families that reflected the national average according to location, type of dwelling, family size, annual income, occupation, and religion.

Menzel and fifteen other world-class photojournalists photographed these families at meals, at work, studying school lessons, and worshiping. But the key image was the Big Picture: "a unique photo of each family with all its possessions outside its dwelling."[23]

Not surprisingly, the differences are striking.

The Thoroddsen family of Hafnarfjördur, Iceland, stand outside their three-bedroom, 2,000-square-foot home in the violet twilight of a December afternoon. They are surrounded by two televisions, a pair of Icelandic horses, two cars in the driveway, a showroom's worth of furnishings, a bevy of kitchen appliances, and two cellos. Still inside the Thoroddsen house are a baby grand piano, hundreds of books, miscellaneous housewares, and six canaries.

The Calabay Sicay family lives in San Antonio de Palopó, a village on the edge of Lake Atitlán in the highlands of Guatemala. They sit on the family bed outside their one room adobe house. A new corrugated metal roof, a glistening porcelain toilet perched above a latrine hole, and a portable two-speaker stereo all point to this family's success. A large floor loom, a smaller loom, and a spinning wheel are tools the mother uses to weave bright scarlet cloth. The father's farming implements—wide-bladed hoes, a single-bit axe, machetes, and a sickle—are in neat piles or hang from the wall. Just outside the separate, small, and smoke-blackened cookhouse are large clay pots, a stone metate, water jugs, and serving jars. A frying pan, a sieve, and a thermos dangle from nails in the adobe wall.

The poorest family photographed in *Material Worlds* is the Getu family of Moulo, Ethiopia. In 1994 Ethiopia ranked 180th in affluence among the 183 U.N. countries. Outside the Getu's 320-square-foot home, the mother and five children, ages eight months to ten years, perch on the family bed. The father stands between his two oxen. One of his three horses is nearby and five cattle are in the corral. There is a waist-tall wooden mortar and long pestle pole for milling grain. An assortment of storage, serving, and winnowing baskets. Pottery water jugs and cooking pots. A tea kettle and cups. Frying pans. Empty tin cans used as drinking cups. The Getu family also has a radio, but the battery is dead.

Each image in *Material World* is a fascinating glimpse of global domestic life, an intimate perspective on the objects that make up home. And although there are marked and obvious disparities in the range and variety of each family's possessions, there is a basic truth common to them all.

No one could carry all their stuff.

This is not a trivial point. After about 15,000 years ago, human societies in different portions of the world increasingly relied on stored food—foodstuffs initially collected, then cultivated, and eventually farmed. With those changes, the configurations of our material culture diversified and our stuff weighed more. When that happened, our homes changed from principally places of temporary shelter into refuges for ourselves and our possessions.

Which is what also happened in the deserts and mountains of the ancient Near East.

. . .

The Near East has been the focus of archaeological excavations—amateurish, piratical, and professional—for more than a century.[24] The first permanent archaeological research group ever established, the Palestine Expedition Fund, was founded in 1865 with the goal of sponsoring sustained programs of excavations. Despite being modeled on the outstanding successes of Austen Henry Layard's multiyear investigations of Nineveh, the Palestine Expedition Fund was not an immediate success. Only after World War I came to its bloody end were sustained archaeological projects developed.

Dorothy Garrod (1892–1968) was an amazing archaeologist whose extensive fieldwork transformed knowledge of the ancient Near East and the Zagros Mountains of eastern Iraq and western Iran.[25] From a distinguished British family of scientists and doctors, Garrod was trained as a Paleolithic archaeologist by the eminent French prehistorian, Abbé Breuil. Garrod excavated Upper Paleolithic deposits in then-lawless Kurdistan, her team accompanied by armed guards. Later, in northern Israel, Garrod directed a multiyear excavation that richly documenting the existence of non-European Neanderthals in the caves surrounding Mt. Carmel—one of the most important excavations in the Near East. Garrod's outstanding accomplishments were recognized in 1939 with her appointment as the Disney Professor of Archaeology at Cambridge University. Garrod was the first female professor at Cambridge (or Oxford, for that matter), a barrier-breaking appointment which was made without significant resistance. She was, as her former student recalled, "a valued member of a valued class."[26]

Garrod's excavations in the Mt. Carmel vicinity began as a salvage archaeology project when the caves were slated to be quarried. Garrod had originally planned to continue excavations at the Cave of Shukbah on the Wadi-en-Natuf in the Judean Desert, where Garrod had found, as she remarks in her clear and understated prose, "a microlithic culture that would not fit exactly into any of the pigeon-holes already existing, and I therefore decided to give it a label of its own."[27] She called it "Natufian" after the Wadi-en-Natuf.

More Natufian materials were uncovered during the Mt. Carmel excavations, including adult skeletons who still wore delicate ringlets of shells around their skulls. The most distinctive Natufian tools were the microlithic blades used on stone sickles. The chipped flints were serrated on one edge, dulled and blunt on their back side, and snapped off at each end into roughly rectangular flakes. The microliths were hafted on bone handles, creating a nearly continuous edge to form sickles. There was other evidence for processing plant foods: heavy mortars, basalt bowls, and other grinding stones. It was an assemblage that could have been used by early farmers.

Yet, all the animal remains were from wild game. None of the Natufian levels had pottery, which prehistorians expected to be associated with agriculture. Garrod concluded, "In the circumstances it may seem surprising that we get evidence of the practice of agriculture at such an early date among a people who possess no pottery and do not appear to have domesticated animals."[28] Garrod's basic assumption was flawed: the Natufians intensively collected wild plants, but they did not farm.

The Natufian tradition is now recognized as a transformative moment in the past. The Natufian strategy of complex hunting and gathering was, in a sense, a conceptual and adaptive bridge between the mobile hunters and gatherers of the late Paleolithic and the early farmers of the Neolithic. Of course, to the Natufians, their "strategy" was a mix of calculated actions, unforeseen consequences, and human responses—a combination of planning and accident that usually characterizes human life.

Since the 1970s, increasingly precise radiocarbon dates and high-resolution data about ancient climate have resulted in a remarkably detailed understanding of the changing post-Pleistocene world of the western portion of the Near East known as the Levant.[29]

In the Levant, rain falls in the winter months between October and May, but annual variations result in frequent droughts. At a longer time scale, the Levant underwent several long-term shifts in climate and vegetation over the last 25,000 years.

As Paleolithic Europeans shivered through the Last Glacial Maximum at approximately 24,050 years ago, climate in the western Near East was cold and dry, although the coastal mountains near the Mediterranean were well watered and forested. After 17,450 years ago, rainfall gradually increased throughout the region, and then precipitation increased dramatically between 16,000 and 13,300 years ago. These damp millennia were followed by a thousand years of drier conditions between 13,000 and 12,000 years ago. After 12,200 years ago, there was a general increase in rainfall in the northern Levant and Anatolia, while the southern Levant remained dry.

It is an oversimplification to summarize 12,000 years of paleoclimate in the language of a weekend forecast from the Weather Channel. Yet, this synopsis captures some of the generous opportunities and stark challenges to which people adapted in the Near East.

During the initial dry and cold period, small groups of mobile hunters and gatherers ranged along the coast and camped by oases, leaving behind an archaeological tradition called the Kebaran (yet another archaeological complex first named by Dorothy Garrod). As the climate became wetter, Kebaran hunters and gatherers migrated into previously uninhabitable regions. Some Kebaran groups used small stone blades, snapped into rectangular and trapezoidal shapes, thus leading to the name "Geometric" Kebaran for this prehistoric culture. Geometric Kebaran sites are found from northern Syria to the Negev and southern Sinai, former deserts transformed into grassland steppes by wetter conditions. Similar to earlier Kebaran sites, the Geometric Kebaran settlements were small, impermanent, and lacked substantial dwellings. They were the camps of mobile hunters who stalked gazelle, ibex, and hare.

The same wetter conditions that allowed for the expansion of mobile Geometric Kebaran groups created environmental opportunities for a significantly different human adaptation, the Early Natufian. The Early Natufians collected nuts in oak and pistachio woodlands, avoiding both the high mountains of Syria and the low steppes to the south. Between 15,450 and 14,750 years ago, permanent and semipermanent encampments were established in the forested hills of the Levant.

The key to Early Natufian success was that old real estate adage: location, location, location. Early Natufian groups established base camps within striking distances of different habitats: nut-bearing pistachio and oak forests, stands of wild cereals and legumes, and the migration routes of gazelles.

And in those strategic locations, the Early Natufians established homes.

Some Early Natufian base camps covered 1000 square meters. Houses were semi-subterranean pit houses, elliptical in plan, and 3–6 meters in diameter.[30] Early Natufian houses were built from upright posts that probably supported roof joists covered with brush. The walls had stone foundations. Cooking hearths were in the center of the house. A particularly large Early Natufian house at Ain Mallaha (Eynan), Israel, was more than 9 meters across and contained multiple hearths, perhaps for communal gatherings.

Diverse strands of evidence suggest that the Early Natufians lived in their base camps for much of the year or year-round, seasonally migrating to short-term encampments and then returning home.[31] Their substantial houses suggest lengthy stays, and heavy plant processing tools—like stone mortars weighing 150 kilograms—indicate a less mobile strategy. Analysis of gazelle teeth recovered from Natufian sites indicate that the gazelles were hunted throughout the year, also suggesting long-stay occupations.[32] Despite the general absence of plant remains (either due to poor preservation or earlier excavations that did not search for smaller objects), two lines of evidence point to food storage in the base camps: storage pits and vermin (especially the bones of house mice and rats).

All of this occurred 2,000 years before the earliest agriculture. Centuries before farming, Early Natufian societies had developed a successful sedentary life.

Until the climate changed.

When drier conditions developed between 12,800 and 11,500 years ago, the oak-pistachio woodland retreated to higher elevations where more rain fell. Wild cereals grew at lower elevations. The habitats exploited by Early Natufians were no longer all within striking distance from permanent settlements. Many Late Natufian sites were smaller, suggesting a return to mobility. At other places people stubbornly persisted in settled life and overexploited the local resources.

The old ways were unsustainable. Only two options existed: become more mobile or change the environment.

Many groups chose mobility, but some people began to modify natural habitats. Wild grains—such as native varieties of barley and rye—were collected and reseeded closer to home. Native legumes, including the ancient ancestor of peas, were collected and planted. Soils were tilled, as indicated by the intrusive species of weeds that rooted in disturbed earth. Fig trees were transplanted. And while these efforts did not result in the genetic transformations that mark domesticated crops, the pathway to agriculture had been taken.[33]

The success of these first innovations is indicated by the development of large granaries by these preagricultural cultivators. In the 1990s, archaeologists Ian Kuijt and Bill Finlayson excavated the site of Dhra', located in Jordan near the Dead Sea, and found the earliest known evidence for massive food storage in human history.[34]

Two types of storage units were built by the people of Dhra': small bins and large communal silos. Although the large silos were not enormous—they were about 3 × 3 meters in size—they were impressive structures because of a unique floor design. The floor was raised above the ground surface in an early example of pier and beam construction. Upright stones, 35–50 centimeters tall, were notched to support crossbeams that were covered by wooden floors and mud-plastered reeds. The raised floors kept stored foods above the damp; air circulated underneath and protected supplies from insects and rodents. Burnt chunks of clay indicate mud-plastered walls and roofs. Built 11,300 and 11,200 years ago, these silos preceded the first agriculture in the Levant by a thousand years.

Dhra' may not be the only site with such silos, Kuijt and Finlayson suggest, and the organization of storage at Dhra' differed dramatically from previous Natufian settlements and later farming communities. At about 10,500 years ago, the communal silos at Dhra' were abandoned and storage moved inside houses. A thousand years later, storerooms and larders were built inside of residences. Writing of the "increasingly 'built world' of the Neolithic," Kuijt and Finlayson observe, "although much debate has focused on the emergence of the home, equally important transition is seen in the appearance of built-in plant food processing and storage features. These practices collectively reflect a significant increase in energy invested in buildings and the permanence of these settlements."[35]

Whether among the Jomon or the Natufian food collectors or early Near Eastern cultivators, sedentism did not wait for agriculture. People lived in permanent houses long before they tilled and plowed domesticated crops. When societies began to base their year's food supply on plants seasonally harvested and stored, or when heavy tools were necessary to render food edible, people became sedentary. And this process occurred in different ways around the world.

Sedentism did not result from agriculture. Sedentism developed when people had too much stuff.

. . .

Like most Americans, I have too much stuff. My wife and I, both of us archaeologists, do not own a lot of consumer products (or at least we do not think we do). Our television is small, our CD player was purchased in 1989, and our cell phones can only be used to make calls. Books are our weightiest weakness; five to ten volumes seem to arrive each week and we rarely get rid of any: scholarly books, mystery novels, cookbooks.

But our largest class of clutter is mementos. Most are folkcrafts and objects we have brought home from fieldwork in Latin America, supplemented by gifts that other anthropological friends have brought home from their fieldwork sites. Objects in wood, pottery, metal, and cloth, these items occupy every flat and vertical surface of our home.

As one small sample, here is a list of objects on the mantelpiece over our fireplace, a flat surface ten inches wide and five feet long. Beginning at the far left:

A small handmade doll fashioned by the Paipai of northern Baja California.

A stone pestle from the Caribbean, a large tear-drop of pecked and smoothed basalt.

A hammered metal cross from southern Mexico.

An ex-voto to the Virgin of Juquila, Oaxaca, from one Jesús Aguirre Morales, thanking the Virgin for her protection during a truck accident in March 1972.

A papier-mâché image of San Simon seated in a wooden chair, holding a baton of authority, smoking a cigar, and wearing a broad-brimmed, black hat; San Simon is the Catholicized version of the prehispanic Guatemalan deity, Maximón.

A carved wooden image of Santiago, the patron saint of the Spanish conquest and of Guatemala, astride a horse with sword raised.

A small tile from Ayacucho, Peru, showing Santiago in full gallop, his rearing horse trampling a prone infidel.

A small retablo from Peru, a shallow upright box with doors that open to disclose a small scene of ceramic figurines. Originally, a portable religious shrine for muleteers guiding pack-trains, the retablo has been adopted as a genre of Andean folk art.

A small Mexican box holding two miniature dioramas depicting the classic calavera skeletons from Day of the Dead. One shows an altar from the Day of the Dead, a minute example of self-reference where figures portraying the dead represent the living. The second is even less reverential, showing a skeleton playing billiards using grinning skulls as pool balls.

And next to this, wrapped in reddish-brown velvet, a small urn holds my mother-in-law's ashes.

. . .

In *The Dominion of the Dead*, Robert Pogue Harrison writes eloquently of the relationship between dwellings of the living and the resting places of the dead.[36] Architecture is, Harrison argues, part of the larger human project of instantiation, in which we create "the places where human time, in its historical and existential modes, takes place. Such places—be they homes, buildings, cities, or landscapes—are recesses of mortal time in which we go about inhabiting the world historically rather than merely naturally." Harrison adds, that "when we build something in nature, be it a dwelling, a monument, or even a fire, we create the rudiments of a world and thereby give a sign of our mortal sojourn on the earth."

While the archaeological record does not support Harrison's claim that "human beings housed their dead before they housed themselves," the link between construction and continuity rings true. "To inhabit the world humanly one must be a creature of legacy," Harrison writes. "[The living] placed [the dead] in graves, coffins, urns—in any case they placed them in something that we call their resting places so that their legacies could be retrieved and their afterlives perpetuated."[37]

We should not assume that such practices are universal. For example, the ethnographer Beth Conklin describes how until the 1950s the Wari' of the Ecuadorian Amazon, commemorated their dead loved ones through ritualized endocannibalism, a ceremonial practice of instantiation by ingestion.[38]

Nonetheless, one of the most common practices in prehistory was the connection between residence and residents, living and dead. *Cemetery* comes, via Latin, from the ancient Greek for *dormitory,* and variations on this metaphoric parallel between death and slumber are common among world cultures. Further, the creation of cemeteries in contrast to isolated burials is an archaeological signature of territory.

This differs from the connection between people and place among mobile hunters and gatherers. For example, Judith Littleton has studied over fifteen hundred precontact aboriginal burials in southeastern Australia, and she has identified specific patterns in the topographic features of burial-places (such as on the tops of dunes, small hummocks, and other raised features). Yet, even when a number of burials occur together, radiocarbon dates suggest that those interments could be separated by centuries. This reflects, Littleton suggests, a situation "where place persists but people do not. . . . Even if a group leaves an area and is eventually replaced by others, the landscape symbols attract similar but new stories and designs. . . . The significance of the landscape persists because people share a model of how to occupy and react to it, rather than a specific knowledge or memory."[39]

The connection between place and people changed with increasing sedentism, and this is equally visible in the archaeological record of Japan and the Near East.

In both the Jomon and Natufian traditions, permanent cemeteries were created after the development of substantial dwellings, but not *immediately* thereafter. The archaeologist Yosuhiro Okada points out that although a sedentary strategy was adopted at approximately 7000–6000 B.C. in the Initial Jomon period, cemeteries were not created until the Middle Jomon at circa 3500–2500 B.C., when the dead were placed in the center of Jomon settlements.[40] At Sannai Maruyama, the Middle Jomon residents built earthen mounds, rectangular raised floor buildings, and dug floors and postholes for dozens of pithouses. The Middle Jomon dwellings cut into Early Jomon features, but carefully avoided the Middle Jomon grave pits and burials in the cemetery. Jar burials contained children; pit graves held adults. "The distribution patterns of these features are not random," Okada writes, "each type tends to be located within a restricted area." Sannai Maruyama was not unique. Cemeteries were common in Middle Jomon sites, leading Okada to quite reasonably suggest that "ancestor worship was an important category of ritual activities to Middle Jomon people." Accompanied by mound building and increased quantities of ceramic figurines, the Middle Jomon appears to be a phase in which place, ceremony, and identity are linked—anchored in place.

A similar trajectory occurred in the Near East. Cemeteries were not created as soon as people built substantial and relatively permanent homes. Natufian people buried their dead in settlements, but either outside dwellings or in graves dug into the floors of abandoned pithouses. Sometimes the graves held a single individual, and sometimes the corpses of several people. At other times and places, secondary burials were interred in Natufian settlements, particularly during the Late Natufian, possibly reflecting a symbolic compromise: during arid centuries the need for more nomadic strategies combined with a sense of continuity and place. People died during the search for food, but their bones were returned home.

The manipulation of bones became more common during the Early Neolithic in the Near East. At 10,300–9,300 years ago, only the skulls of adults and adolescents were removed, and infants and children were buried whole in primary burials. The adult skulls do not exhibit cut marks, and headless but otherwise complete skeletons have been found, suggesting that the crania were removed after the flesh and tendons had decayed. Grave markers may have been placed so the burials could be relocated and the skulls removed. While these practices constituted a form of secondary burial, they do not represent the pressures of mobility. Instead the skulls denote a connection between people and place.

These burial patterns had their origins during the Late Natufian. Ian

Kuijt has discussed some of the implications of changing burial practices.[41] During the Early Natufian (ca. 12,500–11,500 years ago), it was common for people to be buried in groups, either as primary or secondary burials, but always with their skulls. In the Late Natufian (11,500–10,300 years ago), although adults continue to be buried in groups, skulls were removed for the first time, and on rare instances, were reburied in small caches of three to six skulls. By the Early Neolithic/Pre-Pottery Neolithic A (10,300–9,300 years ago), group burials no longer occurred, skull removal became common, yet multiple crania burials remained rare. Finally in Pre-Pottery Neolithic B phase (9,300–8,500 years ago), multiple crania burials became common.

Changes in burial practices were accompanied by variations in villages and houses in the Levant. Beginning in the Late Natufian, the size of settlements increased dramatically, from 2,000-square-meter encampments of 60 people to sizeable towns of more than 3,300 people that sprawled over 140,000 square meters by the Late Pre-Pottery Neolithic B period. Not only did communities grow larger, the settlements became densely built environments. In the Late Natufian, dwellings occupied 20%–50% of the site with the remaining area preserved as open space. In Late Pre-Pottery Neolithic B period sites, houses covered 80%–90% of the sites creating jam-packed settlements.

As houses became more densely packed, two things happened. First, interior space was subdivided into small and smaller components, most notably storage bins. Second, for the first time, two-story buildings were constructed. In other words, space was at a premium, crops, tools, and other things had to be stored, and there was nowhere to go but up.

People living between 9,300–8,500 years ago in the Near East encountered a problem recognizable to the twenty-first-century A.D. dwellers of Los Angeles: Too much stuff.

But what about the skull burials?

Kuijt argues that the accumulation of things resulted in social tensions that Late Pre-Pottery Neolithic B communities tried to address, symbolically referencing earlier and less materialistic times. The burial of multiple crania was a ritual practice that emphasized community over individual.

Similar to the way that in the United States, households earning anywhere from $30,000 to $200,000 may categorize themselves as "middle class," residents of the Late Pre-Pottery Neolithic B communities, Kuijt argues, had good reasons to minimize their socio-economic differences via rituals that underscored common ancestry and faux egalitarianism.

In that process, the connections between people, dwellings, and communities fundamentally changed. Elsewhere in the Near East, the house became an enduring point of human actions, built and remodeled, equipped with ceremonial fittings and wall decorations, and ultimately a repository for human skulls. Writing of the site of Qemerz Dere, an early Neolithic site in northern Iraq contemporary with the Late Pre-Pottery Neolithic B in the Levant, archaeologist Trevor Watkins observes, "The house was now the appropriate place for symbolic constructions, and ultimately for the reception of the skulls of the long dead. In short the house, formerly the shelter for general everyday activities, was being perceived as something more than utilitarian, as the home, the private and concrete expression of a particular family group."[42]

Humans made shelter for thousands of years before they attached complex meanings to dwellings. Further, the symbolic anchoring with architecture did not occur immediately with sedentism. That notion apparently required not just sedentism but a permanent connection to a place. In part this was triggered by the accumulation of goods—gathered foods, harvested grains, heavy tools, and nonportable features—but the real difference was marked by the presence of our ancestors.

. . .

The profuse and complex symbolic associations and cultural meanings associated with home did not immediately emerge once people had a roof overhead. Based on what we know right now, it does not appear that dwellings were imbued with such concerns until some point after sedentism had developed. The archaeology of Japan and the Near East—just two early and well-documented cases—suggest that the transition to sedentism was not immediately marked by this intensely domestic concept.

Based on what we know from archaeology and by analogy with modern and historic traditional societies, people become sedentary either when they rely on stored foods—whether salmon, acorns, or wild wheat—or when the tools required for processing foods became impractical to move. Even under these circumstances, people may have shifted settlements, moving to smaller camps for specific tasks, but returning to a central place. That took place long before the first agricultural harvests, such as on the periglacial steppe occupied by the inhabitants of Mezhrich (discussed in chapter 3). It occurred among the intensive food collectors such as the Natufians and coastal hunters and gatherers like the Jomon and the Chumash of Southern California (discussed in chapter 10).

But while sedentism developed in the absence of agriculture, the complex meanings associated with dwellings appear later in the process of settling down. As the next several chapters discuss, our homes may serve as models of the way we see the world (chapter 5) and be places where the Sacred is encountered (chapter 9). Human homes may contain extended groups of kin that are literally the building blocks of society (chapter 6) or delineate communities that have withdrawn from this world to create their own (chapter 7). Our houses may proclaim the enormous social divides between elites and commoners (chapter 8) or may provide the spatial locus for our encounters with Death, the great equalizer (chapter 11). And finally, our houses may be such a part of our lives that they are imbued with a vital existence (chapter 10).

All these affiliations and meanings appear relatively "recently" in the human experience, roughly in the last 15,000 years. These complex notions attached to home apparently required not only sedentism, but a connection of permanence, a new way to think about place. Initially triggered by the acquisition of durable goods, human homes were profoundly changed by the presence of the departed. Whether we bury our dead in village cemeteries, stack the tender-held skulls of loved ones in caches or shrines, or carefully store the ashes of our dead on a mantelpiece, this fundamental affiliation between dwelling and identity marks a transformation in the ancient creation of home.

CHAPTER 5

Model Homes

But the ancient night is bottomless, like a jar
of brimming water.

—Jorge Luis Borges, *Manuscript Found in a Book of Joseph Conrad*

Shortly before he died, I heard Jorge Luis Borges remark that of the thousands of metaphors deployed by poets, only a few are universal and key: Life is a dream. The stars are eyes. Women are flowers. Time is a river. Death is sleep. These paired metaphors inform in both directions. Time is a river. A river is time.

Shifting from the verbal and written to the material and constructed, one of the most common metaphoric connections in human culture is between the dwelling and the cosmos. The architectural order of home replicates or restates the order of the cosmos. The cosmos is encoded in the home. Domestic order becomes a template for understanding the larger patterns of existence.

In dwellings throughout the world, the order of the home parallels the order of the universe. Humans have built these metaphors for the last ten thousand years. Our homes mirror our worlds. Dwellings denote the cosmic origins of humans, the proper distinctions between people and things, or the borders between culture and nature. Houses physically reflect and materially restate human conceptions of proper order, and those houses become the architectural settings in which humans renegotiate and revive the social order.

And yet, such complex symbolic freightings have not always been part of the human experience. Only after our ancestors began living in relatively permanent structures for extended periods of time do we see the first traces of such associations. At that point, the distinctions become more pronounced and articulated, as ancient people manipulated nature and the cultural and natural realms became distinct if not bifurcated. And we certainly see this when the house of the living is given over to the dead.

From that point in our prehistory, the house becomes a recurrent schema for social order, as durable a metaphoric association as the connections between time and a river or river and time.

. . .

In the rugged provinces of northern Algeria, as Pierre Bourdieu documented, the Kabyle Berbers build houses that collate diverse sets of symbolic themes.[1]

The rectangular Kabyle house is usually constructed on a hillside, forming a split-level dwelling. The front door faces east, and sunlight through the open door illuminates the far wall. Thus, the western wall is "the wall of light" and the eastern wall "the wall of darkness." The wall of light is associated with health and well-being; the wall of darkness is, by extension, the wall "of sleep," "of the invalid," or "of the tomb." The wall of light is also the place of honor. The word *qabel* means "to honor" and also "to face east," and a mistreated guest will complain, "He made me sit before his wall of darkness as in a grave."

The Kabyle house is bisected by an interior half-wall, creating an upper sector where most human activities take place and a lower sector that serves as a stable and storage area. From this constructed separation, the Kabyle derive a complex set of oppositions. The low dividing wall separates "the house of the humans" from "the house of the animals." The upper level is associated with light, warmth, and human activity. The hearth is there, as are the tools for transforming raw matter: the handmill, cooking pots, and loom. The lower area is the shadowy zone where raw matter is stored: firewood, water, animal fodder, and the animals themselves. The upper room is affiliated with light and culture; the lower sector with darkness and nature.

The Kabyle house becomes a spatial template for relations between men and women and for the household and the broader world. Perched above the stable there is a loft where the wife and children sleep, occasionally joined by the husband. The darkened loft is the place for lovemaking and birth, and thus is a female zone. At sunrise, men depart their houses for the broader exterior world of fields, marketplace, town square, and mosque—the public and patriarchal domain of the Berber world. The house, in contrast, is the female realm, *harem* to non-kin

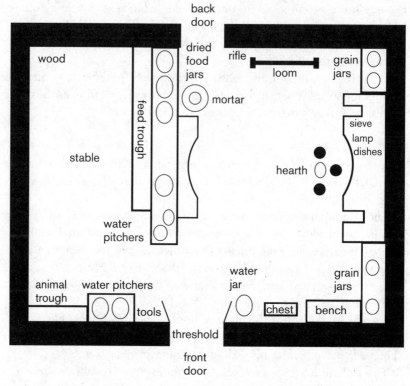

FIGURE 7. Plan of a Kabyle house, Algeria. Redrawn from Bourdieu 1977.

males. It is even somewhat suspicious for a man to stay at home during the day, as this suggests his indolence and femininity.

Even the dwelling's structural elements bear the weight of diverse meanings. The loft is raised and carried by the building just as the corpse is lifted on a stretcher by grave bearers; *tha'richth* names both the loft and the funeral litter. The ridge beam is supported in mid-span by an upright wooden pillar made from a forked tree. The ridge beam is male and protective, the upright pillar splayed and receptive, and the sexual imagery of joining is obvious.

From this, a number of Kabyle sayings are derived—"the woman supports the man," "the woman is the central pillar," and the new bride is told, "May God make of you the pillar firmly planted in the middle of the house." The house, thus, becomes the expression of perfect familial order: the male roof beam that covers all within and protects it from the elements and dishonor, and the female pillar that supports and protects, yet is inherently interior.

The Kabyle dwelling is a metaphoric house of mirrors, reflecting the oppositions of human/animal, culture/nature, male/female, light/dark, health/sickness, life/death, honor/dishonor, public/private, and so on. These associations are expressed in the material plan and construction of the home, but reinforced by traditional maxims and daily actions. The Kabyle house reflects and recreates the Berber world. And the Kabyle are not unique, as humans in different places and various times use their houses as models of their worlds.

. . .

The metaphoric associations between house and cosmos are a subset of the larger domain of human symbol-making. Since the earliest human symbols were gestures and vocalizations that left no direct material traces, we can only infer their existence indirectly. For example, between 2.6 and 1.6 million years ago hominids in eastern and southern Africa were making simple core and flake stone tools, selecting specific types of raw materials based on how the stone would fracture.[2] This behavior probably relied on knowledge conveyed through verbal symbols. Somewhat later (1.6 million to 300,000 years ago), the creation of Acheulian hand-axes and cleavers, double-edged stone tools that became refined and more standardized through time, suggest the verbal communication of established technological knowledge rather than individual trial and error.[3] These artifacts indirectly point to the use of symbols.

At present, the oldest objects that seem to be materialized symbols are simple shell beads and etched chunks of red ochre from Africa and the Near East. Excavations at Blombos Cave on the southernmost tip of Africa uncovered two small pieces of ochre dating to 70,000 years ago that are simple engraved plaques with sets of evenly spaced parallel lines.[4] The excavators also found some forty small beads made from the shells of a common marine snail whose shell is the shape and size of an olive pit. The small shells were punctured so they could be threaded, and they bear faint traces of a dusting of red ochre.[5] Similar beads have been found at the site of Grotte de Pigeons in eastern Morocco that are roughly 82,000 years old, a few millennia older than the Blombos Cave beads. Other similar, but less securely dated shell beads come from the Skhul site in Israel and the site of Oued Djebbama in Algeria.

The etched ochre and shell beads demonstrate that ancient humans were using objects as symbols by 80,000 to 70,000 years ago. The simple, Late Stone Age beads point to a subtle development: The shells are personal adornments, and personal adornments imply a sense of personhood. By 80,000 to 70,000 years ago, the "I" was distinct from the "Other," and the distinction broadly understood over the length of the African continent and in adjacent areas of the Middle East—a development in human history ancestral to modern *fashionistas* in Paris, New York, or Milan.

It was once thought that the earliest use of complex symbols occurred at about 35,000 to 18,000 years ago, as exemplified by the spectacular cave art at Upper Paleolithic sites like Lascaux, Altamira, or Chauvet Cave. "Our knowledge about our ancestors," wrote poet Zbigniew Hebert when contemplating the cave paintings of Lascaux, "is modulated by a violent cry and a deadly hush."[6] The subjects of different interpretations—as hunting magic, backdrops for initiation ceremonies, or depictions of the hunt—the dynamic art-making has led some scholars to propose the existence of an Upper Paleolithic "Creative Explosion" associated with the evolutionary changes in the human mind.[7] And yet this art was restricted to a relatively small portion of western Europe and was preceded by some 30 to 40 millennia of symbol-making.

Everything is older than we once thought. The emergence of what Randall White has called "the material rendering" of symbolic associations took various forms throughout prehistory, employing different media and occurring at different temporal scales.[8] It is worth remembering that more centuries elapsed between the creation of beads and etchings at Blombos Cave and the Upper Paleolithic wall art at Chauvet Cave than separate Chauvet Cave from Picasso's (1907) *Les Demoiselles d'Avignon.*

Most ancient symbols were ephemeral and fleeting, and even enduring material renderings are shaped by time and decay. For example, the oldest known pictographs in open-air sites in the American Southwest, Brazil, Mexico, Australia, the Sahara, and central India are all drawn in red ocher, not because of a pan-human attraction to the color red, but because red ocher is the most durable of the iron minerals used as ancient pigments.[9]

Not everything endures. Caution is required given the uneven materiality of the past. That said, it is plausible to suggest that making symbols *in* place preceded making symbols *of* place, which, in turn, antedated the creation of symbols of home.

Numerous archaeological sites exemplify a specific place or a landform being a recurrent locus for symbol-making, and these prehistoric sites are known from every continent except Antarctica. In Baja California, my students and I have recorded rock-art sites where a distinctive symbol was etched into the rough surfaces of canyon walls. The motif is a pecked, rectangular shape called a *tabla*. We believe these motifs commemorated the eminent but deceased men of wandering bands of hunters and gatherers. According to Spanish missionary accounts, the best hunters, the fastest runners, or the most powerful shamans were recalled in an annual ceremony of remembrance that incorporated wooden tablas, and we have found analogous motifs etched into cliffs. These motifs were inscribed in places with specific properties—freshwater springs and abundant plant foods—although the symbols were not about the place per se.

Prehistoric symbols about places are more rare and elusive. In southern Australia, sets of finger flutings and deeply grooved circles and lines have been found at petroglyph sites in limestone caves and may be some 30,000 years old.[10] They appear similar to recent Aboriginal rock art in which visual art, religious practice, and mythic narrative are combined in specific locales, but it is difficult to prove that similar kinds of place-making also occurred deep in prehistory.

More definitive examples of symbolizing place are votive offerings associated with the sacred caves and peak sanctuaries in Minoan Crete (ca. 3100–1470 B.C.). Of the thousands of caves and hundreds of peaks on the mountainous island of Crete, offerings occur only at certain caves and peaks.[11] Offerings of weapons and metal objects were placed in subterranean pools inside caverns. Stalactites and stalagmites whose natural shapes resembled people or animals were worn smooth by human touch. On peak sanctuaries, the offerings were not placed on the highest promontory but rather on lateral outcrops and terraces or inside fissures in the limestone; the offerings were frequently miniature images of livestock or people or carefully chosen smooth, cool pebbles. Some peak sanctuaries incorporated architecture: stout masonry terrace walls, an altar, screens, and other constructions. Much as the rock art in Baja California denoted the ceremonies held in desert canyons, the constructions associated with peak sanctuaries referenced the rites that occurred there rather than the place itself.

In southern Africa, there is a deep archaeological record for the creation of rock art, dating back 24,000 years. The rock art suggests the hunters and gatherers of the ancient Kalahari occupied a conceptually inhabited environment, populated with people and game, but one in which dwellings were not portrayed. It is an analogical stretch to connect ancient rock art to modern peoples, but it is noteworthy that modern !Kung San social life focuses on outdoor hearths rather than the small temporary huts. Even during the rainy season when !Kung San huts are more substantial, dwellings are for temporary refuge and storage. Since the !Kung San move camp often (rarely occupying a camp for more than a week), their dwellings do not materially anchor complex sets of symbolic associations.[12]

A similar situation is found with the Inuit iglu, which the anthropologist Franz Boas described in 1883 and 1884.[13] Boas provides a detailed account of the construction—"the method of building is very ingenious"—illustrated with multiple plans and sections of an iglu built by Inuit living on the eastern shore of Baffin Island. A multichambered construction, the inner walls of the largest room were screened with hanging furs that trapped cold air against the ice vault and caught melt drops. A pair of soapstone lamps burned blubber oil, heating food and drying damp clothing. A sleeping platform was built on the distant side of the largest room, covered with oars, tent poles and other wooden objects, padded with clumps of heather, and then covered with a thick layer of deerskins—"and thus a very comfortable bed is made" Boas noted. Boas's account is detailed and observant—including in his description of *qaggi*, or singing houses, in which he describes the building, the arrangements of people during the singing feast, detailed accounts supplemented by his own sketches. Thus, it is interesting that Boas makes absolutely no mention of cosmological meanings associated with the Inuit iglu.

So when, then, did human dwellings take on profound symbolic meanings?

I think that the connections between home and cosmos only developed after people began living in structures that had a more extended existence, and thus provided a constructed medium for metaphor. Rather, complex meanings resided in dwellings only when the house became relatively permanent, or at least was a relatively permanent, "reusable" mobile dwelling.

Ephemeral buildings may have fleeting meanings, but even seasonal dwellings may be imbued with notions of the cosmos. The Yolngu of eastern Arnhem Land in northern Australia build a rainy-season house (*gatjawordo*).[14] Constructed from eucalyptus poles and sheets of bark, the gatjawordo consists of an elevated platform, its gabled roof supported by two forked uprights and a ridge-pole wedged into the crotches. This simple and rustic hut is adorned with complex meanings. The gatjawordo was given to humans by the Wagilak sisters who journeyed across the eastern sea and created Arnhem Land. The forked uprights are associated with sexual union, and reference the splayed stance of the human form. Simultaneously the forked posts represent the female principle, the opened mouth of the Rainbow Serpent, and the wombs of the Wagilak sisters.

The gatjawordo becomes a ritual stage during the Kunapipi, a male initiation ceremony. The boys huddle inside the dwelling, which now represents a primordial womb. As the boys crouch under the eucalyptus-bark roof, a line of dancers representing the rainbow serpent snakes into the clearing and surrounds the dwelling, symbolically strangling and swallowing the cowering boys, only to spit them out reborn as men.

Mobile dwellings can anchor complex meanings. The tent, or *kåhte*, used by the mountain Saami of Norway has fascinated travelers since the early eighteenth century for its ingenious construction and its delineations of symbolic space.[15] The bent-pole kåhte incorporates a pair of birch-pole arches and another fifteen to twenty birch poles to form a tipi-like conical frame covered with hides or thick canvas, all of this transported on reindeer-drawn sleds. Whenever the tent was pitched, the main doorway faced south, while a special and rarely used exit in the rear tent wall faced north. A kettle dangled over the central hearth, a square fire-pit with a border of logs.

The kåhte is divided into three principal zones: the central hearth area *(arran),* the area between the hearth and the door *(uksa),* and the area between the hearth and the rear of the tent *(påssjo).* The areas on either side of the hearth box are called *luoito,* and these distinctions results in an internal division of the kåhte into distinct zones.

The påssjo was the male and honored space forbidden to women, and sometimes occupied by a household shrine. The uksa was the female zone, through which men could pass. The luoito was a common zone, but when a woman had to retrieve pots and pans from the other side of the tent, she stepped through the uksa zone and avoided the masculine space. Male objects—such as hunting and fishing gear—were kept in the påssjo, while items associated with women—clothing and footgear—were stored in the uksa zone. Generational differences were ordered within the tent: parents sat on one side of the hearth, older children opposite, infants and young children with their parents. Guests or servants sat and slept by the entrance on the children's side of the tent.

The cosmos was reflected in the Saami tent. The Sun-God (Peive) who vanquished darkness and cold was represented by the hearth-fire,

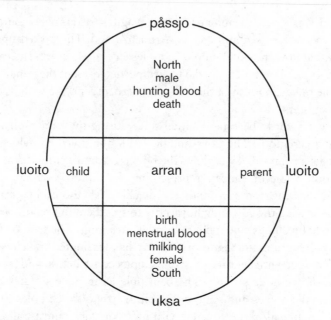

FIGURE 8. Plan of a Saami kähte. Redrawn from Yates 1989.

which was venerated as Peive's living representative. Other deities lived beneath the tent floor. The goddess responsible for the birth of children and reindeer lived beneath the hearth; she received the souls of the dead for later rebirth. The door goddess lived under the uksa entrance, protecting the new born and menstruating women. The goddess of the hunt lived beneath the rear, påssjo door, the area where arrows, bows, and bear spears were stored, the hunting gear smeared with bear blood to counteract possible pollution by menstrual blood. After a successful hunt, men spent three nights in a cleansing ritual before returning to the kåhte and the polluting realm of women. Associated with the feminine, reindeer milk passed through the uksa entrance, while the masculine game meat was slid through the rear påssjo door. Milk and meat met at the hearth.

Given all these symbolic associations, it is not surprising that the Saami tent also demarcated the difference between life and death: a corpse was never removed through the uksa entrance, but only through the påssjo door, passing through the realm of Tiermes, the zone of killing and of death. And thus the Saami tent became a template of the world.

Not one of these meanings would be preserved in the archaeological record. The kåhte is pulled down and packed onto a sled, the Saami lead their draft reindeer off into the forest, and soon the hearth box becomes humus. In northern Australia, the pungent menthol of eucalyptus quickly fades, insects gnaw and fray the sheets of stringbark. The forked poles rot and sag in the mud as rainfall sheets across Arnhem Land. All of this recedes from an archaeological vista.

So we should be cautious in our claims of when dwellings became constructed templates. But I think that these associations were firmly in place by the time humans first farmed.

. . .

The name for the traditional Navaho dwelling, *hogan*, means "home place."[16] The conical forked-pole hogan is the oldest type, a domed circular structure with a central frame made from an interlocked tripod of juniper logs. Stripped of bark, the butts of the main forked logs are set on the south, west, and north sides, and a separate pair of uprights frame the east-facing doorway. Additional logs and branches cover the tripod frame that are chinked with brush, bark, and sod, and finally covered with earth.

The Navahos arrived in the Southwest in the late 1400s and the earliest hogans were built in the 1700s. Since then, other forms of hogans have been devised, including modern hogans built from planed lumber, tarpaper, masonry, and concrete block. The only criteria, as Susan Kent noted, are that a hogan "is to be round and to be blessed during construction. The hogan retains its sacredness even during its mundane use, which comprises most of its occupation and describes most of the activities performed inside. However, within the mundane there is a special property, a spirituality that transcends everyday life and needs."[17]

The hogan is a domestic space and a sacred space. Although the early conical forked-pole constructions have been generally replaced by more spacious stacked-log, vertical-post, and masonry hogans, the size and type of construction doesn't change the sacred elements of a hogan. Hogans are the only appropriate space for Navaho ceremonies. Even Navaho living in rectangular log cabins or frame houses with gabled roofs often build a hogan nearby as a ceremonial space, and larger hogans are built as worship spaces for the Native American Church.

A gift from the Talking God deity, the primordial hogan was shaped in the form of a geological hump on Gobernador Knob, a mountain located in the center of the Navaho's homeland. Built from forked posts made from white shell (east), turquoise (south), abalone (west) and obsidian (north), this original hogan was the model for all conical

FIGURE 9. Navaho hogan, 2009.

forked-stick dwellings. Each post is associated with one of four female deities: Earth Woman (east), Mountain Woman (south), Water Woman (west), and Corn Woman (north).

The east-facing door receives the first blessings of dawn-light. The southern side of the hogan is the male side and the north side is female. The western side is the seat of honor allocated to singers and shamans. In larger hogans, recesses built into the base of the western wall may hold masks and other ritual paraphernalia.

While there are specific spatial associations within the hogan—men should move to the left, women to the right—there are no internal divisions. Just as the Navaho recognize the distinctive but intertwined realms of male and female in the cosmos, the hogan reflects the unity of differences.

Various rituals occur within the hogan. For example, ethnographer Louise Lamphere describes the Male Shooting Way Ugly ceremonial, designed to counteract a man's contact with the "ugly" things in the cosmos, including witches and ghosts.[18] Occurring over two to nine nights, the ceremony removes the ugly and unhealthy forces from the patient's body and inoculates him from further harm. Using prayer sticks and sand-paintings, special arrows and bows, whistles and bullroarers, the curing singer brings the patient in contact with the supernatural and purifies him by expelling harmful "ugliness." This complex rite only can occur in the hogan.

The hogan is a living space and a space that lives. Ritually sanctified during its construction, hogans are alive and must be blessed and fed. Alternatively, bad fortune and death contaminate the hogan, sometimes irreversibly. If someone dies in the hogan, the house is abandoned and avoided. The corpse is removed through a hole chopped in the north or west wall, instead of through the east-facing doorway. A hogan where someone has died is a "ghost hogan" or a "no-hearth home." The entire homestead site may be abandoned until the ghost hogan collapses. No new hogan will be built near the contaminated no-hearth home.

The Kabyle house and the Navaho hogan are very different types of homes. The Kabyle house is divided in plan, vertically distinguished between the upper living area and the lower stable and storeroom. The Navaho hogan is circular and unified, unsectored by interior walls. And yet there are some broad parallels between the symbolic associations. Solar associations make the eastern side significant and the western wall privileged. Interior spaces are defined as male or female. Health and well-being are encoded in their walls. And, perhaps, more fundamental than these detailed homologies is this basic metaphoric symmetry: The house is like the cosmos. The cosmos is like the house.

. . .

Dwelling in a largely desacralized Western world, we may not realize that our own homes encode any principles of cosmic order. Living in Southern California as I do, one is struck by the motley assortment of home styles. As historian Kevin Starr discusses, since the nineteenth century there has been a basic progression of building materials and styles in Southern California, as Mexican adobe houses were replaced by Victorian constructions in wood, brick, and granite, only to be succeeded by wooden Craftsman bungalows of the 1910s, the stucco and roof-tiles of Spanish Revival in the 1920s, and then the competing styles of the 1930s of International Style, *Systeme Moderne,* and Art Deco.[19] Seismically reshuffled by the region's relatively frequent earthquakes, new architectural forms arose from the rubble.

In the face of such magpie diversity of materials, floor plans, and building styles, it seems unlikely that metaphorical statements about the cosmos are materially expressed in the modern American home. But is that true?

Consider a relatively standard contemporary floor plan for one type of American home: the single-story, ranch-style house—ranch *style* because it rarely sits on an actual ranch. At about 1,750 square feet and with "only" three bedrooms and two baths, this house is a relatively modest American home. (As of 2006, the average American home was 2,349 square feet, a growth in house size discussed below.) And while we are "existential insiders" so accustomed to our own domestic habitats that we may overlook their symbolism, the American ranch-style house is as encoded with meanings as the Kabyle house or the Navaho hogan.[20]

Several spatial and symbolic dimensions run through the house. Passing through the paired pillars that support the covered porch, one steps from the outside and public realm into a set of private spaces. Beyond the simple dichotomy between "outside" and "inside," the progressive exclusivity of spaces marks complicated gradations. The patio is "outside" but it is a private "outside," a fair-weather extension of the dining area. The hall bathroom serves bedrooms 2 and 3 and guests using the more public spaces in the house. The most private and exclusive space is the toilet off the master bedroom, which is wedged between two separate bathing areas—a shower stall and the "garden tub," two forms of ablutions undistinguished in the hall bath. The WC associated with the master bedroom is the most hidden space in the entire ranch house plan.

A basic distinction encoded in the ranch-style house is the difference between "family" and "visitors." Usually only family members park their cars in the garage (if there is room among the clutter). Family members can enter directly into the house, passing the dirty laundry piled in the utility room. In contrast, visitors enter through the "front" door of the house, stepping through the transitional covered porch before entering the "great room."

Another symbolic distinction is between the "master" bedroom and the other bedrooms. The smaller rooms are more than twenty feet away from the master bedroom. The physical separation of the master (parents') bedroom from the other (children's) bedrooms only became a feature of American middle-class culture in the mid-nineteenth century; since then, the distance has increased as house size has grown.

This growing distance also reflects the emergence of the "companionate family," a twentieth-century American social institution in which the previous conceptions of patriarchal households were replaced by an ide-

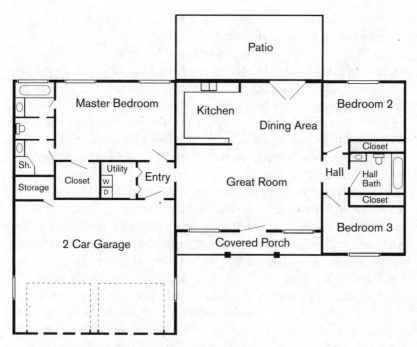

FIGURE 10. Modern American ranch-style house.

alized union between husband and wife in which sexual fulfillment was
essential for harmonious family life. In that process the bedroom was
eroticized and moved further away from the kiddies.[21]

Currently, the designation "master bedroom" is being replaced by the
term "owner's retreat," as a team of interior designers informs us, "both
in compliance with nondiscriminatory language required by US federal
civil rights and fair housing laws, and in order to convey the sense of
sanctuary." A "master's" bedroom implies the existence of a mistress,
servant, serf, or slave, while the term "owner" avoids the ugly suggestion
of gendered social inequalities, even if the house is actually "owned" by
the bank. And finally, "the term 'retreat' implies an increased emphasis
on the privacy and relaxation that the space is designed to offer."[22]

Thus, ranch-style architecture encodes the American notion of the
house as a refuge from the world and the largest bedroom serving as a
sanctum, not only from the broader world, but from one's own children.

An early twenty-first-century trend is the American fortress home.
In a July 4, 2006, report titled "Behind the Ever-Expanding American
Dream Home"[23] National Public Radio reporter Margot Adler profiled

Michael Frisby, the proud owner of a $1 million, 11,000-square-foot home in Fulton County, Maryland.

Mr. Frisby and his wife were raised poor but achieved great material success. In 2001 the Frisbys built a very, very large house—containing gym, sauna, business center, entertainment complex with bar, wine cellar, five bathrooms, four bedrooms, and (inevitably) "an extensive master bedroom suite." Mr. Frisby explained: "I always wanted a house big enough that my kids could be in their room screaming, and my wife could be in a room screaming, and I could be somewhere else and not hear any of them."

But according to Adler, Mr. Frisby is far from unique—not only in his desire to create some peace among his many screaming family members—but in his idea of his house as a fortress and a protective refuge. Architecturally expressing the old principle of English common law, *et domus sua cuique tutissimum refugium* (one's home is the safest refuge for all), Mr. Frisby and other affluent Americans built extremely large houses in the early years of the twenty-first century, particularly after September 11, 2001. Adler quotes a Long Island architect, Anne Surchin, as explaining, "You know, we are very tenuous. No one knows when the next 9/11 will happen. And these houses represent safety—and the bigger the house, the bigger the fortress."

I do not know how broadly representative these opinions are, but it would seem that the ranch-style houses and McMansions express basic principles of the American worldview. The public and private are distinct. The home is a refuge from the outside world. Adult bedrooms are to be separate from children's rooms. Bodily functions should only take place in the most hidden, private spaces. And, of course, a man's home is his castle.

The Kabyle house is divided horizontally and vertically, and its symbolic associations are analogously bilateral. The Navaho hogan is circular and intimate—the average hogan would nestle comfortably within the American master bedroom suite—excuse me, "owner's retreat"—and the spaces within the hogan, although distinguished, are unified with the male and female spaces linked by the solar circuit. The American ranch-style house is a refuge, distancing private spaces from public zones, parents' bedrooms from children's rooms, and secreting bodily functions in the deepest recesses of the house. And as such houses grew larger and larger, the American mega-house became a refuge not only for the family as a social unit protected from the outside world, but as a refuge for individual family members from each other. Various houses and different societies with distinctive views of the cosmos.

. . .

Before the horse was introduced to the Great Plains of North America in the seventeenth and eighteenth centuries, native peoples settled along the Missouri River and its numerous tributaries.[24] Ancestors of the Pawnee and Arikara nations, these people spread across the central Great Plains using big dogs as their largest pack animals. Although they hunted the herds of bison that rumbled across the plains, these prehistoric groups were also farmers, tethered to the arable bottomlands of the Missouri, Niobara, Platte, Republican, Smoky Hill, Arkansas, and Kansas rivers. Tilling the rich soils with hoes made from buffalo shoulder blades, these farmers planted maize, beans, and squashes and lived in small hamlets and homesteads that stretched along the river bluffs. Unlike later communities that lived in palisaded villages, settlements dating to A.D. 1000–1500 showed little concern for defense.

Their houses were earth-lodges eight to nine meters long. During the historic period, these earth-lodges were circular in plan, but prehistorically the buildings were roughly rectangular. A floor was excavated less than a meter into the soil with a sloping entranceway. Upright cottonwood house-posts were spanned by cross-beams. Additional rafters were raised, woven in place by a wicker of saplings, and covered by willow mats. Sod grass was spread over the mats, leaving a space for the smoke-hole.

These Central Plains earth-lodges were snug and substantial. Indoor cache pits held stored maize, raised sleeping platforms circled the hearth fire, and people made tools and cooked meals protected from the cold winds of a long winter. But Pawnee houses were more than just shelters. They were models of the cosmos.

The intricacies of Pawnee cosmology are best known from ethnographic interviews from the late nineteenth and early twentieth centuries. Even after the chaotic changes of the seventeenth to nineteenth centuries—a swirl of events that included the arrival of the horse and firearms, the movement of Indian tribes out into the Plains, warfare and raiding, savage epidemics, Euro-American conquest, and the forced relocation of American Indians onto reservations—the Pawnee retained a stunningly complex concept of the sacred.

The Pawnee were born from the star in the west, and, as the early

American ethnographer Alice C. Fletcher (1838–1923) wrote, "for numberless generations the thought and attention of the entire community have been directed toward a special aspect of nature, the firmament with its stars, clouds, and winds."[25] Individual Pawnee villages descended from stars, and village shrines were dedicated to those astral origins.

"The influence of the star cult," Fletcher wrote, "was manifest in the construction of the earth-lodge of the Pawnee. The circular floor of this dwelling symbolized the earth, and the dome-shaped roof the arching sky. The four posts which supported the framework of the roof represented the four stars of the leading villages, and on occasions were painted in their respective colors. The place of the shrine was at the west in accordance with the position of the star of the west."[26]

For the Pawnee, the star of the west was the Evening Star, the planet Venus. The lodge door opened to the east, towards the Morning Star, the planet Mars. The Morning Star was a warrior. The Evening Star was the maternal deity who oversaw crops and harvests. These two stellar gods united to give birth to the Pawnee.

Oriented to the sacred, the circular Pawnee earth-lodge was both location and template for the elaborate Hako ceremony, a five-day event consisting of more than twenty ritual phases accompanied by nearly one hundred songs in which the Pawnee prayed "for the gift of life, of strength, of plenty, and of peace." Key to the ceremony is the establishment of a place as holy. As a ritual expert *(ku'rahus)* explained to Fletcher:[27]

> The first act of a man must be to set apart a place that can be made sacred and holy, that can be consecrated to Tira'wa; a place where a man can be quiet and think—think about the mighty power and the place where the lesser powers dwell; a place where a man can put his sacred articles, those objects which enable him to approach the powers. Kushara means such a place.
>
> In this [the seventh] stanza we are taught that before a man can build a dwelling he must select a spot and make it sacred and then, about that consecrated spot, he can erect a dwelling where his family can live peaceably. Kushara represents the place where a man can seek the powers and where the powers can come near to man. Such a place is necessary for all ceremonies.

Stanza after stanza restate the significance of the earth-lodge as the appropriate place for the ceremony, a dwelling form given to humans by Tira'wa—"The Expanse of the Heavens"—the most significant deity in Pawnee religion who, through the power of his thought, created the universe and the astral deities who, in turn, created humans.

Working with native experts, Fletcher was able to record an elegant and complex ceremony that expressed and anchored Pawnee cosmology. The descriptions of the Hako ceremony and other nuanced concepts of Pawnee religion would never be completely reflected in the material traces of an archaeological site. Further, there is no reason to assume that Pawnee religion had not changed over the centuries, especially in its sacred associations with the earth-lodge, which we know changed in overall form from rectangular to circular.

Which makes the discovery at the C.C. Witt site all the more fascinating.[28]

Located in northeastern Kansas on a bluff overlooking the confluence of the Smoky Hill, Republican, and Kansas rivers just east of Junction City, the C.C. Witt site (named for the landowner) was excavated in 1973 and 1974 by Patricia O'Brien, a professor of anthropology at Kansas State University. The site contained two areas: a small cemetery mound and the remains of a rectangular earth-lodge.

Measuring about ten by ten meters, the earth-lodge was aligned to an east-west meridian. The excavations recovered evidence of standard household activities: flat limestone slabs (metates) for grinding maize, chipped stone scrapers and knives for working hides and cutting meat, arrow points and fishhooks, sewing awls, a bison scapula hoe, a stone abrader used for making arrow-shafts, and pottery. It was a suite of artifacts commonly found at sites in the Central Plains.

Other objects were not so ordinary. Opposite the door was a feature consisting of four small post-molds that aligned perfectly with the doorway and the central hearth; this feature apparently was a small altar, placed to be illuminated by dawn's light passing through the door.

The right talon of a bald eagle was found just north of the altar, probably the remains of a sacred medicine bundle. Just inside the door, a storage pit ("Feature 2") contained wings of other birds: the right wing of a red-headed woodpecker, the left wing of a blue jay, the lower right wing of the rare long-eared owl, right and left wings from four bobwhite quail, and the wings of an unidentified species of woodpecker.

These bird bones were not the remains of a meal. Rather, these birds were offerings, an inference bolstered by the special placement of the pit, and the fact that the bird bones were accompanied by bone beads and a bracelet inscribed with a sunburst motif. This inference is also supported by the significance of these birds in later Pawnee cosmology.

For the historic Pawnee, the feathers, talons, and wings of eagles were sacred objects. The eagle is the chief of day and represents the warrior deity, Morning Star. The owl is chief of night and a messenger, instruct-

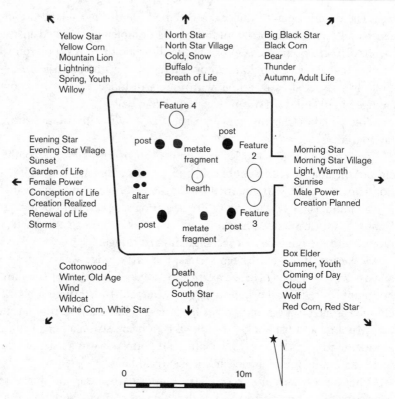

FIGURE 11. C.C. Witt earthlodge and Pawnee cosmology. Redrawn from O'Brien 1986.

ing humans in worship. The blue jay carries humanity's prayers into the sky, an intermediary to Tira'wa, whose blue feathers recall the vast blue celestial dome over the Great Plains. The red-headed woodpecker is the chief of trees, protecting humans from storms and lightening, its guttural rattle crying out fearlessly in the midst of storms.[29]

In addition to the talons and wings of sacred birds, the C.C. Witt earth-lodge had another feature: it was aligned so that the doorway framed the sunrise on the vernal equinox.

As O'Brien showed in her detailed analysis, the earth-lodge occupied at A.D. 1300 exhibits traits found in historic Pawnee cosmologies recorded some six centuries later. Some of complex sets of dual oppositions and symbolic associations found in historic Pawnee earth-lodges were present at the C.C. Witt site: the east-west dichotomy associated with the Morning Star and the Evening Star, the significance of the number "four" in the idea of the four lodge poles and the four-posted altar, the alignment of the door with the vernal equinox, and the remains of sacred birds associated with Tira'wa. All these point to a deep antiquity for Pawnee religious beliefs and worldview, a cosmology that was modeled at home seven centuries ago on the edge of the Central Plains.

. . .

During the seventeenth century, the Dutch developed what historian Simon Schama has called "the most obsessively residential culture in Europe."[30] Alternatively admired and satirized by visitors from other countries, the burnished cleanliness of the Dutch home literally extended out to the paved street, an order achieved through endless hours of scrubbing and sweeping at a time when most European cities were marked by chaos, clatter, and ordure. (It is notable, however, that some of the most beguiling paintings of Dutch maternal tenderness are images of mothers cleaning their children of head lice.) The scrubbed pavement marked the cleansed and sanctified threshold, separating the domestic sanctum from the external hurly-burly.

"Home was where peace, virtue and prosperity were ideally to be found," Schama writes, and even when houses incorporated businesses and workshops, "the division between living space and working space in middle-class households was clearly demarcated and jealously guarded."[31] In turn, the Dutch bourgeois home was a *gemeenschap*, the community in microcosm from which the larger society was constructed and where order, mutual obligation, and prosperity were prized.

The seventeenth-century bourgeois Dutch home was the framework through which the broader world was perceived and measured. It is literally so in the elegant and quiet painting by Jakob Ochtervelt, *Street Musicians at the Door* (1665). The world is framed by the doorway, the outside world with its church spires and solid facades meets the polished regularities of floor tiles and furnishings. Shimmering damask and brocade encounter dun-colored wool. And while the social distinctions are marked, there is an absence of tension in Ochtervelt's vignette: the order of the house is reflected in the order of these different social classes—the street musicians smiling and adoring, the child delighted but seeking the nanny's approval, the mistress of the house reaching forward to tip the street musicians with a discreet coin.

Conversely, the home may be a microcosm of failure, as Jan Steen depicts in his painting, *The Dissolute Household* (1663–64). With a crimson-slippered foot planted on the open pages of a Bible, the woman of the house lurches for more white wine as the maid and husband

FIGURE 12. J. Ochtervelt, *Street Musicians at the Door,* 1665. St. Louis Museum of Art.

intertwine their fingers in a sexual gesture simultaneously explicit and unseen. Anticipations of lechery curl across the slovenly burger's face.

The waning sunlight visible through the leaded glass indicates this wantonness began earlier at midday. The house matron slumbers, unwakened by a young child's pestering. The tablecloth was not ironed before it was laid. The foreground is a chaos of fallen backgammon board, forsaken lute, and broken glass. A pocket-watch lies discarded without care for time. A good haunch of meat is abandoned to a housecat. The older

FIGURE 13. J. Steen, *The Dissolute Household*, ca. 1663–1664. Metropolitan Museum of Art.

son draws his rapier against the beggar at the door instead of offering the hungry man even a taste of uneaten food.

In this dysfunctional domestic microcosm, the very foundations of Dutch society are perverted as social distinction and social obligation are undone in a long day's debauch.

Thus the Dutch house becomes a template against which the beneficial and malevolent dimensions of social life are displayed. Dwellings are constructed delineations of propriety and indecency. In one case the threshold delimits the outside world from the domestic sanctum. In the other case, the chaos of domestic disorder—the open drapery of the bedchamber encourages the short stagger from drunkenness to rut—exemplifies a world turned upside down. Domestic order mirrors social order, which the orgy slurringly mocks.

. . .

Our homes provide the foundation for complex meanings, a significant subset of a larger human propensity to materialize symbols. Antedated for more than 1.5 million years by gestures and words, the earliest material objects, like the beads and etchings from Blombos Cave, date to approximately 70,000 years ago. It seems likely that earlier material symbols might be found. Subsequently, there is a diverse record of humans using symbols to mark places and their associations, whether rock art in the Kalahari, Australia, or Baja California, peak sanctuaries in Minoan Crete, or Upper Paleolithic paintings in Lascaux, Altamira, or Chauvet Cave.

Despite this lengthy ancient history of symbols and signs, the archaeological evidence suggests that the complex symbols associated with dwellings were devised only after humans began to occupy a structure for a length of time—either a portable lodging that they reconstructed as they moved or a permanent house where they lived.

The complex symbolic associations of home are well documented in anthropological studies of modern and historic traditional societies—such as the Kabyle farmers, Saami reindeer herders, and Navaho ranchers discussed above. Perhaps it is more surprising to see the range of meanings associated with home in the domestic traditions of the West, whether in the obsessive domesticity of the seventeenth-century Dutch or the fortress-like twenty-first-century American house with its owner's retreat. Many such meanings would evaporate with time, failing to leave behind a robust material record that an archaeologist could discover and decode. But as the example of the Pawnee earth-lodge suggests, there are often meanings that can be discovered through careful excavation and thoughtful interpretation. Such investigations are central to understanding the prehistory of home.

After ancient humans settled down, our homes became a potent focal point for multiple meanings and distinctions, many posed as binary oppositions: Life/Death, Male/Female, Elder/Youth, Light/Darkness, Public/Private, Safety/Danger, Dawn/Dusk, Order/Chaos. At this point in the human experience, crossing the threshold meant more than simply avoiding the elements. Going home implied a position within a moral landscape.

CHAPTER 6

Apartment Living

I just want to say, you know: Can we, can we all get along?
Can we, can we get along?
—Rodney King, May 1, 1992

In the damp spring of 1806, the Corps of Discovery led by Meriwether Lewis and William Clark arrived at the Nez Perce village of Tumacheootool, which the explorers described as "in fact only a single house one hundred and fifty feet long . . . that contains twenty-four fires, about double that number of families, and might muster a hundred fighting men." While visiting the village of Tumacheootool, Lewis and Clark dined on a supper of "horse-beef and roots," the roots being the staples of camas *(Camassia quamash)* and biscuit-root, "and the noise made by women in pounding them gives the hearer the idea of a nail factory."[1]

Unlike bees or termites, humans do not naturally cluster in dense hives. In the broad view of human history, large communities are relatively rare and unstable. As discussed in chapter 2, archaeological evidence of social life dates to at least 2 million years ago, although the oldest dwelling currently known is about 450,000–350,000 years old. For most of human prehistory, dwellings have been occupied by relatively small groups of people, seldom more than two or three families and often a single nuclear or extended family.

Yet, at certain times and spaces, humans have lived in densely occupied groups either under a single enormous roof in a big house or in separate dwellings packed together as tightly as the chambers of a honeycomb. When that has occurred, specific problems of social life tend to emerge—conflicts, rivalries, and passions—issues that either demand resolution or lead to chaos.

Of course, different societies have distinctive notions of social space, privacy, and retreat. The ethnographer Lorna Marshall wrote of the band of !Kung San, "Conversation in a !Kung werf [i.e., the camp] is a constant sound like the sound of a brook, and as low and lapping, except for shrieks of laughter."[2] Marshall noted the profound desire for social contact among the !Kung San who "are also extremely dependent emotionally on the sense of belonging and companionship." Living in bands of 10 to 60 people and clustering together around campfires in the open savanna of the Kalahari, the !Kung San create these intimate spaces of social contact. "Their need to avoid loneliness," Marshall wrote, "is actually visible in the way families cluster together in the werfs and in the ways people sit, often touching someone else, shoulder against shoulder, ankle across ankle. Comfort and security for them lie in belonging to their group, free from hostility or rejection."

Nine thousand years ago on the rich Anatolian farmlands of central Turkey, a low knoll was once a dense warren of homes. The site of Çatalhöyük was inhabited from 7400 to 6200 B.C. Beginning as a pre-pottery farming community, most of Çatalhöyük was occupied after 7000 B.C., developing into a large settlement, estimated as having 3500 to 8000 inhabitants spread across the 13.5-hectare eastern mound.[3] Çatalhöyük was first excavated by James Mellaart in 1961–1965; a second and ongoing excavation project was begun in 1993 by Ian Hodder. Both projects exposed a densely constructed zone of adobe-walled buildings, many with spectacular artwork, including vivid murals, modeled plaster reliefs, and stacks of horned bull skulls slathered with plaster.

Most of the houses were one- or two-story rectangular constructions, built from mud bricks and timbers. The houses consisted of sets of interconnected rooms and storage pantries, built from 0.4-meter-thick walls that originally were 2.5–3 meters tall. Floor plans varied, but most houses were 4–6 × 8–10 meters in size.

In fact, Hodder claims, "all there is at Çatalhöyük are houses and middens and pens."[4] Although only four percent of the site has been excavated, no plazas or courtyards, alleyways or streets, have been found at Çatalhöyük. People entered their homes via doors on their roofs, and neighbors clambered over each other's roofs to their own homes.

Given the densely packed dwellings, the community of Çatalhöyük must have experienced a variety of social frictions. A slumping wall in one house would damage a neighbor's dwelling. People and animals stomped over neighboring roofs. House mice skittered into food bins and under the reed-covered floors. Household garbage and human feces

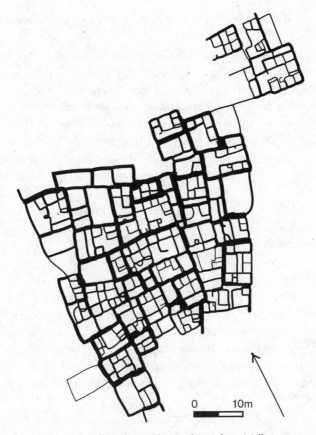

FIGURE 14. Çatalhöyük: site plan. Redrawn from Mellaart 1967.

were swept into small open areas between houses; sometimes an abandoned house was used as a dump. Filled with rotting organic material, the dumps must have attracted swarms of flies to these fetid trash-heaps, especially rank during the warm summer months.

And yet, people continued to live at Çatalhöyük, rebuilding homes, replastering the floors and walls dozens of times in the course of a residency, burying their loved ones in the house floors, covering the graves, and continuing to occupy the spaces. In this dense human hive clouded by cook-smoke and scented with rancid slops, the people of Çatalhöyük lived jammed together in their individual houses. No temples or communal buildings, no clan houses or community granaries—the people of Çatalhöyük lived bunched together in tight domesticity.

So now comes the obvious question: Why? Why did the residents of

Çatalhöyük live so densely packed together and why did they do so over 1,400 years?

The investigators have considered various hypotheses; each has been discarded. There is no evidence of an external threat that herded people together, huddling defensively in response to enemies. No special food-stuffs or other resources were unique to Çatalhöyük's location; residents ventured out to surrounding areas—tended sheep and cattle, grew wheat and other crops, hunted game and collected wild plants—and brought all those resources home. There were no obvious advantages from living in Çatalhöyük: no markets or craft-sellers, no oracle shrines or temple-mounds.

So why did 3,500 to 8,000 people cram themselves together on this knoll in central Anatolia?

No one knows.

. . .

In different places and at different times, people have lived in big houses. The anthropologist Roxana Waterson has studied longhouses built by traditional societies in mainland and insular Southeast Asia. Among a variety of societies living on Borneo, longhouses 150 meters in length may hold twenty or more families, each with an individual apartment linked by a long veranda. A single longhouse may shelter the entire community.[5] On the other side of the Pacific Ocean, on Puget Sound, the protohistoric and historic Suquamish "Old Man House" was more than 160 meters long, 12–18 meters wide, and may have housed 600 people.[6] The best documented big houses in North America, however, were further east, built by the six tribes of the Iroquois confederacy, the Ho-dé-no-sau-nee or "People of the Long House."

When Samuel de Champlain visited the Huron in 1616 he wrote the first detailed description of a northeastern longhouse:

> Their cabins are in the shape of tunnels or arbors, and are covered with the bark of trees. They are from twenty-five to thirty fathoms long, more or less, and six wide, having a passage-way through the middle from ten to twelve feet wide, which extends from one end to the other. On the two sides there is a kind of bench, four feet high, where they sleep in summer, in order to avoid the annoyance of the fleas, of which there were great numbers. In winter they sleep on the ground on mats near the fire, so as to be warmer than they would be on the platform.[7]

The nineteenth-century American anthropologist Lewis Henry Morgan estimated "a house one hundred and twenty feet long would con-

FIGURE 15. Longhouse of the Iroquois. From Morgan 1881.

tain ten fires and twenty families."[8] As Morgan noted, the longhouse developed "in ancient times," and excavations in New York and Ontario suggest the Iroquoian longhouse originated after A.D. 900.[9] Longhouse villages left a robust imprint of post-molds, wall trenches, pits and palisades, resulting in a dense archaeological record. More than 750 village sites are known from south-central Ontario alone, and the overall density of Iroquoian village sites is greater than other well-studied regions of the world, such as the Valley of Mexico or Neolithic Britain.[10]

The antecedents of the longhouse were oval dwellings about 6 × 4 meters in size and housing one or two nuclear families. Between A.D. 900 and the late 1200s, longhouses averaged about 15 meters in length and increased incrementally, perhaps as population increased after the introduction of maize blunted winter famines. After A.D. 1300 longhouses doubled in size, averaging 33 meters in length, and by the early 1400s longhouses became enormous dwellings, averaging 48 meters long and with some gigantic houses up to 124 meters (longer that a football field, including end-zones).

But why did longhouses become long?

Various hypotheses have been considered and rejected. One idea is that longhouses were expressions of conspicuous consumption: like the McMansions erected during booms in the stock market, perhaps Iroquoian houses grew larger as their inhabitants became wealthier. A reasonable hypothesis, but other lines of archaeological evidence indicate that Iroquois society was unranked and reasonably egalitarian. The largest longhouses have no evidence of elaboration or disproportionate accumulations, and prized objects (such as native copper or beads) are found in precontact sites of all sizes—not just in the largest longhouses.

Warfare is alternative explanation. Perhaps longhouses became larger as people banded together for the common defense. There is solid evidence for intensified warfare and raiding, especially in the early 1400s when Iroquoian settlements retreated to defensible positions and behind palisade walls. Yet, longhouses had increased in earlier periods with little evidence of conflict, and subsequently decreased from the 1500s to the 1700s, although war swept Iroquoian territories with unabated ferocity.

In the 1600s, the average Iroquois longhouse had shrunk to 20 meters, and by the late 1600s longhouses were replaced by single-family cabins. In 1881 Morgan wistfully wrote, "The Iroquois longhouses disappeared before the commencement of the present century. . . . A complete understanding of the mode of life of these longhouses will not, probably, ever be recovered."[11]

Despite Morgan's pessimism, archaeologists have recovered important insights into the modes of longhouse life. One insight regards Iroquoian social organization. Iroquois households were matrilocal; a newly wedded couple lived near or with the bride's family. Iroquois kinship was matrilineal; people traced their descent and identity through the mother's line. Whether female or male, an Iroquois belonged to the same lineage as her or his mother, who belonged to the same lineage as her mother, and so on over generations.

Ideally an Iroquois longhouse was occupied by a married woman, her daughters, and all their families—husbands and children—or by founding sisters, their daughters, and all of their families, each nuclear family occupying its own space within the longhouse, but forming a large extended kin group.[12]

Although only a minority of human societies is known to be matrilocal, about eleven percent according to some cross-cultural analyses, this residence pattern is associated with two factors: the importance of women's work, particularly in agriculture, and the extended absences of men from households. Both factors are relevant for understanding Iroquois home life.[13]

As maize agriculture increased in significance, women—who did all the farming except for the initial and laborious clearing of forests for new fields—provided three-fourths of all the food. Iroquois men were away from home often for weeks at a time, away hunting, fishing, on trading ventures, or waging battle campaigns. As the archaeologist and ethnohistorian Bruce Trigger wrote, "women were the guardians of family life and its traditions, men were charged with the responsibility for safety and order."[14]

Matrilineal kinship and matrilocal residence were ties of social unity incorporated into Iroquoian homes.[15] As one archaeologist observed, "The longhouse was the focus of Iroquois matrilyny."[16] Since many different societies live in big houses—societies with very different forms of social order—the development of longhouses per se is not "the result" of matrilocal residence, although it was a fundamental aspect of matrilineal Iroquois society by A.D. 1300 and thereafter.

Multifamily longhouses posed certain advantages. Heating was more efficient with more people collecting firewood for long northern winters. According to Morgan, the Iroquois had a kin-based form of "social welfare," in that "the principle of hospitality . . . came in to relieve the consequences of destitution."[17]

Despite such advantages, living with a hundred housemates must have posed problems and heightened social tensions. As archaeologist Garry Warwick notes, "From a modern perspective, life in an Iroquoian longhouse would have been unpleasant. In addition to being crowded and infested with mice, fleas, and other vermin, longhouses were constantly filled with dust and smoke and commonly caught fire."[18]

Yet, one might think that the real challenges of longhouse life were the social frictions and conflicts that might occur. Such tensions apparently were moderated by the bonds of kinship that linked nuclear families into larger social groupings, networks that united the residents of a longhouse and of different longhouses.

From its matrilineal core, the Iroquois constructed social order and political organization.[19] The matrilineal kin living in longhouses formed a model of nested, progressively inclusive social relations from wife-husband and siblings-cousins and all the way to friend and foe. As Trigger wrote, "Every human being, or group of human beings, whose existence was known to the Huron was considered to be either their enemy or friend."[20] To a large degree that distinction was rooted in the longhouse and the matrix of martilyny.

Beginning in the late 1300s, households, longhouses, and villages united into larger coalitions.[21] For example, oral traditions hold that the Seneca were unified by external threats even before the League of the Iroquois was established. Among the Hurons, multi-community coalitions were marked by the Feast of the Dead, a periodic event in which the bones of the dead were collected from their individual graves and reinterred in large, communal ossuaries.[22] Ossuaries found in Ontario have upwards of 500 individuals buried in a shared and common grave. Ceremonies like the Feast of the Dead tied separate communities into larger social networks.

As the European fur trade expanded, indigenous society was transformed. Long-standing enmities between the Huron and the League of the Iroquois erupted. In the early 1600s epidemics decimated the Iroquois as the Dutch established colonies on the Hudson, the French invaded Quebec, and Britain claimed New England. Smallpox was followed by measles. Longhouse life was a perfect environment for the spread of disease; if one occupant was infected, soon everyone was ill. "The horrendous losses of the middle decades of the seventeenth century," archaeologist Dean Snow writes, "threw the Iroquois into a convulsion of unending retribution against real and imagined enemies."[23]

Villages were occupied by survivors and captives. The authority of traditional leaders eroded. The Iroquois nations fought among themselves and against neighboring Indian nations. As France and England struggled for global domination during the eighteenth century, native nations were ensnared into the conflict as allies and enemies. Near constant battles and raids flared among the Iroquois, when the Seneca allied with the French and the Mohawk with the British. This violent conflict reduced to a simmer at the end of the Seven Years' War (1756–1763), only to boil over as American colonists raided Iroquois villages during the American Revolution (1776–1783). Increasingly, white colonists moved west onto native lands. The territory held by the Iroquois was reduced to miniscule reservations. The descendants of the People of the Longhouse lived in small cabins on tiny reserves. By the 1800s the longhouse was a shadowed memory.

. . .

In 1986 my wife, Janine Gasco, and I excavated a site on the coast of Peru. The coastal desert of Peru is one of the driest regions in the world. In places it receives less than one-eighth of an inch of annual rainfall, making it is drier than the Sahara. Much of the coastal desert is nearly bare of vegetation, in some areas only supporting miniature lichen that tints sand dunes slightly green.

In verdant contrast, this lunar desert is sliced by a series of river valleys, drainages that begin in the Andean cordillera and slope west to the sea. These valleys contain fertile farmland and for that reason attracted human societies throughout Andean prehistory. People settled the val-

FIGURE 16. Archaeological excavations at Quebrada
Santa Cristina, Casma Valley, Peru.

leys; built villages and cities; constructed temples, palaces, and fortresses;
created mausoleums and cemeteries; and, of course, built homes.

The site we excavated, Quebrada Santa Cristina, stretched across a
dry and rocky alluvial fan on the south margin of the Casma Valley,
about two hundred miles north of Lima. Despite covering more than
seven acres, nothing about the site was impressive. No towering mounds;
no massive walls. In fact, Quebrada Santa Cristina was invisible until
you walked across its stony surface and looking down saw the litter of
potsherds and the slight traces of ancient dwellings.[24]

The site was part of the Chimú Empire. After about A.D. 900 the
Chimú created one of the largest cities in the prehispanic Americas, their
sprawling mud-walled capital of Chan Chan in the Moche Valley of
Peru. After consolidating their Moche Valley homeland and neighbor-

ing regions, the Chimú expanded, raiding north to defeat the wealthy Lambayeque kingdom and marching south to conquer smaller villages and chiefdoms. They arrived in the Casma Valley around 1350, where they co-opted local settlements and built new towns. The Chimú ruled this southern frontier until 1470, when they were conquered by the great Andean empire from the south, the Incas.

At the modest site of Quebrada Santa Cristina, the stubs of prehistoric walls poked up in ragged lines among the shards and stones. The walls had been built from a wickerwork of river canes, still a common construction technique on the rainless coast of Peru—especially for poor people unable to afford concrete blocks or adobe bricks. Among the Chimú, buildings constructed from different materials similarly marked the distinctions of class: royalty and nobles lived in adobe-walled houses, commoners occupied dwellings made from canes.

Quebrada Santa Cristina was built from canes. Our team of excavators and workmen swept away sand and cleared rocks; instead of trowels, we used brooms. As the wall-clearing progressed and the layout of Quebrada Santa Cristina was exposed, it became obvious that the site had been constructed at a single moment as a large, planned community.

The collective nature and brief occupation at the site grew clearer during the months we excavated at the site. Quebrada Santa Cristina had been occupied only once: the thin layer of artifacts and food debris covered sterile sand and gravel. The walls were laid out in blocks of rooms. External walls were built in straight lines up to 75 meters long, and then subdivided by interior walls to form small cubby-spaces 9 to 12 square meters in size. In this way, blocks of rooms were quickly defined and built, and the perimeter walls of adjacent room blocks formed long straight corridors and alleys. Some 280 rooms and patios were built, the densest concentration on the southern end of the site. On the northern flanks additional room blocks were planned, but never completed: the stony surface was cleared of rocks and exterior walls were built, but the rooms were never finished.

In this expansive maze of cane-walled rooms, food was prepared in only two or three communal kitchens. Large grinding stones were standard equipment in ancient Peruvian kitchens, huge granite blocks on which corn and other foodstuffs were pulverized. Grinding stones were as ubiquitous in ancient Chimú homes as stoves in a modern American kitchen. In other nearby sites I had excavated, there was one or more grinding stones for each house, literally dozens of large blocks spread across the remains of a prehistoric neighborhood. In contrast, there

FIGURE 17. Quebrada Santa Cristina—Overview of excavations showing extensive cane walls.

were only nine grinding stones at Quebrada Santa Cristina, and these were located in three open patios that also contained dense scatters of food debris—shells, corncobs, and fish bones. Interestingly, the only plant foods we found at Quebrada Santa Cristina were the common staples of corn and beans; there was no trace of the array of avocado pits, fruit seeds, and other fresh foods we uncovered at other sites. At Quebrada Santa Cristina, people ate a narrow diet of stored foods.

The absence of fresh food at the site was puzzling since a vast expanse of prehistoric raised-bed farming fields sits in front of Quebrada Santa Cristina. Visible in air photos, the fields covered more than a square mile of the lower Casma Valley.

Raised fields consist of a mounded bed surrounded by ditches, a farming technique found throughout the tropical regions of the world. In some places people plant crops in the damp soils of the ditches. On the edge of Lake Titicaca, ancient farmers mounded up raised beds to protect potato vines from killing frosts, as the colder air flowed downslope and away. Throughout the Americas, raised fields were used where rivers seasonally overflowed their banks, and farmers planted above the floodwaters. Intriguingly, the prehistoric raised fields in the Casma Valley were the only ones known from the coast of Peru.

So there were several alternative reasons for this type of farming. As part of our project at Quebrada Santa Cristina, we also excavated trenches in the fields to learn how they were used and why they were built.

We cross-trenched the fields and exposed their patterns of soils and sediments. What we discovered was interesting: the tops of the fields were a mottled jumble of clay clods, dark organic humus, and silts. The furrows between the fields were unmixed: a dark layer of organic materials covered intact curved layers of clay and silt. This meant that the tops of the fields had been cultivated, churning the topsoil, but the furrows were not farmed. The farmers planted on top of the fields, above the surrounding floodwater.

There was only one problem with this: the Casma Valley rarely gets "too much" water. Generally, the problem for modern farmers is not enough water. It rarely rains on the desert coast and fields in the lower valleys are often dry.

Except during El Niños.

As most people know, the El Niño phenomenon occurs when sea temperatures, ocean currents, and trade winds in the tropical Pacific vary from their "normal" patterns. When this happens, there are two basic consequences for western South America: the cold waters of the northward-flowing Humboldt Current heat up, and torrential rains pour on the North Coast of Peru. Two lines of evidence indicated Quebrada Santa Cristina was occupied in the aftermath of an El Niño.

First, geological studies of the Casma Valley discovered flood sediments associated with a prehistoric El Niño and radiocarbon dates on organic materials in the sediments pointed to an El Nino at approximately A.D. 1330.[25]

Second, there were no mussels in the kitchen debris at Quebrada Santa Cristina. Mussels are wiped out by El Niños, because the warmer sea waters temporarily destroy phytoplankton the shellfish eat. In normal years, mussels are abundant in the cool waters of the rocky coast. Mussels make up 70%–80% of all the shellfish consumed in Peru, and mussels were ubiquitous in other Casma Valley archaeological sites. But there were none at Quebrada Santa Cristina, even though the community was less than a mile from the sea and despite the presence of the shells of other mollusks.

Collating all these bits of information, it seems that Quebrada Santa Cristina housed prehistoric laborers who built the raised fields in the aftermath of floods and destruction caused by a fourteenth-century El

Niño. A major El Niño would have destroyed large swaths of irrigated farmlands, washing away canal systems and capping fields with layers of gravels and silt. While those irrigation canals and agricultural fields were being rebuilt, people needed food and the raised fields provided a quick alternative. We think the Chimú Empire supported the people who built those fields: quickly erecting the walls of Quebrada Santa Cristina, organizing communal kitchens, and provisioning the workers with ration bowls of beans and corn.

So in this case in prehistory, people lived in this densely occupied camp for a specific reason. The community had no other purpose than constructing the raised fields. No other social framework or cultural rationale held these ancient people to this place. Once their task was completed, the occupants of Quebrada Santa Cristina abandoned the settlement, leaving behind the traces of their presence, soon covered by desert sands.

. . .

Abandonment is recurrent in the ancient American Southwest. The vast reaches of pinyon mesas, scoured dry washes, and mesquite-covered playas were home for distinctive prehistoric traditions, agrarian societies who raised corn on the tenuous edge between aridity and frost.[26]

After the fourth century A.D., the Hohokam of central Arizona developed substantial communities and extensive irrigation systems in the Gila River drainage over a territory of 100,000 square kilometers.[27] As many as 40,000 Hohokam lived in villages and farmsteads, many occupied for multiple generations. The largest site, Snaketown, developed over centuries into a major center. By A.D. 700–1100 Snaketown had a population of as many as 2000 people, and another 1000 people lived at the neighboring Grewe site. The people lived in large pithouses grouped around courtyards, while central Snaketown held plazas and ballcourts that could hold hundreds of people.

At A.D. 1150 Snaketown was abandoned.

Ninety kilometers to the southeast, a large multistoried structure was erected at the Hohokam site of Casa Grande, a distinctive form of architecture that may have housed relatively few residents, serving more as a ritual space, a storage area for esoteric regalia, or even an astronomical observatory. A handful of other Hohokam sites may have had similar structures, but such "Great Houses" were rare and their functions are poorly understood. By A.D. 1450 the Hohokam tradition ended, their once-extensive world depopulated.

Centuries earlier, a similar pattern of development and abandonment occurred in Chaco Canyon, in northwestern New Mexico.[28] The most complex settlement in the Ancestral Pueblo region, Chaco is famous for its dozen Great Houses erected beginning in A.D. 850. Pueblo Bonito was the largest, a D-shaped Great House built in a dozen phases between 1020 and 1125. Covering over two acres and containing nearly seven hundred rooms, Pueblo Bonito was four to five stories tall. Archaeologist Stephen Lekson writes that Pueblo Bonito and the other Great Houses of Chaco Canyon began "as monumentally up-scaled versions of regular domestic structures . . . but Great Houses took a canonical turn in form and function that distinguished them from regular residences."[29] This included the incorporation of kivas, circular subterranean chambers that were ritual spaces that were modeled on the universe.

Despite its hundreds of densely packed rooms, Pueblo Bonito held only a score of families, perhaps fewer than one hundred people. Great Houses were not pueblos but rather multipurpose constructions, combining residences for an elite few, sacred spaces, and storage, "surrounded by loose clusters of much smaller family habitations."[30] In turn, the dozen Great Houses in Chaco Canyon served as architectural templates for settlements over a vast region of the Colorado Plateau. Some of the builders of these Chacoan "outlier" sites were clearly familiar with the hidden details of Bonito-style masonry; other builders had only a superficial knowledge of the style.

While Chacoan peoples built Great Houses, settlements tended to be smaller and simpler across the pine-forested mesas and canyons in the Four Corners area of the Colorado Plateau. Occupied by a single nuclear or extended family, each site was a small group of aboveground structures around a modest subterranean structure or kiva, forming what archaeologist William Lipe has called "a relentlessly modular habitation unit."[31] Built between A.D. 1050 and 1150, these small homesteads were sprinkled across Mesa Verde and other parts of the Colorado Plateau. A few communities had either larger kivas or "outlier Great Houses," local constructions modeled after Chaco, which was abandoned around 1150, but remained a sacred space emulated by others.

In the late 1100s and early 1200s, the settlements grew on the Colorado Plateau. More and more blocks of rooms crowded together around Great Houses or kivas, sites with as many as fifty or more homes of densely packed rooms. After 1240 this process accelerated, as people moved into large pueblos. More and more people lived in fewer and

FIGURE 18. Great House at Chaco Canyon. Photo courtesy Stephanie Hawkins.

fewer sites, many consisting of apartment-like complexes of buildings surrounding plazas, and incorporating small kivas directly into the blocks of rooms.

Superficially like the earlier Chaco Great Houses, these Ancestral Pueblo houses in the Four Corners region seem to represent communities without major differences in family wealth, prestige, or power. Resolutely egalitarian, the families clustered together linked by kin ties, shared faith, and fresh water.

Jammed onto the bench of a naturally carved sandstone vault, the ruins of Cliff Palace are shaded from mid-summer sunlight. The iconic ruin of Mesa Verde National Park, Cliff Palace was built between 1260 and 1280, and although it is the largest cliff dwelling in North America, its 150 rooms probably housed fewer than 100 people. Today tourists dutifully follow park rangers on the guided tours through this Ancestral Pueblo ruin, first discovered in the late 1880s by the Wetherhill brothers of nearby Mancos, Colorado, local boys who combined ranching and trading with pot-hunting and artifact selling. When in 1891 the Swedish naturalist and nobleman Baron Gustaf Nordenskiöld excavated at Cliff Palace and other Mesa Verde sites, he was one of the first prehistorians

FIGURE 19. View of Cliff Palace, Mesa Verde, before excavations. Photographer unknown.

to use rigorous excavation techniques in North America. The resulting monograph was the first major report on archaeological research in the United States.

Just as in the small homesteads, larger communities were composed of clusters of families living around a kiva, a social group of people who knew each other intimately interacting in a face-to-face "first-order community."[32] Sometimes these communities were dispersed, on other occasions tightly clustered, but they were always woven together in a network of social interactions. As settlements grew larger, bringing together numerous first-order communities, conflicts may have intensified (over farmland, for example), and new ways of resolving those conflicts were necessary. Among the Ancestral Puebloan peoples, these tensions were, in part, resolved through rituals conducted by clans in Great Kivas.

Great Kivas had many features in common with smaller, household kivas: they were subterranean, their interiors were organized along a north-south axis, and they were hidden: activities within kivas were only visible to those allowed to enter. A bench ran along the inner perimeter, seating for the select few. The *sipapu,* a covered hole in the kiva floor, represented the place of original emergence through which the ancestors emerged from the underworld.

At their largest, the Great Kivas were less than 15 meters in diameter. At Aztec Ruins for example, the original excavator, Earl Morris, reported in 1921 that the Great Kiva was precisely "41 feet 3 ½ inches in diameter," and even if Morris's population estimate of 700–1000 people is an overestimate —100–200 residents is more reasonable—the Great Kiva was still too small to hold the entire community.[33]

And then the Colorado Plateau was abandoned. Beginning in the mid-1200s people began emigrating from the Four Corners region, and by 1290 the area was largely depopulated. Precisely dated by the tree rings of pine timbers in pueblo houses, the demographic plunge is striking: robust growth across the region from 1200–1210, a boom in house construction and population in 1270–1275, and complete abandonment by 1300.

A laminate of causes produced the Ancestral Puebloans' withdrawal from the Colorado Plateau. Some factors "pushed" people from the region, while others "pulled" people southeast to establish new pueblos along the Little Colorado and Rio Grande drainages. A significant drought in 1276–1299 affected ancient farming communities in the Four Corners region, particularly people who were farming thin upland soils without irrigation. The impacts of drought were intensified by the number of people already living in settled communities with defined territories; it may have been harder for folks to become nomadic. Warfare and conflicts may have intensified among the Ancestral Puebloans, initially contributing to larger communities as people banded together for defense only to make matters worse: more people, fewer resources, followed by more conflicts. It was, as archaeologist Timothy Kohler and colleagues have written, "a cascade of events."[34]

Other factors might have attracted migrants from the Four Corners region to the Little Colorado and Rio Grande drainages.[35] More reliable summer rains and innovative religions may have attracted people to resettle in this region. The exact reasons for the relocation are complex, but the general pattern is relatively clear: over two and a half centuries, humans moved out of an area they had occupied for the previous five hundred years and resettled on the mesas and river valleys of northeastern Arizona and northern New Mexico. The emigrants established new pueblos in some areas, while others sought refuge in already established communities.

Oral histories recall the saga and trauma of emigration. The anthropologist Florence Hawley Ellis records that the ancestors of Laguna Pueblo had come from the north, presumably the Four Corners region, "as a result of a number of years of bad drought brought about by the lack of obedience to Our Mother Nature . . . and insufficient attention to religious practices, a typical Pueblo explanation for failure of natural resources and for group movement."[36]

The people of Acoma Pueblo also had come from the north, refugees in a landscape of death and dissension. A dispirited remnant band settled at the base of a tall snake-infested mesa. Struggling to establish a new home and placate the spirit beings, the people battled giants and a gigantic bird monster with wings of flint. Finally regaining the protection of the spirit beings, medicine men removed the rattlesnakes from the mesa, and the people occupied the mesa top where they constructed a new pueblo. These legends, Ellis suggested, described harrowing events of cultural trauma that were preserved and remembered in "a soul shaking saga."[37]

After A.D. 1300 in the Southwest, a new form of settlement became common: a pueblo with large plazas, smaller kivas, and single and multistory blocks of rooms. Although this settlement form had appeared previously at about 1050 in the Mimbres region to the east, villages occupied by large groups of people became the norm in the fourteenth-century refugia of the Puebloan Southwest.

Not all of these communities were successful. For example, Grasshopper Pueblo in the White Mountains of Arizona was established in 1295–1305, grew rapidly into a town of more than five hundred people by 1330, and then was abandoned by 1350.[38] Elsewhere, though, these communities endured as dense settlements surrounding plazas where masked spirit beings danced.

"One of the hallmarks of Pueblo religion is the performance of ceremonial dances by groups of masked individuals (representing Katsinas, or supernatural beings) in open-air plazas."[39] The katsina religion may have developed in the Mimbres region as early as 1100, although some scholars place its development in west-central Arizona during the fourteenth century. Because every pueblo has its own katsinas and oral histories, it is difficult to point to the religion's specific place of origin. Given the literally hundreds of katsinas depicted in petroglyphs and pottery or associated with historic and modern pueblo communities, it is similarly difficult to make sweeping generalizations. Yet, in essence, katsina religious practices involve different groups of initiated men dedicated to select katsinas. Devotees of specific katsinas were drawn from different kin groups, and thus katsina societies united the pueblo. "This ritual system is characterized by community-wide ceremonies that crosscut lineage groups and fostered village integration," the archaeologist T. J. Ferguson has written.[40] Pueblo plazas became arenas for ceremonies that simultaneously display the magnificence of katsina groups, attract and honor the supernatural beings, and unify the community. Katsina groups and community-wide ceremonials were the weft and warp of Puebloan social fabric.

The katsinas survived the Spanish *entrada* in 1540, the imposition of Christianity, the massive and temporarily successful Pueblo Revolt in 1680, the reassertion of Spanish control in the 1690s, raids by neighboring Navaho and Apache groups, and the repercussions of Manifest Destiny. Pueblo nations built their settlements in ways that held communities together. The Pueblos represent remarkably resilient ways of living in large social groups who were bent but unbroken by Spanish conquest, Catholicism, American imperialism, and modern tourism. Unlike earlier Southwestern societies at Chaco Canyon, Mesa Verde, and elsewhere, the pueblos survived. This is not to suggest that the pueblos are fossilized remnants of an indigenous past, but to recognize that these communities have survived while living in densely packed villages and towns.

In that there is a lesson.

. . .

In 1992 when the beating victim Rodney King famously and plaintively asked, "Can't we just all get along?" after Los Angeles's worst race riots in thirty years, he was posing a question that philosophers and poets, political scientists and novelists have pondered for millennia. From Plato's models of the just society to Cormac McCarthy's dystopian *The Road,* the question "What holds society together?" is one of our most central inquiries. It is also one of the most difficult to answer.

The prehistory of home suggests that human societies are inherently unstable, and especially so when households have unequal shares of wealth and power that make mockery of ideologies of egalitarianism. One possibility is that human societies have innate thresholds of growth, which—once passed—require new ways of dealing with conflicts. As groups become larger, conflicts grow even more rapidly, a truth that any elementary school teacher or chair of an academic department understands.

The cultural anthropologist Roy Rappaport called this phenomenon "the irritation coefficient." Studying the Tsembaga in New Guinea, Rappaport observed that "the frequencies of some kinds of disputes are dependent on population densities" and those "sources of irritation . . . increase at a rate greater than [increases in] population size. If population increase were taken to be linear, the increase in some kinds of dispute might be taken to be roughly geometric."[41]

The archaeologist Gregory Johnson explored this issue in greater precision. Based on a cross-cultural analysis, Johnson concluded that it was not population per se that resulted in increased social irritations, but rather the number of the individual agents or units within a social group. Larger numbers of individuals can coexist, if they are classified into a smaller number of social groupings, such as families, neighborhoods, ethnicities, or katsina groups. Rather than simply a matter of numbers, Johnson found that intolerable stresses are created when everyone's individual demands become collectively overwhelming. There is too much clamor. When that occurs, a social group undergoes what Johnson called "scalar stress." Something must change.

Much of Johnson's argument is so commonsensical it may seem unimpressive, except for two points. First, Johnson showed there was a surprisingly uniform threshold for scalar stress: six. He argued that "there are rather severe limits on the maximum task size of task-oriented groups that are organized . . . nonhierarchically," limits reflecting human capacity to process information. And, Johnson insisted, this was true whether we are discussing individuals, two-person teams, or committees: when there are more than six entities involved, it becomes difficult to accomplish tasks. Once this threshold is crossed, disputes increase and decisions are harder to make.

Second, when human societies cross this barrier, Johnson argued, they deal with scalar stress in one of several ways. They may fission, splintering into smaller groups and reducing tensions in the process. They may develop social hierarchies, delegating specific classes of decision making to particular actors and thus reducing the sources of social tensions. Or they can redefine the essential social unit. For example, in small camps of !Kung San hunters and gatherers, the essential unit was the nuclear family, in more populous bands extended families were the building blocks—but in either case, the number of basal units was around six. So Johnson's research suggests that as human societies become larger, there are essentially two alternative paths other than fissioning: either develop hierarchy or redefine the groups.

This may be borne out by the changing sizes of Iroquoian longhouses. From A.D. 900–1200, longhouses had an average length of 15 meters, housing four to six families, and thus below the threshold of scalar stress. By 1330–1350, longhouses doubled in average length to 30 meters and were occupied by eight to twelve families, who although matrilineally related by female kin also included husbands from other kin-groups, a source of potential social fracture. It may be that moiety affiliation and clan affinities smoothed over these tension points, and it is interesting that while the Oneida and Mohawk had three clan names, other Iroquoian groups had eight clans but these were divided into two moieties, thus reducing the social distinctions below the scalar threshold. When in the 1400s longhouses again increased in size to an average of 45 meters, additional and larger coalitions were developed in Iroquoian society.

A similar process may have happened in American Southwest during the thirteenth and fourteenth centuries. If one assumes that the protohistoric Pueblos were as resolutely nonhierarchical as historic and modern Pueblo societies—with strong cultural constraints inhibiting the accumulations of wealth or power—then how did larger communities deal with scalar stresses, especially when they were living packed together and literally on top of each other? In a community, like the Hopi town of Orayvi, with upwards of a hundred households and a thousand residents, what was the response to scalar stress?

An intersection of human responses. Individual families were linked into more inclusive kin groups, such as clans; when the number of clans grew above the scalar threshold, clans were clustered into two or more sets. Further, katsina sodalities overlay kin-based groupings, binding together people from different parts of the pueblo.

Finally, there was the strong Puebloan emphasis on egalitarianism. In utopian communes the most consistent source of dissension is unequal access to material wealth; other inequalities may be tolerated (gender distinctions, status differences, or access to sexual partners), but glaring disparities in material wealth are intolerable.[42]

In 1906 the Hopi town of Orayvi, originally established in the 1100s and the most conservative Hopi pueblo, fractured in a bitter dispute that split the community in half. The cause? Despite its egalitarian values, in reality some Orayvi clans controlled better farmland, while other clans only had marginal land. Deteriorating environment in the early twentieth century exposed the internal contradiction between an egalitarian ethic and the actual inequalities, leading to "a revolt of the

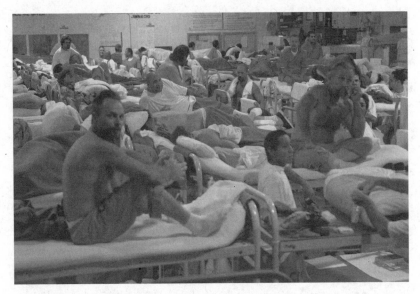

FIGURE 20. California Institution for Men, 2006. California Department of Corrections and Rehabilitation.

landless." Orayvi splintered, the landless half of the community left to establish two other pueblos, and the community began a long, steady decline.[43]

The archaeology of apartment life would suggest that the answer to Rodney King's question, "Can't we all get along?" is "No." When groups of more than fifty to one hundred people live closely packed together in permanent settlements, social frictions intensify. Those tensions may be partially constrained through conceptual sleight-of-hand: regrouping families into larger social units like Pueblo clans and ritual sodalities or Iroquois longhouse groups and matriclans. Ceremonies may rearticulate a vision of cohesion, whether a Snake Dance witnessed in a Pueblo plaza or the massive reburials in Huron ossuaries. A group may cohere around a specific shared task, like the need to rebuild farmlands in the lower Casma Valley, but then evaporate once the immediate task is completed.

Perhaps Çatalhöyük was the great exception, a community of several thousand people living cheek-to-jowl in harmony in the absence of any integrative structures above the individual family, but it seems more probable that this vision of Neolithic Anatolia will be revised as more than the current four percent of the site is excavated. It may also be that the people of Çatalhöyük solved the problems of apartment living in ways that do not leave archaeological traces, perhaps with ribald teasings or prayerful injunctions for harmony.

But what the prehistory of home seems to show is that all these densely packed, ideally egalitarian, ancient communities ultimately are unstable. And that problem is as modern as tomorrow's news.

CHAPTER 7

Gated Communities

There it is. Not just a wall. A wall would be a fact. But this
wall is a philosophy . . .
—David Hare, *Wall: A* Monologue.

The Greek historian Herodotus writes of Deioces the Mede, a canny political leader who "was a man of great ability and ambitious for power."[1]
The Medes had overthrown their Assyrian masters and reverted to the
contentious equality of village life. A respected man in his own village,
Deioces gained fame as an arbitrator of intervillage disputes, chosen by
claimants to judge their merits and failings.

Behind this public facade of fairness, Deioces privately schemed.
Herodotus writes that "once the news of Deioces' integrity got abroad,
everyone was glad to submit cases to his judgment, until in the end he
became the only person they would turn to." As the cases mounted,
so did Deioces' prestige. Ultimately Deioces became the indispensable
man.

Claiming that he was tired of tending to others' matters while ignor-
ing his own affairs, Deioces threatened to "no longer sit in the chair of
judgment." The Medes debated the prospects of a chaotic future, and
in 710 B.C. they chose Deioces as their king. He ruled for the next fifty
years.

Deioces set to building. First, he commanded that a noble palace be
built that would be defended by a select royal guard loyal to him alone.
Next, Deioces commanded that the village-dwelling Medes build a great
walled city on a hill, Ecbatana.

Ecbatana was surrounded by seven concentric walls. Each wall was
progressively taller and painted a different color—white, black, crim-

son, blue, and orange—while the two innermost walls were sheathed in silver and in gold. Deioces' palace stood inside those gilded walls.

The walls of Ecbatana delineated more than just defensive fields. "When the work of building was complete," Herodotus writes, "Deioces introduced for the first time the ceremonies of royalty." Deioces withdrew behind a screen of new protocols.

"Nobody was allowed to see the king," Herodotus records. Messages were relayed through intermediaries; petitions were made and responded to in writing. The new protocols of kingship created a social distance "designed as a safeguard against his contemporaries, men as good as himself in birth and personal quality, with whom he had been brought up in earlier years. There was a risk that if they saw him habitually, it might lead to jealousy and resentment, and plots would follow; but if nobody saw him, the legend would grow that he was a being of a different order from mere men." Deioces punished any act of "arrogance or ostentation" that might rival his own splendor. And thus Deioces the King ruled the Medes and expanded his empire from within the golden walls of Ecbatana.

Twenty-five centuries later, Ecbatana was visited by the British archaeologist Austen H. Layard.[2] Only thirty-four years old and before his excavations at Ninevah and Babylon launched his spectacular Victorian career as archaeologist, author, and diplomat, Layard traveled overland from London to India in 1840, stopping en route at Ecbatana.

For Layard, Ecbatana was a roadblock rather than a destination, the scene of a frustrating month-long delay as he attempted to get travel permits from the local shah. Suspicious of the infidel traveler, the townspeople cursed and stoned Layard as he rode through the streets. Layard huffed, "The population of the city was fanatical, the soldiers were insolent and without discipline, and there were in the irregular cavalry wild fellows from the mountain tribes, who would not have scrupled to take the life of a Christian and a European."

In the face of such frustrations, Layard did what any archaeologist would do: he went out to look at archaeological sites.

The ancient name, Ecbatana, had been transformed by linguistic twistings to Agbatana, then Hagmatana, and ultimately to Hamadan. Hamadan held notable monuments of antiquity, including the tombs of the medieval Arab physician and philosopher Avicennes and of Esther, the Jewish maiden who won the heart of the Persian king, Xerxes, and freedom for the Jews.

But the walled city of Ecbatana was invisible. Layard grumped, "I explored the city and its neighbourhood in search of ruins, but without much success. A few mounds on an eminence at a short distance from the walls may mark the site of an ancient castle or palace, but with the exception of the shafts of some marble columns, and the figure of a lion rudely sculptured in stone, I found nothing to reward my trouble."

Layard knew his Herodotus and was familiar with the descriptions of the glorious walled city built by Deioces the Mede, but with the supreme self-confidence in personal empiricism (another trait Layard shared with modern archaeologists) he doubted the accuracy of the ancient accounts: "[Ecbatana] was renowned for the seven concentric walls of different colours, by which, according to Herodotus, it was surrounded to represent the seven heavenly bodies. That such walls ever existed is more than doubtful. I could find no traces of them."

The only walls Layard saw were the uninspiring, undecorated walls of the town of Hamadan. "The mud-built houses, or rather hovels, inhabited by the poorer classes were mostly in ruins," Layard wrote. "The streets were narrow and unpaved, and deep in mud and filth."

Even in the better neighborhoods, "houses . . . had no exterior architectural ornamentation. The outer walls, built of sun-dried or baked bricks were without windows" because, as Layard added in a footnote, "As the women in Persia are always kept closely concealed, the houses generally have no windows looking into the street which allow them to see, or be seen, by men."

The walls of Hamadan concealed their female occupants from sight, as the walls of Ecbatana had screened Deioces the Mede from scrutiny.

Just as the walls of Ecbatana enclosed a splendid palace, the interiors of the "the dwellings of the principal inhabitants of Hamadan were remarkable for the beauty and richness of their decorations." The inner courtyards had formal gardens and fountains. The rooms were painted, Layard wrote, "with the most intricate and graceful designs," and the scores of small mirrors in the coved ceilings reflected candle light producing "a most enchanting and fairy-like effect."

Secure from the mud streets, cursing residents, and barking dogs, the houses of the elites were constructed islands of order and beauty. Layard acknowledged, "It would, indeed, be difficult to imagine anything more truly enchanting than these abodes of the nobles and the wealthy merchants of Hamadan."

Twenty-five centuries of life behind walls.

. . .

The first walled cities probably sprouted in a landscape of conflict, and one of the earliest places this occurred was in southern Mesopotamia.[3] The first Mesopotamian cities developed between 4000 and 3100 B.C., as centers of religion, trade, and politics that were surrounded by smaller villages and towns. By about 2900 B.C. the majority of Mesopotamians had moved into the cities, all of which were surrounded by walls.

"Mesopotamian cities were usually surrounded by walls," archaeologist Susan Pollock observes. "Although undoubtedly built with an eye to defense, the monumentality and careful construction of at least some city walls attest to a concern with their symbolic value as well. Rulers boasting of their conquest of other cities frequently claimed that they had destroyed the defeated city's walls, a claim that archaeological evidence often indicates to be exaggerated."[4]

The greatest Mesopotamian city was Uruk. A vast wall, several meters thick and seven meters tall, surrounded the city, enclosing some 5.5 square kilometers. The wall was the creation of Gilgamesh, whom the gods made two parts divine and one part human:

> He had the wall of Uruk built, the sheepfold (Uruk-the-Sheepfold)
> Of holiest Eanna, the pure treasury (sacred storehouse)
> See if its wall is not (as straight) as the (craftsman's) string (like a
>   strand of wool),
> Inspect its . . . wall (battlements?), the likes of which no one can
>   equal . . .
> Go up on the wall of Uruk and walk around,
> Examine its foundation inspect its brickwork thoroughly
> Is not its masonry of baked brick,
> Did not the Seven Sages themselves lay out its plans?[5]

From Mesopotamia the creation of walled cities became a common, but not universal human response to conflict. The Athenians built two long defensive walls protecting the access to their port of Piraeus, walls that the victorious Spartans tore down in 404 B.C. at the end of the Peloponnesian War. Initially confident in the strength of their legions, the walls surrounding ancient Rome formed a "ritual and token defensive perimeter" until A.D. 272–280, when more substantial fortifications were built in "the greatest construction project in Roman history"—just as the Pax Romana devolved into chaos and the barbarians attacked the City of the Seven Hills.[6]

Descendants of Roman fortresses, European castles and walled cities responded to the attacks of Vikings in northern and western Europe, as Norsemen captured coastal and riverside cities from Rouen to Provence.

As the brief but influential Carolingian Empire fragmented after Charlemagne's death, the Viking raids intensified. Norsemen sailed up the Seine to sack Paris in 854 as Charlemagne's hapless heir, Charles the Bald, watched the pillage from the hill of Montmarte. Attacked by Vikings from the sea, Magyars from the east, and Saracens from the south, political authority fragmented among the countercurrents of invasion and disorder. Not surprisingly, castle-building and the fortification of cities began in the ninth and tenth centuries as central authority decayed and "walled cities, like walled castles, reflected the insecurities of the countryside."[7] By A.D. 1000 the vast majority of European cities were walled.

Black powder and projectiles transformed the walled city. The earliest European depiction of a cannon, a *pot-de-fer,* occurs in the 1326 manuscript, *De Nobilitatibus Sapientiis Et Prudentiis Regum* (On the Nobility, Wisdom, and Prudence of Kings) by Walter de Milemete, tutor to the future English king Edward III. Originally conceived as an explosive, dart-propelling alternative to the *ballista* (a massive crossbow), as artillery power and precision increased, so did the efforts to reshape defensive walls.[8]

Within two centuries, city walls were reshaped from encircling ramparts to slanting bastions, as fortifications were smithed by cannonades. Michelangelo's designs for the defense walls of Florence formed a classic star fortification, a walled plan so identified with warring Italian city-states that it became known as *il trace italienne.*

Idealized and reformed as bastions were extended, enlarged, and redivided, the walled city evolved into elaborate fractals. An increasingly complex assortment of glacis and counterscarps, hornworks and counterguards was developed to deflect bombardments and expose all frontal assaults.

Yet, each new and more elaborate defensive design carried within it the potentialities of defeat. Thus, the configurations of walls implied their specific routes for breeching, labeled in the 1728 *Encyclopaedia* diagram as "Trenches of Approach." The configurations of defense determined the parameters of assault, as certainly as the chess opening "White King's pawn e4."

The enigmatic architectural historian Austerlitz in W.G. Sebald's novel brilliantly summarizes the history of construction and destruction, in which "it had been forgotten that the largest fortifications will naturally attract the largest enemy forces, and that the more you entrench the more you must remain on the defensive." Austerlitz observed that "as the architectural plans for fortifications became increasingly com-

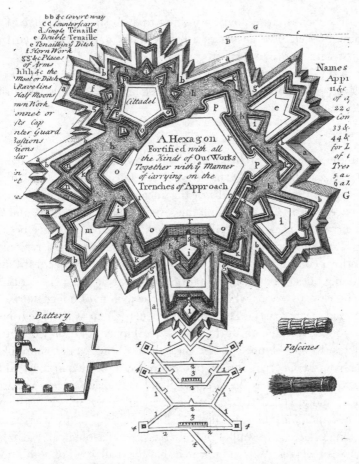

FIGURE 21. Idealized fortifications and their lines of attack. *The Encyclopaedia*, 1728.

plex, the time it took to build them increased as well, and with it the probability that as soon as they were finished, if not before, they would have been overtaken by further developments, both in artillery and in strategic planning."[9]

For example, Antwerp's city walls were destroyed by the French in 1832 only to be reconstructed over the next thirty years—bigger, better, and inevitably outmoded—resulting in an enormous fortification complex that the entire Belgian army was insufficient to hold.

We look at such enormous constructions, Austerlitz concludes, "in wonder, a kind of wonder which is in itself a form of dawning horror, for somehow we know by instinct that outsize buildings cast the shadow of their own destruction before them, and are designed from the first with an eye to their later existence as ruins."[10]

And thus the defensive trajectory that began at Uruk became a progressively brutal and futile process that staggered towards conclusion at Guernica.

. . .

Of all the subjects of archaeological inquiries, walls should be obvious. A wall is a wall is a wall. Therefore, it is a bit unnerving to learn that some of the best-known walls of the ancient world remain enigmatic. It is uncertain if Hadrian's Wall, the seventy-mile line of stone and turf built circa A.D. 122–28, actually held back the barbarous Picts, because many Roman forts along the wall overlooked uninhabited regions of the British countryside. Rather than a trans-insular barrier restraining screaming tides of barbarians, Hadrian's Wall anchored a chain of forts housing Roman troops who settled into the tedium of police work.[11]

On the north coast of Peru, the spectacular Great Wall of Santa was first spotted from the air during the 1931 Shippee-Johnson expedition. Geologist Robert Shippee piloted the Bellanca Peace Maker monoplane while Navy Lt. George Johnson photographed the Peruvian coast with a large-format camera.[12] The Great Wall of Santa snaked over the barren hillsides and graveled arroyos of the Peruvian coast. Shippee estimated that the Santa Wall ran some ninety kilometers, and soon it was dubbed "the longest defensive wall in the Americas." Archaeological research in the 1980s by David Wilson indicated that the wall was not continuous, but consisted of seven segments separated by gaps of two kilometers or more, spaces where walls had never been constructed and gaps unprotected by natural barriers. Instead of a defensive wall, Wilson concluded that the Great Wall of Santa served "as an extensive, visible barrier erected as a symbol of the social, or ethnic, divisions" in the region at circa A.D. 650–900.[13]

And so perhaps the Great Wall of China should not shock us. Despite legends that it was built by the first emperor of China to defend the Ch'in Empire from barbarian hordes, in fact the wall was built in fits, starts, and segments between the fourth century B.C. and A.D. 1500. (It has been suggested that the reason the astute Venetian observer Marco Polo never mentioned the Great Wall of China was because it wasn't yet constructed, while other scholars suggest Polo's omission indicates that he never really went to China.)

FIGURE 22. Great Wall of Santa. Shippee-Johnson Expedition 1931. American Museum of Natural History.

Amazingly, the overall length of the Great Wall is yet uncalculated, with estimates ranging from 4,247 to an impossible 50,292 kilometers; the most accurate current estimate stands at 6,259 kilometers of walls, supplemented by 359 kilometers of trenches and 2,232 kilometers of natural defenses.[14] Or so it is thought. The only indisputable fact about this Great Wall is that it is in China.

But ultimately walls have four essential purposes: to protect, to define, to proclaim, or to hide. And determining the purposes of walls requires going behind them.

. . .

The articulation of walls and the sacred lies at the heart of the Christian monastic tradition. Patterned on Jesus's solitary sojourn in the wilderness, where he resisted Satan's temptations, the compelling logic of monasticism is founded on withdrawal from the world. Derived from the Greek *monos* and literally meaning "dwelling alone," monasticism was initially twined with the idea of the hermit (from *erēmia,* "solitude, desert, wilderness, isolation.").

One of the earliest experiments in monastic life was created in the fourth century in the deserts of Egypt west of the Nile delta. Inspired by he *Life of St. Antony*—written by a near contemporary, Athanasius, the head of the Egyptian church—the tale was a biography that served as "a monastic rule in the form of a narrative."[15]

The son of a wealthy farmer, Antony renounced his possessions and withdrew from the world, initially occupying a necropolis. Walled into a tomb, Antony battled nightly with evil. Foul spirits slithered from the walls that lurched with seismic tremors, as Satan fought for Antony's soul. Night after night, St. Antony resisted the agonies of these malevolent onslaughts, until one night he reached the dark edge of death. At that moment, a beam of heavenly light pierced the tomb. The evil spirits dissipated, Antony's agonies ceased, and his valiant struggles were rewarded with the Lord's enduring blessings.

In A.D. 270, Antony moved into the desert in an act of *anachōrēsis*, or withdrawal. Antony inspired other aspirants to follow him, where they built monasteries in the desert. "And so, from then on," Athanasius writes, "there were monasteries in the mountains, and the desert was made a city by monks, who left their own people and registered themselves for citizenship in the heavens."[16]

An eminent Jesuit scholar has wryly commented, "Later, in the desert, Antony appears as a sort of spiritual land developer, taming the wilderness and reclaiming it from the demonic."[17] As St. Antony's story inspired followers, he withdrew further and further into the desert, seeking the solitude and deprivations of tormented contemplation. He died at the age of 106.

St. Antony inspired a generation of disciples, who built vast concentrations of hermitages in the desert. One of the largest of these is the site of Kellia, named for the monastic cells built in the arid landscape. Many of the hermitages were walled compounds ranging from small enclosures 12 × 15 meters that housed a single elder monk, while others were larger compounds measuring 40 × 60 meters in area, sheltering an entire community of monks.[18]

The concentration of monastic cells is amazing. In the 390s Kellia was home to six hundred monks, living in small and simple compounds. A stunning assortment of crosses, painted in red and gold, decorated the whitewashed mud-brick walls. By the sixth century, the hermitages grew into larger complexes that housed an elder monk, disciples, and the closed quarters of anchorites who had withdrawn from the two sources of temptation, the Devil and the Flesh.

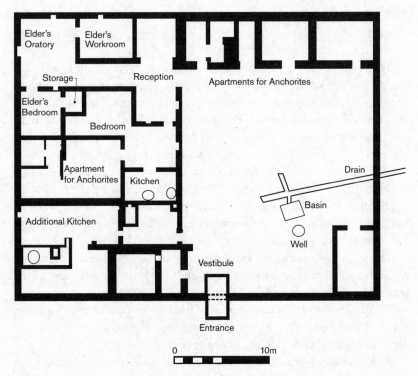

Elder's Oratory

Elder's Workroom

Storage

Reception

Apartments for Anchorites

Elder's Bedroom

Bedroom

Apartment for Anchorites

Kitchen

Additional Kitchen

Drain

Basin

Well

Vestibule

Entrance

0   10m

FIGURE 23. Plan of Hermitage, Kellia, Egypt. Redrawn and modified from Badawy 1978.

When the site of Kellia was discovered by the French archaeologist Antoine Guillamont in 1964, this cellular monastic settlement covered some forty-nine square miles. And although each individual hermitage was separated from each other—its single entrance manned by a gate-keeper—Kellia represented the simultaneous desire for isolation and companionship as monks withdrew into the desert together.

The impulse to renunciation is present in human societies of all scales and complexities. The social anthropologist Victor Turner wrote of the human search for liminality, the experience of being "betwixt and between" social statuses, and showed how this impulse was variegatedly manifest—in initiation ceremonies in traditional hunting and gathering societies or during the like-minded progression of pilgrimages.[19]

But renunciation does not always over-map with residence. Even in cultural traditions in which the religious undergo extended separa-tion and training, it is uncommon for entire reclusive communities to establish themselves behind walls. Explicitly rejected by Islam (with the exception of the Sufi order), Judaism, Zoroastrianism, and Baha'i, monasticism developed among the "world" religions of Christianity, Hinduism, Jainism, and Buddhism.

The conceptual origins of Buddhist monasticism unintentionally paralleled the life of St. Antony. Rejecting the pleasures of a nobleman's life, Siddhartha Gautama spent six ascetic years in the sixth century B.C. dedicated to austerities and bodily mortifications: starving himself, sleeping on thorns, and exposing himself to the broiling sun. These self-tortures were pointless. Taking sustenance, Siddhartha sat under the Bodhi Tree, vowing to sit in meditation until he achieved Supreme Enlightenment. Beset by demons sent by Mâra, the ruler of sensuality, Siddhartha remained unmoved. Gaining knowledge of his previous lives and obtaining a supernatural insight into suffering and existence, Siddhartha became Buddha.

The initial cadre of ascetics who became the Buddha's disciples formed a *sangha,* a monastic community and engaged ministry who spread the teachings of the Eightfold Path and periodically retreated to monasteries. Contributing to the construction of monasteries *(vahara)* was a pious act, and kings and wealthy patrons sponsored their construction, along with those of other Buddhist monuments.

As Buddhism spread from India across Asia—ultimately found from Samarkand to Japan and from Mongolia to Java—the construction of religious buildings became co-opted by local rulers and elites. Archaeologist Gina Barnes has noted that although Siddhartha renounced his throne and "became a wandering ascetic and preached rejection of this world, other rulers supported his disciples in order to enhance their own karma. The symbiotic relationships that developed between the sangha monkish community and the rulers of many different states throughout historic Asia accounts for the more magnificent Buddhist establishments that still exist today, either as ongoing monasteries or as stupendous archaeological sites."[20]

But while St. Antony and Siddhartha retreated behind walls to forgo wealth and worldly temptation, ancient kings like Deioces lived behind walls as a symbol of their power and secluded otherness. And this latter strategy of withdrawal and mystery not only occurred in ancient Persia, but also on the North Coast of Peru.

. . .

The vast site of Chan Chan sits on the edge of the Pacific Ocean on a dry pampa on the outskirts of Trujillo, Peru. The capital of the prehispanic

FIGURE 24. Aerial view, Chan Chan, Peru. Shippee-Johnson Expedition, 1931. American Museum of Natural History.

Chimú Empire, between A.D. 900 and 1470 Chan Chan developed into the one of the largest cities in ancient South America, spreading over 20 square kilometers. Chan Chan was by far the largest city in the Chimú Empire, whose territory stretched over 500 kilometers of the Peruvian coast.[21]

Some 30,000–40,000 people lived in Chan Chan. Most of them were poor. The lower class of Chan Chan lived in modest dwellings with cane walls, cobblestone foundations, and flat roofs of bulrush matting. Their homes were also their workshops, as most of Chan Chan's lower classes were artisans and craftspeople. They wove cloth from cotton threads and llama wool. The commoners pounded copper and copper-arsenic bronze into needles and fishhooks, jewelry and funerary masks. They carved the hard, dark wood of the algarrobo tree, making everything from hairpins to statuettes depicting gift-bearing courtiers, arm-bound prisoners, musicians, hunchbacks, and kings.

The commoners' houses sprawled in unplanned neighborhoods without main avenues or central plazas, a residential jumble of cane walls and hearth-smoke on the southern and western margins of Chan Chan's urban core. The commoners' cemeteries formed an irregular swath along the southern margin of the city, their burial grounds today scarred by the pockmarks of looters' pits.

And in the center of the city stood the walls. In brute contrast to the fragile walls of cane and cobbles, the center of Chan Chan was dominated by ten large royal compounds called "ciudadelas," each enclosed by solid spans of walls. The compound walls stood up to 9 meters tall, built from adobe bricks and a concrete-like conglomerate of slurried gravel and mud. The smallest ciudadela covered slightly less than 15 acres (6.7 hectares), the largest almost 46 acres (21.2 hectares).

The ciudadelas were the palaces, administrative centers, and mausoleums of the kings of Chimor. The royal ciudadelas are only found at Chan Chan, suggesting their unique role in the Chimú state. The compounds enclosed open plazas, banks of storerooms, open-air kitchens, and smaller structures that may have been sleeping quarters, shrines, or administrative areas. Most of the ciudadelas also housed a platform mound that probably served as the tomb for the Chimú king. The target of looters over centuries, none of the platform mounds were intact when the first archaeologist saw the site of Chan Chan.

Chan Chan has been known and visited for the last four hundred years. In the late eighteenth century, the bishop of Trujillo commissioned a map of the site and an architectural plan of one of the ciudadelas. During the nineteenth century, antiquarian travelers like the American E. G. Squier, the French Charles Weiner, and the German explorer Jakob von Tschudi made partial maps of the site and speculated on its history. The Swiss-born archaeologist and historian Adolph Bandelier—who had spent decades engaged in ethnographic and archaeological research in the American Southwest—studied Chan Chan in 1891, during a larger survey of Andean archaeological sites for the American Museum of Natural History. And when Shippee and Johnson flew over the coast of Peru, they were certain to take several pictures of Chan Chan from the air.

Despite all this information, the first detailed knowledge of Chan Chan was obtained only in 1969–1973 when a major archaeological project—the Chan Chan–Moche Valley Project, directed by Michael Moseley and Carol Mackey—gave sustained scrutiny to Chan Chan and surrounding sites in the heartland of the Chimú Empire.

But the large compounds posed an archaeological challenge. Extensive clearings of fallen rubble preceded mapping the compounds, and the research team produced extremely detailed plans of the ciudadelas.

Yet the specific activities that occurred within the compounds were elusive. Few objects were found in the banks of storerooms. In the rear of the compounds, there were open areas that contained traces of informal structures and domestic debris, possibly the place where servants lived. The burial platforms had been thoroughly and intensely looted. The ambiguous archaeology of the Chan Chan compounds led one eminent scholar to question whether they were, in fact, the palaces of the Chimú kings.

But two very different pieces of information have illuminated, at least in part, what occurred within the compound walls.

The first is a wooden model, arguably the single-most informative artifact ever found on the North Coast of Peru. Since the early 1990s, archaeologist Santiago Uceda has directed excavations at the enormous site of Moche, located ten kilometers east of Chan Chan.[22] Flanked by two massive constructions, the Pyramid of the Sun and the Pyramid of the Moon, the site of Moche was a major city by A.D. 200–500. Although largely abandoned as Chan Chan grew in significance, Moche retained ritual significance for the later Chimú and their descendants.

In 1995 Uceda and his team were excavating in the Pyramid of the Moon when they uncovered a pair of burials. The burials had been disturbed by looters, probably during the Colonial Period. The most intact burial contained the skeleton of a very high status young person, ten to fifteen years old, surrounded by offerings of llama, precious shells, and a suite of remarkable objects.

Among those objects was a model depicting an ancient ceremony occurring inside one of Chan Chan's royal compounds. Carved from wood, the model represents a plaza with its distinctive architectural features of ramp, bench, and slant-roofed portico, corresponding precisely to spaces excavated and mapped by the Chan Chan project. Inside the model were three principal figurines, carved from wood and inlaid with shell, that depict the mummy bundles of a Chimú king and two wives. In a surprising detail, the earlobes of the wives are different—one has a large, round Chimú-style ear-spool while the other wife has the split-lobed style associated with the Lambayeque, a North Coast kingdom that the Chimú conquered and incorporated in the fourteenth century. The miniature mummy bundles hint at dynastic linkages and calculated marriages.

The king presides over a vibrant ceremony. Two groups of musicians play drums and flutes, led by a conductor waving a large staff or rattle. A brewer wields a ladle in front of a large jar of maize beer *(chicha)*

FIGURE 25. Chimú wooden architectural model, Moche Valley, Peru. Photo courtesy of Santiago Uceda.

while a hunchbacked servant offers a large beaker. The plaza is filled with miniature baskets and chests representing offerings to the royal mummies, including a small model of a temple. It is a remarkable depiction of what occurred behind compound walls.

But, amazingly, these Chimú burials at the Pyramid of the Moon held other artifacts that told other stories. Uceda and his team found five small trays made from canes and covered with coarse cotton cloth on which other carved miniatures had been placed. A needle-bore through the heels of the figures was strung with cotton thread and each figure had been stitched into place.

These five complex artifacts are iconic tableaux portraying passages in the funeral ceremony. Two of the scenes are funeral corteges, showing a procession conveying mummy bundles to the ceremony. In another scene, a prisoner, arms bound behind his back, is marched to sacrifice accompanied by a trumpeter and staff-bearing guard. Another trumpeter leads a train of llamas, probably to their sacrifice as well. Another processional bears gifts to the dead Chimú king and queens.

In his book *The Savage Mind*, anthropologist Claude Lévi-Strauss asked:

What is the virtue of reduction either of scale or in the number of properties? It seems to result from a sort of reversal in the process of understanding. To understand a real object in its totality we always tend to work from its parts. The resistance it offers us is overcome by dividing it. Reduction in scale reverses this situation. Being smaller, the object as a whole seems less formidable. But being quantitatively diminished it seems to us qualitatively simpler. More exactly, this quantitative transposition extends and diversifies our power over a homologue of the thing, and by means of it the latter can be grasped, assessed and apprehended at a glance.[23]

I think this is precisely why the Chimú models from the Pyramid of the Moon are so informative. We can look at these icons and grasp a moment in the past. We can imagine the throaty drone of the trumpets and the pounding of drums echoing within the compound walls. The sweet smell of maize beer floats in the air. The padded clatter of llama feet. The approach of the prisoner and the final groan of agony. We glimpse what happened behind the tall compound walls.

The walled compounds at Chan Chan descended from an architectural tradition that first appeared on the North Coast of Peru at circa A.D. 700–900. Similar compounds, for example, do not occur at the earlier sites associated with Moche. Elite walled compounds are a North Coast architectural creation, like those at the site of Pacatnamú, a major site associated with the Late Lambayeque culture at circa A.D. 1100–1370/1400.

Pacatnamú sits on a large wedge-shaped terrace between the Pacific Ocean and Rio Jequetepeque flood plain, and the northern edge of the settlement was protected by dry moats and massive walls 5–7 meters tall. Between the terrace edges and the vast walls sits one of the largest concentrations of ceremonial architecture in ancient Peru. Fifty-three truncated pyramids with mound-top constructions dot the site. The largest pyramid, 70 × 70 meters at its base and 10 meters tall, is adjoined by a large quadrangle 175 × 170 meters in area that is surrounded by a wall 5 meters tall. Similar to the burial platform inside the Chan Chan royal compounds, a mortuary complex lies deep within the quadrangle hidden by the walls.

The origins of the Lambayeque dynasty were preserved in legends recorded in early Colonial documents. The remembered fragments of the legend tell of the arrival of Ñamlap, a lord from the far north of coastal Ecuador who, defeated in battle, sailed south to establish a new kingdom. Accompanied by a vast retinue of wives and concubines, courtiers and vassals, Ñamlap landed at the mouth of the Lambayeque Valley, at a place called Chot, where he founded his dynasty, built his palaces, and installed an idol, Yampallec, an green stone carved in his own image, which gives the Lambayeque Valley its name.

Ñamlap's rule was long and he fathered many children, but finally, as death approached, "so his vassals would not know that death had juris-diction over him," Ñamlap was secretly buried within his palace walls and it was announced throughout his kingdom that, due to his great virtue, Ñamlap had been transformed into a bird, taken wing, and thus escaped death.

His loyal courtiers, worried and saddened, could not understand why their beloved lord Ñamlap had abandoned them. Leaving behind their homes, families, and lands, the courtiers went forward, without guide or plan, to search for Ñamlap, swearing to not return until they had found him and brought him back. These loyal vassals ventured where no one had gone before. Nothing more is known of them.

The throne was inherited by Cium, Ñamlap's eldest son, who also ruled for many years. At the end of his life, Cium—in a mortality-deny-ing act similar to his father's—had himself placed in a crypt where he died, hidden behind walls, so that his people of Lambayeque would take him for an immortal and a god.

The legends describe a notion regarding the conceptual divide be-tween kings and commoners that was articulated in the Lambayeque culture and echoed in later Chimú practice. In this sense, the walled compounds of Lambayeque and Chimú societies served as architectural models of the social and existential divide between royals and ruled.

Mystery may be a source of power. The kings of Chimor, like Ñamlap and his heir, were buried behind the tall walls of Chan Chan, and were honored as being beyond death and thus sacred.

. . .

In western Europe, the monastic ideal meant retreat from this world, and new worlds were created behind walls. From its birthplace in the deserts that flank the Nile, Christianity's eremitic monasticism was introduced by Athanasius to Rome in 339 and by Martin to Gaul in 361. From these initial communities, monasticism was spread westward to Ireland by St. Patrick in 432, and the monastic life was adopted in Scotland and western Britain, before diffusing to mainland Europe and penetrating the northern frontiers of the waning Roman Empire in territories ruled by barbarian tribes. As competing forms of Christian monasticism vied for place and papal recognition, the construction of monasteries was stimulated by the teachings of St. Benedict. The Rule of St. Benedict

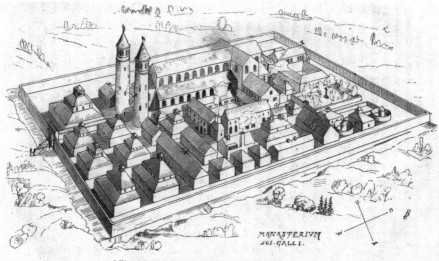

* Kloster Sanct Gallen nach dem Grundrisse vom Jahre 830. (Lasius).

FIGURE 26. Reconstruction of the Benedictine monastery of Saint Gall. From J. Rudolf Rahn, *Geschichte der Bildenden Künste in der Schweiz. Von den Ältesten Zeiten bis zum Schlusse des Mittelalters.* Zurich 1876.

"formed such a complete departure from the prevailing types of monarchism that it has been termed a revolution rather that a development from the earlier forms"; it was characterized by "a deliberate rejection of the individual rivalry in ascetic achievement, which had been the keynote of Egyptian monasticism, and the complete submersion of the individual in the community."[24]

A paragon of the Benedictine monastic tradition was the Abbey of St. Gall, located in northeastern Switzerland. In A.D. 830 the monastery was planned in red ink on a large vellum sheet.

The Plan of St. Gall was a masterpiece of design, outlining a model for a self-sustaining community of 270 men in an area of only 146 × 195 meters (or 480 × 640 feet). It was an architectural embodiment of the central Benedictine injunction: *ora et labora*. Pray and work.

The walls of St. Gall enclosed everything necessary for the moderate monastic life outlined by St. Benedict. Of course, the church was the largest structure, flanked by bell towers named for the archangels Michael and Gabriel. The cloister contained, as St. Benedict had instructed, "all necessary things such as water, mill, garden and various crafts . . . within the enclosure."[25] The bakery and brewery sat next to the gristmill. Monks copied manuscripts in the scriptorium; the handwritten books were housed in the abbey's library. The cloister contained no fewer than six kitchens: one each for the abbot, the monks, the novices, distinguished guests, the sick, and for pilgrims and paupers. There were workshops for barrel-coopers and wheelwrights. A small garden of medicinal herbs contained rosemary, mint, and fennel. An orchard of apple, pear, and quince grew among the burial plots in the monks' cemetery.

There is a profound difference between St. Gall and the dispersed compounds of Kellia. Although both were inspired by a withdrawal from the everyday world and devotion to spiritual pursuits, the moderate community of monks exemplified by the Plan of St. Gall was a conceptual world away from the individual asceticism and anchoritic retreat of the desert monks. The variations in monastic architecture reflect the divergent conceptions of the religious life.

Although an abbey stands at St. Gall, the monastery, as designed, was never actually built. Rather, the Plan of St. Gall served as a model of monastic life. This magnificent artifact of vellum and ink conveyed an entire worldview, inspiring the construction of the cathedral at Cologne and serving as paradigm of monastic life during the rule of Charlemagne.

In the Christian monastic tradition, withdrawal from the temptations of Satan and of the Flesh also entailed the segregation of communities based on gender. The establishment of convents for nuns, however, lagged behind the creation of monasteries in western Europe until the eighth to tenth centuries. In A.D. 320 and 327, St. Pachomius the Great (a disciple of St. Antony) had established nine coenobitic monasteries in Upper Egypt—two of them being for women—shared communities that contrasted with eremitic individualism. As ascetic monasticism spread to Ireland and western England, Anglo-Saxon England saw the development of "double minsters," religious communities composed of men and women under monastic rule. While some of these communities had cohabiting men and women, most consisted of distinct male and female cloisters separated and defined by walls.

As archaeologist Roberta Gilchrist has shown, the double minsters were replaced by distinct monasteries and convents by the tenth century in England, a trend that increased after the Norman Conquest and peaked in the late eleventh century.[26] The construction of nunneries lagged behind monasteries as they were considered a less favored object of noble patronage. Although the relative poverty of convents compared to monasteries is debated, the archaeology of convents indicates a basic similarity in plans. Like monasteries, convents enclosed and defined the faithful, separating them from the temptations of the world.

For nuns, this separation was more explicitly sexual. Gilchrist writes that the transformation of a secular woman into a nun "began with a ceremony in which the postulant donned bridal garments to commit her virginity to Christ. This union was symbolized by the wearing of the nun's finger-ring. Afterwards, the nun's hair, as a symbol of sensuality, was cut and she adopted the uniform common to each member of her order. Henceforward the nun shared a common identity with her sisters."[27]

The rejection of sexuality also required substituting individual identity with *communitas,* a spiritual objective shared by nuns and monks.

> Entry to a monastic community involved renunciation of all aspects of personal identity, including sexuality, family ties, and social status. The monastic rule used by the majority of communities, that of St. Benedict, warned initiates that "thenceforward he will not have disposition even of his own body. . . . " A medieval nun committed her celibacy to the church as a Bride of Christ, beginning with an initiation ceremony that involved adornment in bridal clothes and acceptance of a wedding ring. After having her hair shorn, and donning the identical habit of the nun, she forfeited individuality. The medieval religious woman embraced celibacy as a union with Christ, and her body became their shared, private space.[28]

But for medieval European women, this experience was conceptualized and spatialized in manners divergent from those of men. Gilchrest writes: "The metaphor of the female body, more specifically, provides the connotations of safe, contained spaces. . . . Conversely, medieval medicine explained the physiology of the body through architectural metaphors, with the body's interior perceived as contained, domestic and feminine. In his *Chirurgie* (1306–1320), for example, Henri de Mondeville explained that 'interior space, be it of the house or of the body, is a feminine place; for the first dwelling place of man is buried deep in the secret places of women.'"[29]

The ideas linking the body and building were expressed in spatial separations. A modern reader, nurtured on beliefs of individual will and free movement, might mistake separation for imprisonment. This would be an error.

In the medieval world, spatial separation marked distinctions of class. Kings and queens, for example, were separated from the masses. In castle architecture, Gilchrist writes, "the actual and metaphoric spaces of the castle enclosed both the female and male body. Indeed, its inner spaces were reserved for the man and woman of the highest status, with the chambers of the lord and lady, or king and queen, usually joined."[30]

The separation and seclusion of women was most evident "in ceremonial settings: church services, feasts, tournaments, pageants, funerals—but notably not in burial and commemoration."[31] Women of noble and royal birth were isolated for portions of their life, if for no other reason than to insure chastity, fidelity, and the purity of patrimony. The seclusion of monks was analogous to the sheltered existence of princesses, a point made by the medieval writer Orderic Vitalis who wrote, "True monks are enclosed in royal cloisters as if they were king's daughters, for fear that if they should wander abroad, they may be shamefully defiled."[32]

Despite such similarities, the architecture of gender separation marked distinct patterns and implications visible in the archaeology of monasteries and convents.

Access patterns channeled movements, preventing and encouraging different kinds of interactions. In the monasteries, the most deeply recessed place, the area at the greatest remove from the outside world, was the chapter house, the place where the business of a monastery was organized and conducted. In convents, the most secluded place was "the *dorter*, the communal sleeping areas of the nuns," Gilchrist writes, and "medieval nuns were contained within a private domain, not dissimilar to that of their secular counterparts [i.e., princesses and queens], which emphasized their chaste fidelity as Brides of Christ."

Such protective segregation of women is not unique to the Christian tradition. In secular dwellings—such as the Kabyle house—the pattern is most commonly expressed as a desire to protect women from "strange men," males from outside the family. When the scale of seclusion is an individual dwelling, the separation of women is correlated with a more general demarcation between the outside and public realm vs. the interior private refuge of the home. Archaeologists excavating a broad of array of sites from different regions and times have explored the way living space is divided based on gender, but one of the most fascinating and detailed insights come from the archaeology of Swahili houses.[33]

The Swahili have lived in eastern Africa since circa A.D. 500, occupying the seaboard from Somalia to Mozambique and the islands redolent in tropical mystique—Zanzibar, the Comoros, and the northern jut of Madagascar.[34] Since the days of the Roman Republic, the east African coast had been involved in trade with the Mediterranean. Between A.D.

700 and 1000, the Swahili were integrated into the long-distance trade networks that coursed the rim of the Indian Ocean. Large towns were established by 1000, commercial centers linking the villages of interior Africa to the trading dhows that coasted from India to southern Arabia and sailed on to Java and Sumatra.

Islam spread along these trade routes. By the eighth century, the Swahili were constructing mosques from upright timbers, mud daub, and thatch. Stone mosques appeared in the early to mid-tenth century. The "stone" was calcareous lumps of porites coral cut from the shallow sea floor. An upsurge in long-distance trade around A.D. 1000 triggered a building boom in houses as well, and dwellings of wood posts, wattle, and daub were complemented by two-story coral houses.

The coral houses, Linda Donley-Reid writes, "were built and lived in by an elite class of Swahili people called the *wa-ungwana*, but the power of the house affected all the people living in its shadow."[35] The wa-ungwana were high status, freeborn plantation owners and traders, middlemen between the broader networks of trade and local, mainland communities of hunters, pastoralists, agriculturalists, and slaves.

The wa-ungwana lived within a nested set of enclosing walls. The settlement was surrounded by an enclosing wall, its gates opened during the day but sealed each evening. Within the town walls, the coral houses "reflected an image that the wa-ungwana still try to project—proud, tall, powerful, and reserved, at least on the interior." The substantial houses of stone visible above the settlement walls "must have appeared fortress-like compared to the grass or mud and thatch houses in which other coastal people were living."[36]

Today as in the past, the walls of the wa-ungwana houses delineated the lives of the occupants, defining distinctions based on family, caste, and gender. The houses were relatively narrow and deep. The first story was built and occupied and the second floor added later. Slaves lived on the lower floor; masters on the upper floor. On the lower floor, the entrance of the house had a covered porch with stone benches called the *madaka*, where foreign traders would meet with the household head to haggle and exchange. A strange man, unrelated by kinship, was seldom permitted inside.

The Swahili house was a closed space and a protected female realm. Traditionally, the house was a wedding present to a wa-ungwana bride and it remained her property. Until recently, Swahili houses could not be sold and were inherited only by daughters. Because ideally a woman married her father's brother's son,[37] neighborhoods tended to be occupied by closely related kin. When sisters lived in adjacent dwellings, bridges connected the upper levels of houses, spanning the streets below, or passageways were cut through shared walls, creating a complex warren of domestic spaces.

The *ndani* was the most deeply secluded space in a Swahili coral house. It was, as Donley-Reid describes, "the ritual area of the house, a sacred and polluted area." Goats or sheep were sacrificed in the ndani; when their necks were slit, jugular blood spurted into a pit dug into the floor. Some rites symbolically protected the house from outside threats. Other sacrifices in the ndani protected children. During excavations of a nineteenth-century Swahili house, Donley-Reid found pits for goat sacrifices as well as other pits containing metal, human hair, and chicken bones, archaeological features associated with sexuality and love charms. While goat, sheep, and cattle were "cold" animals, chicken and other fowl were "hot" and sexual. For this reason, a wa-ungwana bridegroom was fed chicken or dove before he first made love to his bride. The marriage was consummated in the dark space of the ndani.

The ndani was also a space where infants were buried. Stillborn infants were not humans, the Swahili believed, but angels whose corporal remnants were buried. Yet, only the angelic corpses of freeborn infants could be buried in the ndani. The stillborn of slave women were buried away from the house in a slave cemetery, segregated in death as in life.

Another class of funeral treatment occurred within the ndami: the *ufuko*. This was the ritual washing of a deceased family member, someone above the age of maturity (minimally a girl who had had her first menses or a boy of twelve or thirteen years). The corpse was washed over a trench dug in the ndami floor. The body was placed on a bed consisting of a wooden frame and woven netting of coconut rope. A hole through the coconut weave allowed the intestines to be evacuated into the trench, along with all the impure washings. The corpse's orifices were plugged with scented cotton, the body was wrapped in a funeral shroud, and the dead family member was carried to the cemetery.

Wa-ungwana women were not allowed to accompany the funeral procession. They remained indoors as the ufuko trench was filled in, a substitute for the distant grave, and the ndami was a dark and hidden place where women honored the dead.

The Swahili house enclosed a complex world, structured by distinction and nuance. And, perhaps not surprisingly, it protected and constrained wa-ungwana women.

It was not unusual for a freeborn, upper-status woman to never leave her house. When she conducted her ethnoarchaeological fieldwork in 1979–1981 in Lamu, off the Kenya coast, Donley-Reid encountered three wa-ungwana women who had been born inside their houses and spent their entire lives within those walls. They would leave the house only when their own bodies were carried to the graveyard.

Despite their obvious differences, the cultural logics of Swahili seclusions bear a general resemblance to those of the Christian convent. In both cases, women were secluded to preserve chastity and prevent defilement. In the Christian tradition, the nun was the "Bride of Christ." In the Swahili tradition, the wa-ungwana woman was the bride of the household male, and he was intent upon preserving the lines of descent, clan membership, and inheritance. In both cases these concepts were reinforced by architectural forms that secluded women behind walls.

. . .

A community may exist behind walls for various reasons. From ancient Mesopotamia to medieval Europe, walls have defended townsfolk from barbarians. Walled palaces declaimed the otherworldliness of kings in Ecbatana and Chan Chan. Christ's withdrawal into the desert inspired the individualistic hermitages of St. Antony and the complex communality of the Plan of St. Gall. Female chastity was preserved behind convent walls and within Swahili houses. The archaeology of gated communities indicates the different rationales for lives lived behind tall walls.

Since the mid-1990s in the United States, the number of gated communities has increased exponentially. In 1997 an estimated three million housing units were enclosed in gated communities; by 2007 there were an estimated ten million housing units behind walls.[38] The construction of gated communities far outpaces the construction of other classes of new home developments within the United States.

Not surprisingly, the creation of new gated communities in the United States has been accompanied by critical analysis, scholarly and otherwise. The explanations fall into two camps.

One set of models sees gated communities as neighborhoods of likeminded people, freely associating to obtain the benefits of living with others who share their values and interests. For example, the first American retirement community, Leisure World in Orange County, California, opened in 1962, and it provides the benefits of recreation centers, swimming pools, a nine-hole golf course, and other amenities to its nine thousand residents in an "age-restricted" community. Such communities, the argument goes, are relatively innocuous crystallizations of shared interests. One of the more charming examples of such a community is the Chiefland Astronomy Village, a community of some twenty families of amateur astronomers founded by a passionate stargazer who sought really dark skies and found them in northwestern Florida, one of the darkest regions in the eastern United States.[39]

An alternative explanation takes a less innocent perspective on gated communities. According to this model, gated communities are responses to fear: Americans are terrified by gang violence, street crime, and terrorist attacks, and even more so after the events of September 11, 2001, now as much an iconic phrase as a historic and tragic moment. The anthropologist Setha Low has written of gated communities as expressing anxieties about race and poverty, articulated in what she calls "a discourse of fear of violence and crime."[40] This discourse, the argument goes, is used to justify exclusionary practices that recreate the segregations of race and class otherwise outlawed by fair housing legislation, producing a "spatialized sociology of inequality."[41] Although this analysis of the development of gated communities has stimulated a large academic literature, its basic tone is captured by the title of an article by Barbara Ehrenreich: "Hell is a Gated Community."[42] (But, of course, so is Heaven.)

Not unexpectedly, the reality of gated communities is more complex than either of these models captures. For example, an analysis of U.S. census data for gated communities found that a high proportion of the occupants tend to be low- to middle-income Hispanic renters—a result counterintuitive to either model.[43] Further, gated communities are neither limited to the United States nor are they uniform expressions of American fears or aspirations. Gated communities have been studied in Mexico, the United Kingdom, China, Argentina, Trinidad, Ghana, Brazil, Turkey, and New Zealand—a global phenomenon dubbed "The New Enclavism." Some of these cases express a fortress mentality, others reflect a search for shared values and lifestyles, and so on, reflecting an amazing array of historical causes and social concerns.

Thus, the gated community, the walled-in domestic experience, may arise from various social processes. Similar architectural configurations may result from different cultural logics. Similar cultural logics may produce different architectonic patterns. Explaining the communities living behind walls defies glib conclusions.

But given what we know about the archaeology of gated communities, perhaps we should not be surprised.

CHAPTER 8

Noble Houses

For a man's house is his castle,
et domus sua cuique tutissimum refugium.
—Sir Edward Coke, 1644

The Rio Tumbes curves down the western slopes of the northern Andes and flattens into a broad ox-bowed river as it nears the Pacific Ocean. The river's delta was once a tangled swamp of mudflats and lagoons where black crocodiles floated in the thick brown waters. Since the 1970s, the swamplands have been dredged and drained for vast rice paddies and large lobster-raising ponds. In the equatorial spring, the rice fields stretch toward the coast in a broad emerald plain fringed by a narrow stand of mangroves that fences the beach strand.

A dry terrace rises on the southern bank of the Rio Tumbes. Vultures coil in the warm updrafts, circling over the thin scrub of thorn forest that covers the terrace. Modern houses crawl up the terrace, mostly modest houses of cane wattle and mud daub and a few more substantial dwellings of adobe brick. These houses were built beginning in the 1970s when major floods in El Niño years washed away villages and homes on the Tumbes floodplain below. Few families hold legal title to their house lots, building as squatters on unoccupied lands.

Their houses sit on the ruins of the Palace of Chilimassa.

When I first walked onto the site in July 1996, I didn't realize it was a palace. I was taken there by my Peruvian archaeological colleagues, Bernardino Olaya and Wilson Puell Mendoza, both native *tumbesinos*. We walked through the thorn scrub and dry grasses onto the edge of the terrace. Bernardino and Wilson showed me the partially filled test-pit they had excavated two years before. In the profile you could see the

rectangular outlines of adobes, large sun-dried bricks nearly sixty centimeters long and twice the size people make today. In a few places, lines
of cobblestone foundations hinted at walls, but there was no standing
architecture. It looked to me like just a natural landform with a few
buildings on top. Nothing palatial.

But I had been working in Tumbes less than two weeks, and I was still
learning how to see. I wasn't a novice archaeologist, having spent years
of fieldwork in the United States, Baja California, southern Mexico, and
further south on the desert coast of Peru. But seeing an archaeological
site involves more than opening one's eyes: it involves discerning patterns at the intersection of two dimensions.

On the one hand, every region has distinctive sets of archaeological signatures depending on the types of prehistoric societies who lived
there (for example, mobile hunters and gatherers or ancient urbanites),
their activities (slaughtering reindeer or building temples), and the materials they used to accomplish those tasks (flint hand-axes or marble
blocks).

On the other hand, different parts of the world transform the archaeological traces people leave behind in different ways. Not only are there
no "Paleolithic Pompeiis" (as discussed in chapter 2), but all archaeological sites are reshaped by different sets of natural processes and most
by later human activities. Each time you begin a new archaeological
project in a new area, you must relearn how to see the traces of the past.

Or at least this is how I justified it to myself at the time.

Frankly, if I had done a bit more homework, I would have known
about the Palace of Chilimassa. It—and the Tumbes region—figures
prominently in the chronicles of the Spanish conquest of the Andes.
Francisco Pizarro mounted several expeditions before successfully con-
quering South America. In 1526–1528 Pizarro organized a two-pronged
expedition, in which one Bartolome de Ruiz captained an ocean voyage along the Peruvian coast as Pizarro led an overland expedition that
struggled down the Colombian coast. Ruiz intercepted a native ship at
sea, a sailing raft manned by ocean-going traders. The native merchants
were returning from the south and their cargo sparkled with treasures.
Pieces of gold and silver. Strings of emeralds. Drinking tankards in silver and gold. Piles of fine cloth—some painted, others intricately woven.
These southern riches had been traded for beads and small objects made
from white and pink shells, the lustrous valves of the thorny oyster,
which were prized throughout the Andes. Taking two of the natives
on board as potential translators, Ruiz sailed north, retrieved Pizarro's

desperate contingent, and after other setbacks and delays, Pizarro and his men finally sailed south and anchored near the mouth of the Rio Tumbes.

After the months of near starvation and desperate voyages, the Spaniards thought Tumbes was a marvel. The tumbesinos sailed twelve rafts filled with food and drink to the Spanish vessel. Pizarro sent two men with the returning rafts to reconnoiter. One Alonso de Molina and an unnamed "black" were the first foreigners to visit Tumbes. Crossing rich farmlands and seeing herds of llamas for the first time, the men marched towards "the fortress," undoubtedly the Palace of Chilimassa.

And there Spaniards first glimpsed the impressive wealth of the Inca Empire.

The foreigners were led through three gates before entering the presence of the Lord of Tumbes, Chilimassa. The walls of Chilimassa's palace were sheathed in gold and silver. Admist this splendor, the foreigners were offered tankards of the maize beer, *chicha*. Lord Chilimassa was attended by scores of "chosen women" who wove fine cloth, brewed chicha, and were given to loyal subjects as wives (one was offered to Molina). The palace also contained a Temple of the Sun, a gilded wonder. By far the most detailed and intriguing account of Tumbes comes from Juan Ruiz de Arce, one of the original conquistadors.

> This town had one thousand houses. . . . In this pueblo there is a fortified house, made with greater skill than ever seen that had five doorways before one arrives to the inner apartments. . . . From one door to the next is more than a hundred paces, it has many terraces, all from hand-made adobes, it has many inner spaces with many murals. In the middle there was a good-sized plaza, and beyond this there were other spaces which contained a patio. In the middle of this patio there was a garden and next to the garden a fountain. The Indians say that the founder of this house was called Gutimaaynacava[1] and they say that he was lord of all that land and he commanded to make this house and that took a year, and with his innovations he made water rise up to that fountain. It seems an impossible thing to make water rise but the Indians swear that it was so.[2]

The report brought back by Molina and the unnamed black man was so spectacular that Pizarro did not believe them, and sent a trusted lieutenant, the Greek artilleryman Pedro de Candia, as a separate witness. Candia was just as amazed as the other men had been. The tumbesinos were also impressed by Candia. In a first demonstration of European firepower, Candia set up his harquebus and fired a harmless round. The tumbesinos dropped in fright, but then gathered in wonder around the weapon, finally honoring the gun with a tankard of chicha that was poured down its barrel, an offering to a power both awesome and feared.

Pizarro returned to Spain to obtain royal authorization for the conquest. At that point, Tumbes was the largest city the conquistadors had seen in South America. The city was considered a prize and figured prominently in the royal charter of conquest. Three years later, Pizarro landed again on the South American coast.

Tumbes was in ruins, yet another disappointment in Pizarro's efforts at glorious conquest and riches. Long-standing animosities between the Tumbis and their archrivals, the people of Puná Island, had erupted in war, and Tumbes was set aflame, leaving little but charred wreckage. Even worse, from Pizarro's point of view, the Tumbis had correctly surmised that the Spaniards had come to conquer. Hostility replaced hospitality. The land was in revolt, and the resistance was led by Chilimassa.

The natives retreated to "secret places in the valley" and Chilimassa sent warriors to harass foraging Spanish troops. According to one Spanish chronicler, Pizarro "for a whole fortnight waged cruel war with fire and sword" until Chilimassa finally sued for peace.[3]

In Tumbes Pizarro first heard tales of the greater riches to the south, although his men did not believe the stories about the riches of the Inca capital, Cusco. Speaking through an interpreter, a local man mentioned that there had been a war with Cusco:

> Then, the Indian being asked what Cusco might be, he said it was a great town where the Lord of all of them dwelt, and that it had many vessels of gold and silver and things inlaid with plates of gold. And certainly the Indian told the truth, and less than he might have said. But as the men were so downcast, they did not believe him, saying it was a stratagem of the governor, who had taught the Indian what to say in order to encourage the soldiers, and so they believed nothing of the news as to what manner of land it was.[4]

In fact, the news was true. The Inca Empire had been embroiled in civil war, and the victor, Atahualpa, and his army were camped in the mountains to the south. The treasures of Cusco would prove richer than any other booty taken during the Spanish conquest of the New World. Pizarro and his men left Tumbes, following the Inca road up into the moss-covered forests of the Cerro de Amotape and then south to the coast before marching into the sierra to capture the Inca king.

Tumbes faded from the Spaniards' intents, lacking the gold and silver conquistadors desired, and becoming a small humid port. For a while it retained some of its luster, and in the spring of 1535 the conquistador

Don Alonso Enriquez de Guzman observed, "The great city of Tumbes is inhabited entirely by Indians. It is on the sea-shore; and in it there is a great house, belonging to the lord of the country, with walls built of adobes, like bricks, very beautifully painted with many colors and varnished so that I never saw anything more beautiful. The roof is of straw, also painted, so that it looks like gold, very strong and handsome."[5]

When I walked across the site in 1996, here were no traces of this opulence. Decades previously a local petroleum engineer and avocational historian had mapped the site, and his sketch showed a nested set of rectangular rooms. But all I saw in 1996 was a possible courtyard attached to a patio, a small bench leading up to another modest complex of rooms, and hints of prehistoric terraces. In fact, the archaeological traces were so faint and modest, I concluded that the Spanish accounts of the Palace of Chilimassa were examples of conquest hyperbole, mere exaggerations of exotic glories.

So when my colleague, the Peruvian archaeologist Carolina Vílchez, began excavations at the site of Chilimassa's palace in 2004, I doubted that she would find much. During her first small-scale field season, she didn't. But beginning in 2007, with a larger budget, Vílchez's team made astounding discoveries in zones of the site not covered by squatters' houses. What looked like a natural landform was actually the slumped-in debris from once-enormous walls, walls that towered twenty feet high, made from huge adobes. The distinctive Inca-style trapezoidal niches in the walls clearly marked the building as an Inca construction, as did quantities of classic Inca polychrome pottery. But even more remarkable was that the walls were painted, bearing traces of brick-red and saffron murals that once made the Palace of Chilimassa just as spectacular as the Spaniards had described.

. . .

For the last few decades, archaeologists have rarely used the word *palace*. As the archaeologist Jeffrey Quilter has written, there has been an "active mistrust of employing the term 'palace' for a Pre-Columbian case."[6] Rather, archaeologists, and especially those working in the Americas, have employed various rough synonyms: "elite residences," "administrative units," "noble residential complexes," and so on. Our reticence is a reaction to several legitimate objections.

In the nineteenth and early twentieth centuries, archaeologists generally focused on temples, tombs, and palaces. For example, Heinrich Schliemann's efforts to establish the historical reality of the *Iliad* led him

to excavate quickly and infer immediately. To cite just one of the con-
troversies that surround his legacy, Schliemann's discovery of a cache
of vessels, weapons, and ornaments made from precious metals was
erroneously (or fraudulently) claimed to be found within the walls of
Priam's palace, when in fact the discoveries were made outside the walls
of Troy.[7] Even a scholar broadly sympathetic to Schliemann has written, "He was not very good at separating fact from interpretation. It is a
recurrent problem in Schliemann. The burnt citadel of Troy II *was* Troy;
the gate *was* the Scaean Gate; the building inside the gate *was* Priam's
palace, and the treasure *was* Priam's Treasure."[8]

Even a more self-effacing scholar like the British archaeologist Arthur J.
Evans could elide the distinction between description and interpretation. During the five seasons in which he completely excavated the Palace at Knossos—a white-hot pace of excavation that makes a modern
archaeologist cringe (although Schliemann had once boasted that, if
given the chance and fifty workmen, he could excavate the entire palace in a week!)—Evans regularly extended inference beyond evidence.[9]
For example, a room contained an alabaster seat built into one wall
and flanked by stone benches; to Evans this was obviously the "Throne
Room," although subsequent scholars have suggested its use as a shrine.
Another broad hallway was dubbed "The Corridor of the Procession,"
and Evans described a life-size mural depicting a parade of men "no
doubt princely, priestly or official personages" and of one woman "a
Queen surely" accompanied by a half-dozen male attendants." The image
of the mural associated with the hallway would seem to bolster Evans's
calling it "The Corridor of the Procession," until one realizes that the
mural was all but destroyed and the intact portions only displayed the
lower hem of a few garments and the people's feet. (Male feet were
brown, according to Evans, female feet white.)[10] And so it goes, as Evans
combined careful excavation with exuberant inferences and sometimes
fanciful reconstructions of the palace. For such reasons, the Mediterranean archaeologists Susan Alcock and John Cherry have noted, "There
are those who would say that the Minoan civilizations is more the inven-
tion of its discoverer, Sir Arthur Evans, than a past reality."[11]

A similar rush to judgment characterized the American explorer Hiram
Bingham's July 1911 work at the now-iconic Peruvian site of Machu
Picchu. Climbing past ancient terraces cleared and cultivated by local
farmers, Bingham was led to the ruins by a young campesino. "Suddenly I
found myself confronted with the walls of ruined houses built of the finest
quality Inca stone work," Bingham wrote. Peering through the tangle of

bamboo and draping mosses, Bingham saw "walls of white granite ash-lars carefully cut and exquisitely fitted together." The boy led Bingham "to a cave beautifully lined with the finest cut stone," of which the explorer immediately exclaimed, "It had evidently been a Royal Mausoleum." A curved wall of fine-cut stone reminded Bingham of a similar curving wall at the Temple of the Sun in Cusco. Within moments Bingham went from a relatively cautious, "This might also be a Temple of the Sun," to the confident conclusion "that this wall and its adjoining semicircular temple . . . were as fine as the finest stonework in the world."[12]

Probably every archaeologist has jumped to an unwarranted conclusion sometime in their career; I know I have. Usually, this is a matter of thinking out loud: coming up with various possible interpretations, casting them aside as new bits of data appear, and winnowing the possible from the unlikely before publication. That does not seem to have occurred in the early researches of these archaeologists.

Which is one reason modern archaeologists are reluctant to write of palaces, as Alcock and Cherry warn in an aside: "(The term 'palace' must be used with caution given its later associations; 'regional center' may be preferable.)"[13]

. . .

Our homes reflect who we are, the ways we are the same, and the manners in which we differ. Among the many cultural dimensions encoded by our homes, dwellings often bear the stamp of material differences. When my wife and I married, our first home was a twenty-foot-long aluminum trailer without running water or heat that we lived in as impoverished graduate students. Thirty years later, we live in a four-bedroom, two-bath house that also contains a living room, a dining room, three offices, a kitchen, garage, and laundry room with outside patio and gardens. The difference between those two points on our domestic trajectory represent more than variations in "style." Our current house reflects who we are: two university professors with a teenage son. And obviously, the difference between the aluminum trailer and our current house indicates the changes in our wealth as we clambered from poverty into the American upper middle class.

In a broadly analogous manner, archaeologists compare the ancient traces of home as a way of understanding the emergence of social differences. One of the fundamental questions that archaeology explores was articulated by Jean-Jacques Rousseau in the opening lines of *The Social Contract*: "Man is born free, and everywhere he is in chains." As far as we can tell, human societies were largely egalitarian from their Lower Paleolithic inceptions until approximately 8,000–10,000 years ago, when we first discern hints of difference in prehistoric societies. Some individuals were buried in more elaborate tombs or with a greater wealth of grave goods than were others. Some people pursued specific crafts or economic activities instead of exclusively food collecting or farming. New forms of architecture appeared: shrines, temples, or fortresses. And people began living in different types of homes.

On the eastern coast of the Peloponnese in southern Greece, the site of Lerna sits near the deep blue waters of the Argolic Gulf.[14] Excavations in the 1950s directed by the American classical archaeologist John Caskey exposed a 5,000-year occupation stretching from the sixth to the first millennium B.C. Lerna was an ideal location with abundant arable land, a good freshwater spring, and fronted by the Aegean Sea. Beginning as a small Neolithic community, Lerna grew modestly. At its peak, Lerna was essentially a small town of perhaps eight hundred families. Most of these families lived in humble houses with walls of either packed clay or sun-dried bricks roofed by layers of clay spread over a lattice of branches or thatched with reeds. As houses were abandoned or felled by fire, Lerna's occupants knocked down the standing walls, filled in low areas, and built again, producing a deep archaeological record.

But one house was different. At 2500–2300 B.C. a large house was built that was 25 meters long, 12 meters wide, and had walls nearly one meter thick. A staircase leading up from the ground floor demonstrates this was a two-story construction. Balconies may have rimmed the second floor. Not only was it the largest dwelling at Lerna, but in its day it was one of the largest houses anywhere along the Aegean Sea. And beyond its enormous size, it had another distinctive feature: it was roofed with ceramic tiles.

The tiles were terracotta rectangles about as thick as your pinkie finger. Hard-fired and flat, the tiles were set into a damp layer of roof mud, the edges overlapping like shingles on the low-pitched roof. The excavators recovered thousands of fragments and named the dwelling the "House of Tiles."

As the House of Tiles was built, Lerna became a citadel, surrounded by a double ring of walls with gates and defensive towers, that as Caskey wrote "was a very powerful protection to the inhabitants, whose possessions must have been valuable enough to attract covetous eyes and therefore to warrant defense on a monumental and costly scale."[15]

Two other intriguing points about the House of Tiles. First, the building apparently was in the last stages of construction when it was torched. Some of the walls were coated with a final layer of plaster and stucco, others walls only had a base coat of plaster that was scored with a comb-like tool but lacked the finishing layer. The House of Tiles was not quite finished when it burned.

Second, it is not clear what wealth or treasure might have made the House of Tiles a target. Copper axes and pottery vessels were present but not elaborate. Aside from a large lump of molten lead, there was no hint of precious metals.

The only artifacts hinting of wealth were more than one hundred clay sealings. Essentially these were lumps of clay that had been stuck onto jars and large wooden chests, and then one or two impressions were stamped into the still-wet clay, much in the way a wax seal stamped with a signet ring marks an unopened letter. The firestorm at the House of Tiles had destroyed all traces of wooden boxes and the valuable contents of jars, but left behind the more durable clay evidence of commerce and trade.

The seals were more than "tamper-proof" tops; they probably were some kind of brands. Given the variety of motifs, there are more than a single producer's mark; these either indicated objects from different craftsmen or possibly were designations for distant customers. Regardless, the clay sealings suggest that the owner was involved in commerce, and this is reflected in the size, richness, and artifacts of the House of Tiles.

Subsequent excavations at other sites and re-examination of buildings from earlier digs indicate that the House of Tiles was an example of a specific type of dwelling, the corridor house. This form of domestic architecture had specific characteristics. Corridor houses are two-storied buildings with long narrow hallways and second-floor verandas, Benches were built into the outside walls; inside, one room had a large hearth, unnecessarily large for cooking but useful for warming a room-full of people on a cold winter day. As the art historian Joseph Shaw observed, "From the architectural point of view, one can note that the size of the corridor houses, the exterior benches, and the occasional presence of a hearth imply that groups of people might have gathered in them."[16]

Who were these people and why would they gather in a place like the House of Tiles? Martha Heath Wiencke summarizes the changes in society and economy that preceded the construction of the House of Tiles and other corridor houses.[17] Population in the Argolid countryside had increased. Agriculture had intensified. Bronze metallurgy became more sophisticated and widespread, and other forms of craft production—in large storage vessels *(pithoi)* for example—became more specialized. There was little evidence for political centralization and none for marked social classes.

Although all these trends began before the construction of the House of Tiles, the pace of those trends accelerated as Lerna developed. Corridor houses combined family residence (especially in the more private second floor) with public zones, such as the outside benches or the hearth-warmed large room on the ground floor. Wiencke suggests that corridor houses were "a kind of residence and headquarters for the elite, perhaps a 'chief.'" The pottery vessels discovered at the House of Tiles may have been used in feasts, a common strategy in so-called "commensal politics." The silver and gold vessels, bronze weapons, and adornments of precious metals found with corridor houses are not, Wiencke contends, "simple declarative statements about the status of a relatively few 'chiefly' persons, but apparently reflect a staking to claims of elite status by a greater number of persons in competition with each other."

These Early Bronze Age houses of the Aegean tell us a great deal about a changing ancient society. Agriculture and trade expanded. Some families achieved either control over resources or the fealty of followers. New prestige items were made, exchanged, and displayed. Partners in trade or politics were feasted around the fire. And all this occurred at home.

The House of Tiles was destroyed in flames, and although Lerna continued as a settlement, after about 2300 B.C. no more corridor houses were built either there or at any other Aegean site. The architectural style of these houses did not continue in Aegean prehistory. But what did continue was the combination of activities in a large house, the intersection of dwelling, meeting room, storerooms, and feasting hall in a single elite residence.

This pattern is well documented in ancient Crete. Despite the uncertain reconstructions made by Evans, a reasonably clear picture emerges about the palaces of Minoan culture on Crete. Beginning at about 1900 B.C., a number of elite residences were built across the island, stimulated by Crete's central position in the eastern Mediterranean between Egypt, Anatolia, and the Aegean. Compared to the dense urban throngs in Mesopotamian cities, the Cretan settlements associated with the palaces were miniscule.[18] Stretched across Crete, as the archaeologist John Cherry has argued, these five palaces were the centers of different and roughly equivalent polities at Galatas, Malia, Phaistos, Zakros, and of course, the largest at Knossos.[19]

The art historian John McEnroe has recently written that the ancient experience of a Minoan palace would have been regulated by social role; a modern visitor to the site sees more than any single ancient visitor ever did. "What they would have seen," McEnroe writes, "would have depended on who they were and what specific business had brought them to the Palace. The Palace seen by visiting dignitaries was different from that inhabited by craft workers, pilgrims, slaves and scribes. The public Palace that staged official or ritual celebrations was not the same as the private chambers."[20]

Actually more than elite residences, the Minoan palaces were architectural complexes where multiple activities took place. The art historians Donald Preziosi and Louise Hitchcock have written:

> The Minoan palaces were distinctly multifunctional centers of their respective cities, combining what we might designate today as religious, commercial, manufacturing, social, political, ceremonial and other activities, some public, others private in a common structural framework with many different gradations of separation from and connection to the rest of the urban fabric. Although the openness and accessibility of the buildings to the rest of their cities has often been exaggerated, the fact is that many different kinds and sizes of interior spaces, terraces, stepped platforms, and courtyards comprise a complex articulated mosaic of interwoven activities; these are porous monuments rather than castles.[21]

Although separated by several centuries and housed in distinct types of buildings, the House of Tiles and the Minoan palaces were seats of power at a time when the lineaments of class and position were still under construction. Commerce and ceremony, ritual and feasting co-occurred because they were the activities through which power was gained, sustained, exercised, and displayed. And this takes place in the houses of leaders and elites throughout the human experience.

. . .

Three and a half millennia after the Cretan palaces were destroyed and on the opposite side of the globe, food and politics mix in traditional tribes in Amazonia. The village of Conambo is located in the Ecuadorian Amazon, nearly two hundred kilometers from the nearest road.[22] The community coalesced in the 1980s around an abandoned airstrip built by the Unocal Oil Company. Conambo consists of about two hundred people from three different ethnic groups, the Achuar, the Quichua, and the Zapara. All three groups speak Quichua, a language of the Inca conquest in the northern Andes, which serves as a lingua franca in this portion of western Amazonia.

The region has a history of conflicts, with high homicide rates resulting from long-term feuds that lasted well into the 1970s. Historically fifty percent of men died violent deaths. Even today in this egalitarian society without institutionalized political positions and lacking a police presence, conflicts are settled by individuals, men and women.

And many of those conflicts are resolved at home.

Over the last two decades, the husband and wife team of John Patton, an evolutionary anthropologist, and Brenda Bowser, an ethnoarchaeologist, have been working in Conambo, trying to unravel the complexities of social life in this multiethnic small-scale group. Patton's research has focused on the way men create coalitions by sharing game meat, exchanging labor in projects such as house construction, canoe-building, or clearing forest for gardens, and by solidifying ties between kinsmen. Bowser's research has examined the coalitions that women create and women's roles in conflict resolution. Central to this is a beer, a manioc chicha that women brew from tubers they have raised in their gardens, which they serve in elegant drinking bowls they make and intricately decorate.

Every one of the twenty-five households in Conambo has a visiting area, which is a roofed open space with benches and a cooking hearth. For nearly half the households, this is the principal dwelling and may contain a small sleeping platform. In other households the roofed visiting area is surrounded by other single-room dwellings or storerooms. In all cases, the visiting area is the center stage of social life.

The space is divided into male and female zones. The space where men sit is somewhat larger than the female area that holds the large jars from which chicha is served. The women of the house serve the male kinsmen and visitors, and serving chicha is as nuanced as a Japanese tea ceremony. If chicha is not served, a serious affront is intended; this rarely occurs. More subtly, a pause before serving chicha may signal disapproval. Whether the chicha is served in a fine-painted bowl or an undecorated calabash indicates the perceived status of the guest and his importance within the family's coalition.

No one speaks until after chicha is served, and then men speak to men, women to women. "Minor disputes are resolved," Bowser writes, "and life or death decisions are made, while drinking bowls of chicha. In Conambo, the public/private and political/domestic contexts are insepa-

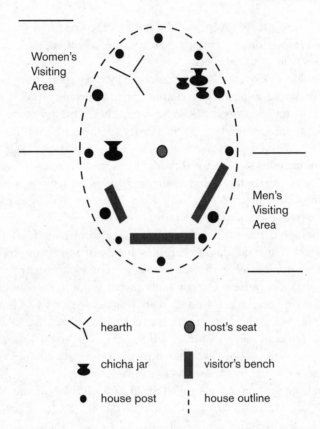

Women's
Visiting
Area

Men's
Visiting
Area

hearth   host's seat

chicha jar   visitor's bench

house post   house outline

FIGURE 27. House plan, Conambo, Ecuador. Redrawn from
Bowser and Patton 2004.

rable, and each woman uses her chicha bowls on a daily basis to bridge
those domains."[23]

The intersection of politics, feasting, and residence occurs at various
points in human prehistory. In *Beowulf,* King Hrothgar, having been
favored by the fortunes of war, attracted a retinue of kinsfolk and followers. He decided to build a great house to serve as his throne room and
mead-hall where he could dispense gifts and secure loyalties. Hrothgar's
great house was simultaneously a dwelling and seat of power. Although
Beowulf is an epic legend, the creation of great houses has been con-
firmed by archaeological evidence. For example, excavations conducted
by the Roskilde Museum near Lejre, Denmark, uncovered a hall 48 meters
long and 7 meters wide dating to A.D. 400–500. Associated with a boat-
shaped longhouse, the great hall was built from huge oak beams, leaving

postholes over a meter deep, and the floor of the great hall was littered with broken bits of exquisite jewelry, smashed drinking tankards, and stone piles from cooking ovens.[24]

On the North Coast of Peru, Ñamlap, the stranger-king who founded the Lambayeque dynasty (see chapter 7), was accompanied by forty courtiers, including a royal chicha brewer, a chef, a master of the throne and litter, a steward of face paint, master of the bath, and a valet in charge of feathered cloth garments. This retinue was in charge of the various items used to adorn Ñamlap's "body and his house." Ñamlap's "house" was clearly more than a shelter: it was, in a sense, a political corporation in which ruler and royal kin, courtiers and servants, lived and interacted as a social unit, a noble household.

An analogous fusion of politics, feasting, and display developed independently along the damp evergreen fjords of northwestern North America. A number of Native American groups living between southern Alaska and southern Oregon constructed wood houses built from huge cedar timbers, large post-and-beam frames covered by split planks. Despite regional and tribal variations in construction techniques and the symbolic associations with the dwellings, the Northwest Coast plank house was a very broadly distributed form of domestic architecture. In some places these plank houses were enormous.[25]

When Captain James Cook sailed the H.M.S. *Resolution* into Nootka Sound in late March 1778, his ship was surrounded by dozens of canoes as the Nootka welcomed the British navigators to their villages and homes.

Cook's description has been accurately described as "mixed," as he alternates between biased abhorrence and grudging admiration. The Nootka houses, Cook wrote, "are built of very long and broad planks, resting upon the edges of each other, fastened or tied by withes of pine bark," yet he complained "They are however, upon the whole, miserable dwellings, and constructed with little care or ingenuity. For though the side-planks be made to fit pretty closely in some places, in others they are quite open; and there are no regular doors into them." Inside, Cook declared "is a complete scene of confusion" and said that "the nastiness and stench of their houses are, however at least equal to the confusion," as the Nootka cleaned and dried fish indoors. "In a word," the navigator shuddered, "their houses are as filthy as hog-sties; every thing in and about them stinking of fish, train-oil, and smoke."[26]

Despite his olfactory revulsion, Cook understood that important events occurred within the Nootka houses. He wrote that the Nootka

FIGURE 28. J. Webber, *Interior of a Nootka House*, 1778. Archives of the State of New South Wales, Australia.

plank house contained "a great number of chests and boxes of all sizes . . . and contain their spare garments, skins, masks, and other things which they set a value on." These wooden chests were "often painted black, studded with the teeth of different animals, or carved with a kind of frieze-work, and figures of birds or animals as decorations." Cook also observed that "amidst all the filth and confusion that are found in the houses, many of them are decorated with images. These are nothing more than the trunks of very large trees, four or five feet high, set up singly, or by pairs, . . . with the front carved into a human face; the arms and hands cut out upon the sides, and variously painted; so the whole is a truly monstrous figure." These sacred objects were usually curtained by hanging mats "which the natives were not willing to remove; and when they did unveil them, they seemed to speak of them in a very mysterious manner." The sacred nature of these totems was made clear to Cook, as the British navigators were entreated through sign language "to give something to these images when they drew aside the mats that covered them."

When the expedition artist John Webber wanted to draw the inside of a Nootka house, one of its occupants, Webber wrote, "approached me with a large knife in his hand, seemingly displeased, when he observed that my eyes were fixed on two representations of human figures, . . . carved on planks of a gigantic proportion, and painted after their custom." Webber attempted to ignore the irate man, who hung a mat to block the artist's view. Webber recalled, "Being pretty certain that I could have no future opportunity to finish my drawing, and the object being too interesting to be omitted, I considered that a little bribery might probably have some effect." Webber offered one of his metal buttons; the man removed the mat. Webber settled himself to continue sketching. The man rehung the mat, again blocking Webber's view. Webber offered another button, and another, and another "continuing till I parted with every single button, and when he saw that he had completely stripped me, I met with no farther obstruction."[27]

The plank house Cook described and Webber illustrated descended from an architectural legacy more than two thousand years old.[28] The earliest known examples of rectangular plank houses come from three widely spaced archaeological sites in northwestern and southwestern British Columbia and on the southwest Oregon coast. The oldest of these sites, dating to 1250–750 B.C., has relatively small houses 8–10 meters long and 6–7 meters wide. Sometime between 650 B.C. and A.D. 350, plank houses doubled in length. After A.D. 1300 houses grew again, and by the sixteenth to nineteenth centuries some plank houses were over 100 meters long. According to the archaeologist Kenneth Ames, historic houses built by the Chinook nation of southwestern Washington fell into two groups: "common" houses (6–18 meters long) and "extreme" houses up to 144 meters long.

So what went on in these enormous houses? First and not surprisingly, a number of people lived in the largest plank houses. The largest plank houses sheltered 200 people, but unlike other "big houses"—such as the Iroquoian longhouse (see chapter 6)—this was not an egalitarian, extended kin group.

Rather, Northwest Coast tribes were among the few hunting and gathering societies that were stratified and class-based. The Pacific Northwest's rich environment and the predictability of salmon and other marine resources (which could be processed and stored, as Captain Cook observed with wrinkled nose) were significant factors that allowed Northwest Coast peoples to live in large settlements with permanent houses. Abundant food resources supported the craft specialists—the carvers, weavers, and sculptors—who made the fabulous objects of Northwest Coast art. These and other variables resulted in stratified societies with social elites by about 3,000 to 2,000 years ago.[29]

When the first Europeans arrived on the Northwest Coast, native society was divided into three strata: title-holders, commoners, and slaves.

Over the ensuing decades, the exposure to Europeans and involvement in global trade dramatically intensified those social divides, but did not create them.

For example, slavery may have developed as early as 4,000 years ago, and slavery was certainly part of Northwest Coast societies when the first Europeans arrived. The ethnographer Leland Donald has written, "Every traditional Northwest Coast community contained at least a few slaves," although the significance of slavery increased from south to north. Donald writes, "A word translatable as 'slave' is found in all languages spoken in the culture area, and in many communities outsiders could distinguish slaves from the other inhabitants because of special haircuts or other external markers. In all of the region's cultures, slavery was regarded as shameful and degrading. Slave status was hereditary: the children of slaves were slaves. As they were without kin group membership, slaves had no rights or privileges. Masters exercised complete physical control over their slaves, and could even kill them if they chose."[30]

Slave raids targeted women and children, although men were also taken, and the raiders attacked neighboring communities and took captives from all social classes. Elite title-holders could be ransomed by their families, but some captives were never freed. There was also a market in slaves. Although some villages had small numbers of slaves, other communities had numerous slaves. It was common for 15%–20% of a permanent village's population to be slaves, with in some communities as many as 30% of the residents were in bondage. At those proportions, the significance of slavery on the Northwest Coast was broadly similar to ancient Greece. Undoubtedly Northwest Coast elites would have agreed with Aristotle's statement in the *Politics* that "the household in its perfect form consists of slaves and freemen."[31]

Slaves were held by houses and houses were ruled by chiefs. The power of house chiefs came from several sources. First, houses were more than massive plank dwellings: houses had "estates," and functioned as corporate entities that held rights and property. Houses owned fishing streams, hunting ranges, and plant gathering areas. The house chief controlled access to these estates though he did not personally own them. House chiefs declared the opening of hunting and fishing seasons, organized raids, declared war against enemies and interlopers, and mustered trading missions. Also, house chiefs directly controlled the labor of slaves, the only members of the house over whom house chiefs had uncontested authority.

In addition to such tangible property, houses held expressive property, having the right to display particular crests and other fine objects and owning the rights to songs, dances, narratives, and rituals. Significant to these displays were the fine objects made by craft specialists who also were members of the house. Born into the house and inheriting a particular craft from their parents, these specialists—master canoe builders or expert wood carvers—were themselves elites, producing objects that enriched and ennobled the house of which they were members. House chiefs did not command or control the production of elite artisans. However, the house chief coordinated the ways ceremonials were organized and the rites where the richness of a house was displayed. Ames writes that "organizing and participating in the public rituals in which the House's privileges were shown was a central part of the chief's job. The continued stature and prestige of the House depended on his taking part in potlatches and/or other public rituals."[32]

While a house chief's *status* was based on birth and rules of succession, a house chief's *standing* had to be continuously reasserted through public displays, the most famous of which was the potlatch. A complex competitive event involving feasting, chiefly oratory, and conspicuous consumption, the potlatch was where a chief's ability to amass, give away, or even destroy possessions demonstrated his status and enlarged his renown.

As the ethnographer Franz Boas wrote, the giving of gifts in potlatch required the recipient to repay "with interest" the gift at some future point, enhancing the wealth of the wealthiest. "Possession of wealth is considered honorable," Boas wrote, "and it is the endeavor of each Indian to acquire a fortune. But it is not as much the possession of wealth as the ability to give great festivals which makes wealth a desirable object to the Indian."[33]

The potlatch has been called "fighting with property." By the late nineteenth century, fortunes of trade goods were exchanged: woolen blankets and copper plaques, canoes and foods. In some potlatches, a chief executed a house slave simply to show a chiefly indifference to wealth. At other potlatches, guests were served vast quantities of the flammable oil of candlefish, a highly prized cooking oil, but entire vats of oil were dumped on the central hearth in an act of conspicuous destruction. The house chief would sit seemingly unperturbed as the burst of flames threatened to burn down his entire plank house.

A house chief's status was also the "house's" status, and the protocols of potlatch made this obvious. Boas and his Tlingit consultant, George

Hunt, recorded the opening speech of a potlatch in the winter of 1894–
1895. The house chief Mā'Xua opens the feast by saying:

> Come, tribe, to my house. This is the house of the first Mā'Xua
>   at G'agaxsdals.
> This is the feast house of Mā'Xua here. . . .
> This is the house to which my father invited at Tsā'xîs.
> I take the place of my father now.
> I invited you, tribes, that you should come and see my house here.
> I am proud to speak of my ancestor, the chief who in the beginning
>   of the world had the name Mā'Xua.[34]

As the French anthropologist Marcel Mauss later observed, the gifts
of the potlatch were surrounded by a triad of obligations: the obligation
to give, the obligation to accept, and the obligation to repay. Faced with
"an offer he couldn't refuse," the recipient had to accept and repay at a
later date, sometimes a hundred-fold. Individuals vied with each other.
Houses competed with other houses.

Despite the flamboyance of the potlatch itself, the practice signals a
subtle connection: the "house" was the social group. The Kwakiutl are
what the late anthropologist Claude Levi-Strauss called a "house society," in which a fundamental unit is the "dwelling" (even if it includes
several buildings) and all its occupants and affiliates, including those of
different statuses whether chief, wood carver, or slave. Like the House
of Tudor or the House of York, the House of Mā'Xua was more than a
residence; it was a social entity that combined politics and commerce,
social strivings and competition enacted through intrigue and validated
with pageantries.[35]

But the house chiefs of the Northwest Coast could not command freeborn individuals. They had life-or-death power over slaves, but over no
one else. Fundamentally, the power of chiefs rested on their ability to be
a good leader for the house by managing resources and enhancing the
house's reputation with potlatch and ceremonials.

Those feasts and ceremonies occurred inside the plank house. Cleaned
of fish scales and decorated with the house's crests and heraldry, the
huge interior spaces of plank houses became stages for impressive the-
atrical events. Elaborately masked dance societies performed. Complex
wooden puppets flew from the rafters. Trap doors opened revealing cos-
tumed deities.

The goal of all this drama was an effort to validate and enhance priv-
ilege and position. Kenneth Ames writes about the central challenges all
house chiefs faced: "On the one hand their position depended on their

place within the household, on their ability to 'manage' the House's estate . . . and their continued ability to cajole, manipulate, and wheedle their household into doing what they, the chiefs, wanted them to do. On the other hand, their position depended on a steady supply of slave labor stolen from outside the House."[36]

In a sense, both issues resolve into a single problem: the problem of recruitment. How can a leader acquire power in a fluid social setting? In the absence of fixed political positions or of strong coercive authority, power must be regularly renegotiated. Followers must be recruited. Coalitions must be constructed, alliances mobilized, and rivals thwarted.

This can occur in different ways and different places, but over the last ten thousand years it regularly has occurred at home.

. . .

Despite archaeologists' reluctance to use the word "palace," it remains a useful term. Perhaps more interesting, however, is the idea that elite houses often accommodate multiple functions, including political spaces. The way that occurs tells us a great deal about different human societies. The open space of a house in the Ecuadorian Amazon lacks the formal meeting hall of a Minoan palace, but in both places people met and power was negotiated. The fact that Minoan palaces were significantly different from everyday Minoan dwellings informs us about the contours of wealth and power in ancient Crete. Inversely, the lack of major differences among houses in Conambo and the ubiquity of open areas where manioc chicha is served reflect the rough egalitarianism of Achuar, Quichua, and Zapara households.

The development of corridor houses, such as the House of Tiles at Lerna, was a material statement of wealth and prestige in the ancient Aegean, and the clay seals are artifactual evidence of commerce and trade, the probable sources of the wealth. Like the houses at Conambo, the lower floors of the House of Tiles were places where people gathered and were served. Food sharing is a universal way that humans solidify social ties, and one with a deep antiquity. However, the creation of spaces regularly used for feasts is a relatively "recent" phenomenon—probably less than 8,000 years old—and one frequently linked to the creation of coalitions and the struggles for power.

When Hrothgar built his guild-hall and hoisted tankards of mead with his followers and allies, it was more than the Neolithic equivalent of a "Man Room" or "Dude Den"[37] (although drunkenness and sports-talk certainly occurred there). The guild-hall was an essential part of a

Norse leader's political establishment, a tangible expression of his status, and a place where old allies were rewarded and new recruits gained.

The Northwest Coast plank house, at times, was used in a similar manner, becoming a space for feasts and theatricals that showed the power and enhanced the status of the "house society" and of the "house chief." This merging correspondence of dwelling and social group, as seen on the Northwest Coast societies, is also known from other cases, separated by time, space, and culture—such as the House of Tudor or the House of Ñamlap.

The dynamic fusion of politics and feastings, residence and ceremonies did not only occur in "regional centers" or in palaces like that occupied by Chilimassa on the Tumbes coast. We have seen that broadly analogous practices occur in settings of radically different scales and complexities, but I think it is fascinating to understand that such cultural practices ennobled a house and they often occurred at home.

CHAPTER 9

Sacred Homes

For religious man, space is not homogeneous.

—M. Eliade, *The Sacred and the Profane*

The Tabernacle was a tent. An audacious and elaborate tent, whose materials and design were stipulated in divine detail to Moses on Mount Sinai. Jehovah commanded that the wandering tribe of Israel, unsteady pastoralists tempted to backslide into idolatry, were to "make me a sanctuary that I may dwell among them." Apparently the children of Israel required the concrete materialization of the Divine, a specific place that anchored the presence of God and allowed for the Sacred to be approached, if not seen.

In the Old Testament book of Exodus, fifteen chapters detail the construction of the Tabernacle, the religious objects it contained, and the priestly rituals that took place there. The tent itself was made from the finest textiles and hides. Curtained walls of linen and fine-spun goat wool dyed deep blue, purple, and crimson hung by golden clasps and loops, linking the different hanging curtains "that it may be one" (Exodus 26:11). The entire Tabernacle was covered by an enormous quilting of red-dyed ram hides, in turn covered by badger pelts.

Although the furnishings of the Tabernacle—the Ark of the Covenant, the Mercy Seat, the Golden menorah, and altars for burning incense and for burning offerings—were entrusted to two outstanding craftsmen, the bulk of the materials for the Tabernacle were made and contributed by the entire tribe of Israel. In this sense, it was a collective offering. Ironically, the Israelites, thinking that one can't have too much of a good thing, overdid their contributions until Moses ultimately commanded, "'Let neither man nor woman make any more work for the offering of the sanctuary.' So the people were restrained from bringing; for the stuff they had was sufficient for all the work to make it, and too much." (Exodus 36:6–7).

A year later, on the first day of the first month, the Tabernacle was raised.

The detailed instructions in Exodus allow for a reconstruction of the Tabernacle's plan: a hundred-cubit-long, curtained rectangular court-yard, progressively divided into more restricted and more sacred spaces. The Ark of the Covenant sat in the innermost sanctum of the Tabernacle, the Holy of Holies, approached only by the high priest as intermediary and representative of the Children of Israel.

The Tabernacle was a sacred dwelling built by a nomadic, pastoral people destined to wander through the deserts of Sinai. A cloud covered the Tabernacle by day and glowed like firelight at night. As long as the cloud remained over the Tabernacle, the Israelites remained encamped; when the cloud lifted, the people followed Jehovah into the wilderness.

The Children of Israel spent forty years in the desert, leaving Egypt for the Red Sea and the dry wastes of the Wilderness of Zin. Finally, on the plains of Moab, the wanderers looked across the River Jordan into Canaan, the land Jehovah gave them. Over the next generations the Israelites conquered city-states and tribes, the people became dwellers of towns and cities.

And later when their warrior-king, David of Bethlehem, had conquered Zion and made Jerusalem his capital, Jehovah spoke to the prophet Nathan and commanded him:

"Go and tell my servant, David, 'Thus saith the Lord, Shalt thou build me a house for me to dwell in? Whereas I have not dwelt in any house since the time that I brought up the children of Israel out of Egypt, even to this day, but have walked in a tent and a Tabernacle.'"

David, Jehovah commanded, "shall build a house for my name, and I will establish the throne of his kingdom forever."

After forty years on the road, even God Almighty wanted to settle down.

. . .

There is no inevitable relationship between the sacred and the domestic. The amateur British folklorist, Lord Raglan, was simply incorrect when he asserted in his encyclopedic and eccentric book, *The Temple and the House,* that human dwellings have their origins as altars and temples.[1]

However, Raglan was correct in arguing that our dwellings are more than shelters. Our homes are one of the media humans use express ideas about the sacred realm. As the social anthropologist Edmund Leach wrote:

> The members of all societies, complex as well as primitive, externalize the ideas they hold about the physical and metaphysical universes, and about the social relations within their own society, by making and manipulating artifacts. The clothes we wear, the houses we live in, the decorated structures with which we surround ourselves, the paths we construct through such human worlds, are all expressive of human ideas, some of which are perfectly well known at a conscious level of experience, while others are only dimly perceived and exist only as sets of relations within the artificially constructed world of culture.[2]

At key points in prehistory, humans have made their dwellings sacred, but we have done so in surprisingly different ways. This broad process is what the archaeologist Richard Bradley has called "the ritualization of the domestic realm." "Ritualization," Bradley argues, "is both a way of acting which reveals some of the dominant concerns of society, and a process by which certain parts of life are selected and provided with an added emphasis."[3]

Obviously this occurs all the time. For example, we give Thanksgiving dinners special emphases—certain foods, selected guests, a specific time to eat—while we do not celebrate drive-in meals eaten in our cars. We celebrate a couple's wedding, but usually not their first date. We make distinctions.

Ritualization "is a process by which certain actions gain an added emphasis through particular kinds of performance," Bradley writes, a varying process in which "certain transactions may be attended by a greater degree of formality than others," extending "from the private to the public domains and from the local, even personal, to those which involve large numbers of participants."

In a sample of archaeological sites from Neolithic, Bronze Age, and Iron Age Europe, Bradley argues there was a change in the way the domestic realm was perceived. Initially, burials were placed in homes, in much the way that Late Natufian and Early Neolithic people in the Near East buried their loved ones (as discussed in chapter 4). Later the corpses were buried in storage pits that once held grain, which may have been a materialized "potent metaphor for human fertility and also for the continuity of life." Hoards and offerings were placed in these Iron Age houses, as houses began to be occupied for multiple generations, acquiring their own social existence.

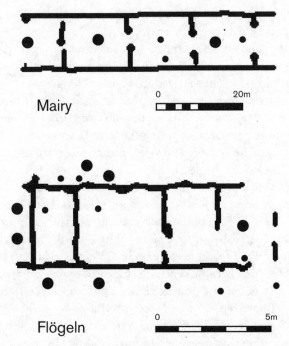

FIGURE 29. Plans of Early and Middle Neolithic houses from Mairy, France, and Flögeln, Germany. Redrawn from Bradley 2003.

As another example, Bradley discusses timber buildings from two different sites, the early Neolithic house from Flögeln on the low coastal plain of northern Germany and two later Middle Neolithic buildings from Mairy in the Ardennes, France, more than five hundred kilometers to the south. A quick glance at the plans suggests that these are three very similar buildings: long rectangular constructions built from large posts with interiors divided by inner walls and floors pocked with storage pits.

But then look at the scales: the constructions at Mairy were three to six times larger than the similar house in Flögeln. Further, the storage pits in the Mairy structures were not filled with stored grain or household garbage, but contained cattle skulls, joints of meat, whole ceramic vessels, and other extraordinary artifacts. At Mairy, Bradley writes, "normal domestic transactions gained an enhanced significance because of the ways they were deployed. Everyday objects were placed ceremoniously in the ground; timber buildings were erected which were greatly enlarged versions of normal dwellings. People were not so much living domestic life as performing it."

Just as the Jehovah's Tabernacle paralleled the nomadic tents of the wandering children of Israel, the enormous timbered buildings of late prehistoric Europe were oversized icons of dwellings.

This transformation of dwelling and domestic life into ritual spaces and ritual practice, Bradley argues, began during the Neolithic and became even more pronounced during the later Bronze Age and Iron Age sites of northern and western Europe. Storage pits were used for buried offerings. People were buried in their homes.

Perhaps even more intriguing, offerings were made before a house was constructed and after a house was abandoned. The very process of building a home and the home itself became intertwined in ritual.

This leads to an obvious question: "Why did this transformation of dwelling into religious architecture occur?" Bradley points to two sets of factors. As farming became central to survival, crops and farm animals gained greater economic and symbolic significance. Thus cow skulls became offerings, replacing red deer sacrificed by earlier Mesolithic peoples.[4] Concurrently, social changes accompanied those subsistence changes, including new social institutions solidified by feasting and new identities that linked place and ancestors (as discussed in chapter 4). With the advent of farming, Bradley argues, domestic life underwent "symbolic elaboration."

Obviously, this does not mean that earlier hunters and gatherers lacked ritual; the locus of ritual practice was elsewhere. As homes became more enduring, they presented an obvious template for thinking about the cosmos—and the cosmos an obvious model for thinking about the home (as explored in chapter 5).

Further, the archaeological data from late prehistoric Europe indicate that there was not a rigid divide between sacred and profane, nor an impermeable barrier between the supernatural and the everyday. Those two realms overlapped and intersected at home.

. . .

On the eastern shore of Baja California, the sand broils in mid-August along the Sea of Cortez. In the southeastern sky, muddy plumes of thunderstorms rise over Sonora. The seawater is dull green slate and slow waves slap in the hot wind.

It is August 2010 and I am trying to begin an archaeological survey south of San Felipe, fieldwork modeled after a research project I directed in the 1990s on the opposite Pacific Coast of Baja California. The field-work is an attempt to understand how ancient peoples adapted to and made sense of the landscape of the Baja California peninsula, how they lived in the desert between the seas.

At least that is the idea.

But the heat is like another form of gravity, weighing every step and slowing each breath. When I set out to look for sites at 7 A.M., it was 87 degrees. By 9 A.M. it is 104 degrees Fahrenheit and with 66% humidity, the heat index is equivalent to 154 degrees.

I cannot drink enough water. My body leaks sweat, staining my clothes in the thick humidity. I guzzle a liter of water every hour and still I stumble back to my jeep, thick-headed and short of breath, as my body exhibits the first symptoms of heat exhaustion. I find my five-gallon jerry can of water, douse my head and neck, clamber into the jeep and drive away. Archaeology will have to wait. I leave for home.

Yet, this desert coast was one part of the homeland of the Kiliwa, an indigenous group in Baja California who transited the peninsula from the Gulf of California, across the mountainous interior, and over to the Pacific Ocean. Their homeland stretched from the cold, western *xa?tay* "large water" fronted by the desert land "that which was sun," across the "Spine of the Earth" (which the Spanish renamed the Sierra of San Pedro Martir), and down to low deserts of the Gulf of California coast.

The archaeological traces of the Kiliwa and their predecessors are found across the width of northern Baja California. As the Kiliwa eth-nographic consultant, Rufino Ochurte, recalled in 1969: "Only these remain; there are no other Indians left. Yet their deeds are there and where they did their things are still there. The villages, the trails, the places where they used to cook, the blackened pits, they are there. Their broken pots are strewn over the land; here still are the metates, manos and bedrock mortars with which they prepared their food." Ochurte remembered, "The places where they pit-roasted and ate are there. Their water jars are there still. Their mountains are there still. And yet it happened that these people came to an end."[5]

Like other native inhabitants of Baja California, the Kiliwa and their ancestors were mobile hunters and gatherers. Unlike the Mesoamerican cultures of mainland Mexico and Central America, the people of Baja California did not establish cities. With very few exceptions, the vast majority of archaeological sites are the remains of seasonal encampments by mobile bands probably comprised of five to fifteen families.[6]

Given the mobility of these people, it is surprising to realize how important "house" was in Kiliwa worldview. This contrasts markedly with the way Jesuit missionaries viewed the cultural landscape of Baja California. The German Jesuit Jakob Baegert wrote: "The Californians were entirely barbarous and savage. Neither architecture, agriculture, nor the many arts useful to human life were known to them. In all that peninsula there was not a house, nor the vestige of one; not even a hut."[7]

Despite the Jesuit's declaration, the aboriginal Kiliwa house did have houses—relatively small, oval structures no more than three or four meters across. By the late 1920s, the cultural geographer Peveril Meigs recorded that the Kiliwa oval house had been nearly replaced by rectangular thatched houses with gabled roofs; only the elderly people still lived in the elliptical dwellings (called *wa?*). The *wa?* was framed by two upright forked posts that supported a ridgepole or "house spine." Willow poles were planted in the ground roughly eighteen-inch intervals and then thatched with tule reeds and yucca stalks. The wall bases were anchored with stones, completing a house that, according to Meigs, could last a decade.[8]

In a symbolic and metaphoric sense, this raw landscape of desert, broken mountains, and unstable seas was a land filled with dwellings. When the deity, The-Sky-Sculptor, made the firmament, he set forked house posts on mountain tops in the four corners of the cosmos, bent rainbows into roof beams, and covered them with the dome of heaven. The center of the sky held The-House-of-Clouds-of-the-Distant-Heaven-Being that was, in turn, bordered by the smaller Spirit-Houses. This cosmic arrangement was made plain on the domed carapace of the desert tortoise on which the larger plates of cartilaginous bone in the center are surrounded by the smaller peripheral osteoderms around the edge.

When the god Being-Here-About ventured out to create the world, he passed through a distant land in the south, stabbing his walking staff into the ground to make volcanoes and planting stands of wild tobacco until he arrived at the sea. At the water's edge, the god underwent a horrid transformation, changing from a human-like form into a sea creature the color of a "crow-black seashell." The god sunk into the sea, completing his metamorphosis into another deity, The-Ancient-One-of-Extended-Kelp, before swimming off to a far-away spirit house, the Spirit-House-Under-the-Shadow-of-the-Distant-Land-in-the-Southern-Sea.

When a Kiliwa died, runners were sent to bring relatives to the homestead. A circular corral of brush was built. The dead person was removed from his or her house through a ragged opening torn through the thatching opposite the door. The corpse was placed in the corral. The deceased's closest relatives wept constantly for the next three days, sitting in the corral with the body. Small fires surrounded the corpse. Before dawn on the third day, a deep pit was dug and filled with firewood. The body was placed on top, along with food and clothing. The funeral pyre flamed. The body smoked and blackened. When the fire cooled, the ashes were swept back into the pit, the cremation fire was covered with topsoil and smoothed until all traces of the funeral were erased.

The dead person's house was torched. The tule reeds and yucca stalks burned quickly, the timbers and thatching collapsing into embers. Once the house of the dead was reduced to ashes, the house site was avoided. The ghost would haunt their home site, lingering about instead of journeying to *ukâ'wá'wéy,* the Crow's-House-Mountain, and then ascending to *úmá'wá,* the House-Where-the-Dead-Live.

In the late summer heat near San Felipe, I am far away from home, just as the Jesuits were five centuries ago. I can imagine their longing for temperate broadleaf forests and cultivated fields and pastures, wistfully remembering the sounds of village markets and the distant tolls of church bells. The Jesuits, missionaries sworn to leave home for distant lands and lost souls, had forsaken home. In the process, they denied the very existence of houses to the people who made this peninsula home and whose houses were transformed into special and sacred places by the cleansing purge of flames.

. . .

Humans connect the sacred and the domestic realms with a broad array of conceptual metaphors, but several symbolic connections are common. One method is via a household shrine, a material focus that connected the home to the sacred. In the ancient Roman houses excavated at Pompeii and Herculaneum, dwellings contained a wall niche, a *lararium,* either in the atrium or in the kitchen, where the household gods, the *lares familiares,* were worshipped. Some of the niches were undecorated and may have served as cupboards rather than shrines. Others were relatively elaborate, incorporating miniature columns and the triangular pediment that clearly alludes to the facade of a Roman temple.

Some niches held figures of the household gods, often depicted as spry figures in short tunics holding offering bowls and drinking horns (cornucopia), symbols of plenty. At the House of Vettii in Pompeii, the household shrine shows a sinuous snake (an emblem of household protection and fertility) under a pair of lares with raised drinking horns who flank a man making offerings ashes to the lares. Offerings included grains, grapes, wine, or blood. Roosters were often sacrificed, particularly the feet and head (suggesting the rest of the bird was cooked and eaten). The offerings were cremated either in the nearby hearth (vesta) or on braziers set in front of the lararium. As the classicist Mary Beard has observed, Roman religion "was demonstrated through action and ritual rather than words." The lararium was the physical focus of a ritual action connecting humans to the gods and bridging house and temple. Notably, the most commonly used Latin word for the temple was not templum, but rather aedes, or "house."[9]

Another way to connect the sacred and the domestic is to never divide them in the first place. From insular Southeast Asia across the islands of the Pacific, a broad swath of cultures contend that the cosmos is animated by a vital force found not only in "living" things, but also within objects and materials that Westerners consider "inanimate." In the Austronesian and Polynesian languages of Oceania this vital force is referred to as mana, while in the Malay and Indonesian languages it is referred to as semangat or other related terms.[10]

Mana is present through all existence, although in varying intensities, densities, and dangers. Not surprisingly, it also imbues homes. In her masterful survey of Southeast Asian traditional architecture, ethnographer Roxana Waterson writes about "the living house," in which dwellings are regarded "as having a vitality of their own, interdependent with the vitality of their occupants." Given a world view predicated on mana or semangat, "it is possible for humans to perceive themselves not as alienated from the rest of the cosmos, but as participating in existence on much the same terms as everything else. The relationship between persons and things may also be much more intimate since concentrations of vital force may be transferred between them."[11]

As the anthropologist Douglas Oliver summarized, "Mana was supernatural power. Objects and individuals might possess it in varying degrees. The tool which invariably turned out fine production had mana, as had the skilled craftsman—his 'skill' and mana being the same thing. Gods, of course, had mana to a superlative degree, and their direct human descendants, the chiefs and their high-ranking families, partook of that concentration of power."[12]

The study of Austronesian languages suggests that the original seafarers who colonized the Pacific shared a notion of mana.[13] The broad distribution of the concept of mana points to a common cosmologi-

FIGURE 30. Lararium, House of Vettii, Pompeii. Photo courtesy of Patricio Lorente.

cal notion. Based on archaeological excavations, it appears that people expanded from insular Southeast Asia after about 2200 B.C., colonized the western Pacific between 1350 and 900 B.C., paused, and then set sail again, landing in New Zealand, the Hawaiian Islands, and Easter Island between A.D. 700 and 1200.[14] These settlers carried a suite of crops and domesticated animals (pigs, dogs, and chickens), sailing and fishing technologies, and pottery and other artifacts that made these bold excursions possible.

· They also had well-defined ideas about their houses. Based on his study of Austronesian vocabularies, the linguist Robert Blust has discussed how these early settlers lived in permanent villages of house built on raised pilings, clambered into on a notched log ladder.[15] This inference from linguistic data is substantiated by excavations at the site of Talepakemalai, located on a small coral island in the Bismarck Archipelago; posts from a stilt house were recovered that date to ca. 1350 B.C. and are associated with Lapita pottery, a distinctive ceramic style associated with the first colonizers of Melanesia and Oceania.[16]

Based on Blust's analysis, the linguistic data contain other insights. Reconstructed from the vocabularies, the houses had a ridgepole and sloping gabled roofs, probably thatched with sago or other palm fronds. A hearth was built in one corner of the floor. The walls held shelves for containers, firewood, and other supplies. Villages also contained other structures—meeting houses, canoe sheds—but used a particular word for dwellings that simultaneously meant "house/family/home."

House design and mana intersect in the building materials, particularly in the posts. Since posts are cut from living trees, it is both logical and scientifically accurate to associate them with a vital force. Across Southeast Asia and Oceania, the transformation from tree to post is surrounded by rituals.

For example, the Jörai highlanders of southern Vietnam deploy a series of rituals to convert the wild, vital force of trees into the domesticated, safe power of house timbers. Chants entreat the trees to be happy and cool when they become part of the house, to become a benevolent force in their new human realm.

The Mingangkabu of western Sumatra hold that mature trees are occupied by dangerous spirits, and a ritual specialist must entreat the spirits to relocate elsewhere before a tree can be felled. Another Sumatran society, the Sa'dan Toraja, construct noble longhouses with swooping saddleback roofs; the central upright post is the "navel post," transported to the building site with the top of the tree held higher than the roots, dressed the post either as a male or female depending on the gender of the founding ancestor of the kin group who live in the longhouse.

As Waterson observes, "The frequency with which house posts are personified or become the focus of ritual attention . . . doubtless reflects the attitude to the trees in the first place. There is a pervasive idea that the timber continues to be animated, albeit in a new form. Secondly, the process of construction itself must be viewed as contributing to the efficacy of an object. It is this process, after all, which brings the object into being."[17]

Related concepts linking dwellings and deities were carried eastward to Hawaii and Tahiti. The ancestral creator-god Ta'aroa placed the celestial dome upon pillars, specific upright supports: the front pillar, the back pillar, the inner pillar, "the pillar to stand by, the pillar to sit by, the pillar to blacken by, the pillar to debate by, the elocution pillar, and the pillar of exit." Through the placement of these cosmogonic posts, "The sky was extended, it was widened with the pillars of the land of Havai'i."[18]

The myth of "The First God's House" was recorded in the early 1800s at several places in the Tahitian islands.[19] The myth begins, "The first god's house in the temple was the empty body of Ta'aroa's own person, and it became a model for all other god's houses." The tale concludes when Ta'aroa dismembers himself and transforms his bones into the frame of the house: "The backbone was the ridgepole, the ribs were the supporters of the god's house, the breast-bone was the capping of the roof, and the thigh-bones became the carved ornaments around the god's house."

European accounts from the early contact period (ca. 1776–ca. 1820) describe the construction of a sacred "god's house" *(fare)*. Originally the fare was little more than a common house, but over time it became a ritual space particularly upon the burial of ancestors in the dwelling, which transformed the space and its mana. Further, god's houses were usually adjacent to an open space or plaza *(marae)* where people assembled. In various Polynesian societies, this essential combination of fare and marae was complemented by a display of posts or upright stone slabs that marked the graves of chiefly ancestors or represented an assembly of gods.[20]

Thus posts were more than structural elements in Polynesian dwellings. In 1809 the Methodist missionary John Davies described the rituals surrounding a sacred fare on Tahiti:

> The house of the gods is according to the fashion of this country an elegant and costly one, it is what is called a Fare pota ... the length is about 56 ft. and width about 28 it is supported by 32 strong pillars well wrought two or three of the middle ones which support the Tahuhu or main beam, that has the upper end of the rafters resting upon [it] are curiously wrapt round with matting & sinnet of various colours, almost most of the rafters are wrapt nearly to the top with the same, the making of this matting and sinnet has been chiefly the work of the women & it has cost them much time.[21]

The special attention given to posts included the careful selection of wood, particularly in the dwellings for gods and elites that radiated particularly intense mana. Jennifer Kahn and James Coil conducted meticulous analysis of the charred remains of posts recovered during excavations in late prehistoric houses in Mo'orea. The functions of different structures could be identified by other characteristics: the size and layout of houses were distinct for elites and commoners, and everyday dwellings were different from special structures where ritual objects were stored or used, known as *fare ia manaha,* or "house of sacred treasures."[22]

Such differences were indicated by house posts. The postholes in ritual structures were larger and more substantial than those used in everyday houses, whether of elites or commoners. More significantly, the tree species chosen for posts varied between houses. The houses of elites and the buildings used in rituals had posts carved from breadfruit wood; the lower status dwellings did not.

Breadfruit timbers were particularly sacred. Although coconut and breadfruit posts were used in elite houses, only the breadfruit seems to have been particularly imbued with mana. "Breadfruit was both an economically important and ritually significant tree," Kahn and Coil write, "and its wood was highly prized and used to fashion diverse objects" including temple altars and sacred figures used in temples and on canoes.[23] Because the house posts "served as important social symbols, embodying relations between the living, the ancestors, and the gods," the wood used for those posts was carefully chosen. Finding the charred remains of breadfruit posts in elite dwellings and sacred structures indicate the significance of those buildings and the intensity of their mana. Such buildings not only were expressions of the power of their occupants, but were structures where the sacred and the domestic were fused in the wooden beams of home.

. . .

Another way to connect the sacred and the domestic is to invite supernatural beings into one's house. An example of this is the "shaking tent ceremony," found among a broad range of subarctic peoples from northern Scandinavia to Siberia and across North America from Alaska to Greenland. This intercontinental distribution may reflect a core set of religious practices transmitted by Paleolithic hunters as they moved from the Old World into the New World; it may also reflect more recent diffusion of religious beliefs as Siberian fur hunters came into contact with Inuit and other North American groups during the seventeenth and eighteenth centuries.[24]

The shaking tent ceremony involves a key set of elements. Inside a tent or specially constructed hut, shamans beat on a flat drum, the drumbeats building into a rapid crescendo as supernatural beings—whether the shaman's spirit helpers or contrary forces—swirl around the tent that pulses and vibrates in this encounter between the shaman and the supernatural.

The shaking tent ceremony leaves few distinctive archaeological traces that would survive the conditions of the far north. Small huts built from birch logs and hides would not be well preserved, and tents transformed by shamanic incantations would be indistinguishable from other dwellings. One of the best archaeological evidence for a shamanic ritual in a tent are two historic petroglyphs from the Altai mountains of central Asia depicting shamans drumming and attracting spirit beings.[25]

Eleven thousand kilometers away and several centuries later, in 1938 the anthropologist Regina Flannery observed a shaking tent ceremony

FIGURE 31. H. Schoolcraft, *Ojibwa Shaking Tent,* 1855. Reproduced courtesy of Wisconsin Historical Society.

among a group of Montagnais living on the southern coast of Canada's Hudson Bay.[26] The tent was made from a framework of fresh-cut poles stuck into the ground, forming a circle about four feet across. Two hoops made from saplings—the first large, the second small—were slipped over the uprights and lashed in place, tightening the frame like barrel staves. The frame was completely covered with canvas that was staked down tight. The shaman crawled into the tent and began to sing.

His first song was the song of the trees, Flannery writes, but "it could not be translated for very few can understand the language of the trees." As the shaman sang, the tent began to vibrate, gently at first but more violently as the spirits entered the tent. The spirit of clawed animals arrived, as did the spirit of fish and all things in the water. The crow spirit came followed by a procession of other spirits. When Mistabeo, the chief spirit who served as "master of ceremonies" arrived, the tent lurched violently. Mistabeo had been a long way away when the ceremony began, so it took him some time to get there. Mistabeo complained that the tent was too small.

With men and women seated on opposite sides of the shaking tent, the Montagnais shouted questions to Mistabeo. Most of the queries were from elderly men who asked about hunting. Mistabeo answered some but not all of the questions, before demanding a cigarette, which was slid under the tent flap. At one point in the ceremony, Mistabeo battled with the spirit of clawed animals, and as the grunts and growls echoed and the tent shook violently, the Montagnais drew closer to the tent and shouted encouragements to Mistabeo, who finally vanquished the spirit of clawed animals, ensuring a future successful bear hunt.

After midnight, the spirits began leaving the tent, which shook violently as they left. Mistabeo was the last to go, singing song after song, until he finally flew away from the shaking tent.

A number of American Indian groups of the northern Great Plains practiced similar ceremonies, although under the pressure of Christian missionaries and Euro-American aggression, the shaking tent ceremony was generally abandoned or reduced by the time the anthropologists arrived.[27]

A similar situation occurred among the Evenkis, who live in the Russian arctic. The Evenkis are mobile reindeer hunters and herders who live in conical lodges, similar to the North American plains teepees or the Saami kåhte (described in chapter 5). Battered by the Russian Revolution, the Stalinist political project, perestroika, and post-Soviet economic and political changes, the Evenkis still move with their herds.[28]

In 1929–1931 and 1937 the Soviet ethnographer A.F. Ansimov recorded a detailed description of the Evenki shaking tent ceremony.[29] Although the ceremony sometimes took place inside a normal dwelling, Ansimov illustrates an impressive architectural complex that elaborated the dwelling and created a remarkable mise-en-scène.

The Evenki word for the shaman's tent (shevenchedek) is glossed as "the locale where the activity of spirits or totems takes place," signaling that the shaman's tent was not an inert shelter, but a place of spiritual encounter. Whether this encounter took place in an everyday dwelling or in the shevenchedek, a larch post was planted in the center of the structure and symbolized the world-tree. The shaman would clamber up the world-tree to journey to the upper worlds. His spirit-helpers rested in its branches.

As the shaman meditated and fasted, his kinsmen built complex enclosures and totemic posts surrounding the tent. Two galleries projected from either side of the tent, bordered by posts and carved figures representing ancestors and shamanistic spirits. The east-facing gallery represented the river of the upper world, the central tent was the shaman's island, and the west-facing gallery symbolized the river of the dead. While the eastern gallery was lined by living larch trees, the western gallery was built from downed snag-wood that bordered the river of the dead. The great clan-river flowed from east to west, from life to death.

The world-tree and the great clan-river formed perpendicular axes that linked three worlds: the upper world, the middle "earthly" realm, and the underworld. These intersected in the shaman's tent.

The road to the underworld was guarded by carved figures representing spirits of birds (loons, owls, geese), the burbot (a voracious fish [Lota lota] who gulps down frogs or other evil spirits who try to swim upstream from the lower realm into the middle earth), and a cow elk protected by Siberian stags. When the shaman captured evil spirits launched by shamans from rival clans, the evil spirits were imprisoned in a sapling-fence pen that resembled a fish weir from which no evil spirit could escape.

In the eastern river of the upper world, the Evenki built a small raised platform made from planks carved to represent salmon. The shaman sat on the platform and rode his raft of wooden fish down the "watery river-road" to do battle with evil spirits of the lower world.

Ansimov described a specific ritual he observed in 1931. The shaman's tent stood in semi-darkness. A small fire flickered inside. Clansmen filled the tent, expectant in the night. The shaman sat at the tent's door, surrounded by the carved spirit images. His face was pale and pinched. His hands trembled. The shaman's assistant brought out ceremonial robes and headdress and dressed the shaman. The shaman's drum was heated over the fire, tightening the skin and improving its tone.

The shaman sat on the raft of wooden salmon, struck the drum with a rattle-stick, and his cosmic journey began.

The shaman began with a well-known song. The clansmen replied in chorus. The shaman improvised new verses, calling out to his spirit-helpers and enlisting them in his struggle. The shaman described the spirit-helpers, sang out whether they were willing or resistant allies. The drumbeats slowed into a low roll.

The voices of the spirit-helpers broke the night. They growled and snorted. The bird spirits cawed and whistled; their wings whirred. The drumbeat paused and then pounded into an incessant roll. The shaman deployed his spirit-helpers, some to defend against the onslaught of evil, others to join him as he battle-charged into the lower world.

The shaman's animal-double spirit led the attack, charging down the world-tree into the underworld. The shaman's army of spirit-helpers scouted for evil spirits sent by enemy shamans, and attacked the malevolent forces.

The deadly struggle between good and evil was described, as Ansimov recalled, "in the shaman's songs in such fantastic form, so deftly accompanied by motions, imitations of spirit-voices, comic and dramatic dialogues, wild screams, snorts, noises, and the like, that it startled and amazed even this far from superstitious onlooker."

The battle raged. The drum moaned. The shaman leaped from the salmon raft and "let loose such a torrent of sounds that it seemed everything hummed, beginning with the poles of the tent, and ending with the buttons on the clothing." Tossing his drum to his assistant, the shaman marched on into ecstasy, channeling the cries and snorts of beasts and spirits and entrancing his kinsmen into the otherworldly moment.

The shaman grabbed the tent ropes and jumped, twisting into the air as his spirit-helpers fought, fled, and counterattacked.

The shaman and his spirit helpers were victorious. The battle won, the shaman fell to earth, his mouth foaming.

The shaman's assistant bent over the shaman's lifeless body, begging for him to return from the lower world. The tent-fire was stoked as a beacon to guide the shaman back from darkness. The shaman murmured in a faint babble, channeling the muffled voices of his exhausted but victorious spirit-helpers. The shaman's assistant called out to the shaman's animal-double spirit, and drummed to guide the spirit back from the lower world and towards the fire's light.

The dramatic encounter between the shaman and the forces of the lower world continued for hours as the shaman marshaled his spirit-helpers, launched attacks against the forces of ruin and sickness, consulted his animal double, healed ailing kinfolk, and retaliated against the enemy clan and their spirit army. A reindeer was sacrificed. The shaman foretold the future by cutting out the reindeer's shoulder bone, placing hot hearth coals on the fresh bone, and interpreting the patterns of the fissures and crazings.

With the clan restored and the future visible, the ceremony ended. The shaman's tent was taken down, but the enclosure, the world-tree, the wooden salmon raft were all left behind as the Evenki and their reindeer herds moved off into the boreal forest.

. . .

The sacred may dwell at home. Given the pivotal place dwellings have in the human experience and the capacity of our houses to shelter both mundane tasks and complicated meanings, it is not surprising that people make their dwellings into sacred homes. What is surprising are the elaborate and diverse ways in which we do this.

On the one hand, we can propose complex domestic analogies: if we live in houses, then our gods must also. If the Children of Israel lived in tent during their four decades of wandering, so did Yahweh; when they settled into city, they built God a permanent temple. Based on this logic, humans build temples that serve as houses of gods and provide deities with food and diversions, an architectural extrapolation from the domestic to the sacred.

Or we may simply state that since the gods are in the heavens, their houses must be there also and therefore we imagine the sky to be a vast celestial ceiling. Even a highly mobile society like the Kiliwa of Baja California may create this symbolic parallel between the houses of the living and the houses of the spirits.

Alternatively, we may separate a portion of our own residences to the service of the sacred, creating household altars or following rituals that ask for blessings or protections for the household. The household altar in a Roman house served as a conduit between the family and the gods, a focal point for offerings and prayers that connected the everyday and the divine.

Perhaps more subtly, we may consider our homes to contain sacred power, incorporating into walls and roofs the same vital essence that flows through the universe. Just as the posts of a Polynesian dwelling subtly vibrated with mana, our dwellings may be seen as architecture contiguous with the sacred.

Another way humans make their homes sacred is by inviting the supernatural to visit. In this case, the shaking tent ceremony is a striking example in that the dwelling is literally tenanted spirits, at least for a few days.

Just as our homes may serve as constructed templates for other aspects of our worldviews, our dwellings can encapsulate and represent our engagements with the supernatural. If it is more common in modern American society for us to encounter the divine in our churches, synagogues, mosques, and temples, it is worth remembering that in other cultures and other times, the gods are often at home.

CHAPTER 10

Home Fires

Not marble, nor the gilded monuments
Of princes, shall outlive this powerful rime;
But you shall shine more bright in these contents
Than unswept, stone besemear'd with sluttish time
When wasteful war shall statues overturn,
And broils root out the work of masonry,
Nor Mars his sword nor war's quick fires shall burn
The living record of your memory.

—Shakespeare, Sonnet 55.

A little after 2 A.M. on March 8, 2010, I woke to crackling wood and the quivering gold of fire. From my bedroom window, I saw a nearby house blazing. I threw on some clothes, ran outside and around the corner to the house as a piston of flames burst through the roof.

Fire chewed the eaves.

A night watchman driving home from his swing shift had smelled the smoke, called 911, and tried to knock on the front door, but the heat was too intense.

It was the home of our neighborhood misanthrope. The house was a wood-framed building from the early twentieth century. His front yard was an overgrown tangle of shrubs and trees, an unkempt anomaly on a street of neat lawns.

In the sixteen years we had been neighbors, he had never spoken a word to me. My next-door neighbor claimed that during the forty-five years she has been living here, only once did the misanthrope speak to her; she was walking her dog on the opposite site of the street from the misanthrope's house when he barked, "Don't let that dog piss in my yard!"

When we moved into the neighborhood, our realtor warned us about him, telling the story of the skateboard ramp. The previous summer some kids had built a skateboard ramp from plywood and two-by-fours, an improvised diversion on a long summer afternoon. Unfortunately, the kids decided to build this in front of the misanthrope's house. After an hour of skateboard-grinding and loud kids, the misanthrope came out with an axe. He hacked the ramp to kindling as the kids cowered behind their parents, who looked on in silence.

Or at least that's what we were told.

Over the years I had learned that the misanthrope was an artist, a painter of delicate watercolors of plants and landscapes. A longtime instructor at a community college, this man who never spoke to his neighbors was a cherished teacher loved by his students.

As I ran up, the house fire intensified, and the windows shattered in a crystal rain. Fire trucks arrived and sprayed foam retardant over the neighboring houses to keep the flames from spreading. Coal-black smoke poured through the broken windows as fire hoses streamed water onto the house.

Firemen crashed through the back door and tried to enter the house, but there was no room to move.

The misanthrope was a hoarder. Pillars of magazines and newspapers crowded the rooms. Debris blocked the hallways. Old furniture exploded and flared. The firemen could not get into the house until they threw out the burning piles.

The fire was out in less than twenty minutes, but by then it was too late.

When the covered body was rolled out on a gurney, I left and walked back to my house. I thought about how little it would take—a stove left on, an unattended candle, a loose electrical wire—to set my home ablaze. I crawled back into bed, told my wife what I had seen, and thought about the fragility of the dwelling that contains our uncertain lives.

. . .

Fire usually destroys, but sometimes it preserves. The best-known case of an archaeological site preserved by fire is, of course, the Roman city of Pompeii.[1] A humpbacked peak on the western caldera that holds the Bay of Naples, Mt. Vesuvius is one of an arc of volcanoes that Pliny the Elder previously had named *campi phlegraei*, or "fields of fire." (Ironically, Pliny the Elder would be killed when Mt. Vesuvius erupted.)

Mt. Vesuvius is the only one of these volcanoes to erupt in historic times. Preceded by some seventeen years of tremors and earthquakes, the volcano had not had a major eruption since about 1200 B.C. Over the next thirteen centuries, a ferocious mix of sulfurous gases and molten lava built up in Vesuvius's main magma chamber.

In late August A.D. 79, after several weeks of severe earthquakes and ventings—including "fires and the smell of sulfur forewarning of fires"— the blocked chamber burst.

Pompeii and the neighboring city of Herculaneum were blanketed in pumice and ash, driven by fire from the earth's core. The eruption released a 20-kilometer-tall column of ash, pumice, and gas with a volume of 2.6 cubic kilometers. A rain of air-fall pumice was followed by "a turbulent cloud of volcanic ash and hot gases, which hugs the ground and travels at speeds often exceeding 100 km per hour" accompanied seconds later by pyroclastic flows—"hot, chaotic avalanches of pumice, ash and gases"—that tumbled down the flanks of Vesuvius and covered the cities below.[2]

Within a half hour of the eruption, a rain of ash began to fall on the cities, accumulating at a rate of 15 centimeters per hour until a uniform layer of pumice 2.8 meters thick covered streets, gardens, and buildings.

The 25,000 inhabitants of Pompeii and Herculaneum vacillated between staying indoors, where they were protected from volcanic bombs, or fleeing outside as seismic jolts tumbled their dwellings, frantic attempts to escape in darkness long before sunset. Bread loaves still sat inside ovens. Vineyards faded from summer green to ash gray. Images of gods and goddesses were concealed by pumice; so were the brothels.

The roofs on many houses collapsed from the weight of ash and pumice. Atria and amphitheaters, baths and bakeries, the houses of the rich and the cramped quarters of the poor—all were silted over with a thick and deadly layer of pumice.

Accompanied by an earthquake-triggered tsunami that left marine animals stranded inland, Vesuvius emitted a *nuée ardente,* an incandescent cloud of deadly gas and ash that flowed in a glowing avalanche. This "hot dense mixture of fine ash and gases instantly buried the victims of the ground surge and suffocated any survivors."[3]

The houses of Pompeii and Herculaneum and more than a thousand residents were preserved in "a state of arrested development . . . [on] the fateful August day [when] its life was cut short."[4] The tragic catastrophe of A.D. 79 resulted in "a remarkable snapshot of an ancient city frozen in time."

Beneath the layers of pumice and under the cooled pyroclastic flow,

FIGURE 32. Reconstruction of the House of Vettii, Pompeii. Photo courtesy of Mattes.

corpses were molded by volcanic debris. In 1863 the archaeologist Giuseppe Fiorelli devised a technique of filling these vacuums of death with plaster, capturing in disturbing and fascinating detail the gruesome deaths of the residents of Pompeii and Herculaneum. When the American consul in Naples, the man-of-letters William Dean Howells, observed the site a year later, he wrote conversationally to the imagined reader of his book, *Italian Journey:*

> You have read, no doubt, of their discovering, a year or two since, in making an excavation in a Pompeian street, the molds of four human bodies, three women and a man, who fell down, blind and writhing, in the storm of fire eighteen hundred years ago; whose shape the settling and hardening ashes took; whose flesh wasted away, and whose bones lay there in the hollow of the matrix till the cunning of this time found them, and, pouring liquid plaster round the skeletons, clothed them with human form again, and drew them forth into the world once more. There are many things in Pompeii which bring back the gay life of the city, but nothing which so vividly reports the terrible manner of her death as these effigies of the creatures that actually shared it.[5]

More recently, classicist Mary Beard has written about how "the impact of these victims . . . comes also from the sense of immediate contact with the ancient world that they offer, the human narratives they allow us to reconstruct, as well as the choices, decisions and hopes of real people with whom we can empathize across the millennia."[6]

Even before Fiorelli devised his casting procedure, Pompeii attracted tourists on the "Great Tour" of the glories of the Classical World. As Goethe wryly, but somewhat callously, observed in 1787, "On Sunday we went to Pompeii again. There have been many disasters in this world, but few which have given so much delight to posterity, and I have seldom seen anything so interesting."[7]

Ten thousand kilometers away on the other side of the earth, the archaeological site of Cerén has been called the "New World Pompeii" as it was buried in ash around A.D. 590.[8] Located in the Zapotitán Valley of El Salvador, Cerén sits between major volcanic complexes that are active and have erupted during various prehistoric and historic events. The regular eruptions have created the fertile soils of the Zapotitán Valley, and the caldera slopes are emerald with thick vegetation thriving on nutrients created by earlier devastations. These volcano-enriched soils supported dense human populations in prehistory, and El Salvador now is more densely occupied than any other mainland nation in the Américas.

Sometime between A.D. 410 and 535, a massive eruption occurred at the Ilopango volcano, today a 8 × 11 kilometer water-filled caldera and one of El Salvador's largest lakes. The fifth-century Ilopango eruption covered some 10,000 square kilometers—all of central and western El Salvador—with over 50 centimeters of ash, cinders, and volcanic bombs. The area within 25 kilometers of the Ilopango Volcano was completely devastated. The ancient "survivors in western El Salvador were left with a sterile, denuded landscape. This ash-choked region could not support any significant agricultural production for some decades after the eruption."[9]

The ancient inhabitants of Cerén were early pioneers, who had resettled this tephra-swathed landscape less than a century later. Cerén was a modest village of perhaps one hundred people, living in households clustered around a small plaza. The households were about 50 meters apart, encircled by small kitchen gardens and farm plots (milpas). The dwellings were surrounded by storehouses, kitchens, and ramadas. Other structures had more specialized purposes. A large sweat-bath could have held a dozen people. One building seems to have been used for ceremonial feasting, another for "civic functions," based on the presence of long benches. Another building, painted white and decorated with red pigment, was where a female diviner peered into the future.

FIGURE 33. House preserved in volcanic ash, Joya el Cerén. Photo courtesy of Janine Gasco.

And then Cerén was entombed in ash.

The eruption occurred with little warning. The eruption did not explode from a major volcano, nor was it preceded by strong earthquakes. Glowing basaltic magma slowly rose through a fissure under the Rio Sucio, less than a half-mile north of the village. The first clear warning was the explosion of steam as lava hit water, and with that every resident of the village fled to the south, as Cerén was quickly covered by five meters of ash.

The site lay deeply buried for the next thirteen centuries. In the mid-1970s a construction crew cut through the northern edge of the site with a bulldozer. When the machine operator saw ancient buildings and pottery, he stopped and notified an archaeologist at a local museum. The archaeologist visited the site, and seeing the well-preserved buildings assumed that they were recent dwellings buried by a nineteenth- or twentieth-century eruption, and thus "insignificant." The archaeologist authorized the bulldozer to continue. At least a dozen ancient houses were destroyed, including one building cross-cut by the bulldozer blade and left exposed in the borrow pit.

But the remaining portion of the site contained marvels.

The investigations at Cerén have been directed by the archaeologist Payson Sheets. In 1978 Sheets saw the remnants of the bulldozed dwelling in the borrow pit and began his research project. El Salvador's tragic civil war prevented archaeological research for most of the 1980s, but excavations resumed in 1989. These investigations resulted in an amazing vision of ancient life in Mesoamerica.

Like Pompeii and Herculaneum, the volcanic ash has preserved the houses and other buildings of Cerén. Unlike those Roman cities, no human bodies have been found at Cerén. The villagers seem to have escaped, but leaving everything they owned behind.

The ash was wet and relatively cool, and it silted over the houses and fields of Cerén. The steamy tephra settled around the young corn stalks in the milpas; in a technique borrowed and modified from Pompeii, the corn casts were injected with dental plaster. Based on the height of the corn, the eruption occurred in August. The ash enshrouded the thatched roofs and wattle and daubed walls without igniting these normally perishable materials. The tephra settled inside the houses, covering dinner plates of food not yet cleared away. Sheets suggests that the eruption occurred between 6 and 7 P.M., right around sunset and during the evening meal.

The objects left behind that August evening fourteen centuries ago provide an unequaled vista into daily life during the Classic period of the Southern Maya world. The architectural details of the houses—the thick roofs of grass thatching, the upright wattles intertwined with vines—normally would have rotted away long ago in the humid tropics of Central America. Because of this ancient disaster, fascinating insights were preserved.

The houses were built on an earthen platform constructed in two layers. The first layer was simply a low clay mound sloped to channel rainwater away from the building, essential in the rainy season. A second rectangular or square mound was built on top of the initial mound, and columns of adobe were built in the four corners. This second rectangular platform was finished with a coat of fine clay. A fire was kindled on this surface, baking the clay to make a durable solid floor. In each corner a stood an upright column less than 1.5 meters tall built from adobes.

The wattle-and-daub walls were constructed from thin vertical poles placed at four to six inch intervals between the upright adobe columns. Smaller horizontal poles were woven between the verticals. Since the four adobe columns were relatively short, the roof may have sat on posts on top of the columns. Although the lower walls were plastered on both sides with a thick layer of mud, the upper portions of the walls were left open but protected by the sloping thatched roofs, letting light penetrate and air circulate into the houses of Cerén.

This fine-scaled vision of daily life produced details that are alternatively familiar and odd. The households of Cerén were surrounded by fruit trees—avocado, guava, and cacao—similar to the orange, lime, and fig trees I tend in my back yard. At Cerén the busted sherds of clay pots that tumbled and shattered when the earth shook, remind me of the precariously perched dishes and plates in upper shelves of my own house. In a clever bit of homemaking, the people of Cerén recycled large ceramic strap handles (probably from broken water jugs) and plastered them into their house walls, reusing them as rod supports for hanging mats or cloth doors, similar to the Venetian blinds that hang in my living room. And the storerooms' jumble of obsidian blades, storage jars, manos, and metates inevitably reminds me of my garage, although the people of Cerén were much better organized.

But other things are breathtakingly different. A scatter of seeds from strings of dried chiles sprinkled over a prized greenstone celt. A domesticated duck was found inside one structure, the bird still leashed by a cord to a house post. A niche in another building contained a painted calabash, an oyster shell, and a trio of polychrome vessels including one that still had fingerprints from the last supper at Cerén.

A number of objects had been stored in the roofs, objects stuck into the thatching that tumbled to the floor during the eruption. Among these fallen artifacts were numerous storage vessels, chunks of red pigment, and obsidian blades. One of the obsidian blades tested positive for human blood.

The bloodied obsidian blade came from a small structure, just a few yards from the other houses at Cerén. Built of the same wattle-and-daub walls, thatched roof, and fired clay platform as the other dwellings, this dwelling contained objects and features indicating an additional, ritual function. Although the building had hearths and metates like the other houses and contained everyday domestic items, it also held numerous polychrome vessels—several of them fitted with ceramic lids—and a pot made in the shape of a caiman that held a red pile of achiote seeds.

Among the ancient and modern Maya, achiote is used as a food coloring—for example, in the Yucatan it is added to stewed pork to make the savory, copper-colored stew *cochinita pibil*—and it is used as a pigment. The archaeologists Linda Brown and Andrea Gerstle, who studied the architecture and objects of this building, noted that among the contemporary Lacandon Maya of the jungles of Chiapas, achiote is used "to make red paint, symbolic of human blood and sacrifice, which is applied to beams in ceremonial structures, ritual clothing, *incensarios* (censers), and the bodies of ritual participants as a means to activate and animate objects with a life force."[10]

In this same building, the wall of one room was painted red—the east-facing wall in the easternmost room—as were several objects found inside this room, including an amazing headdress made from the skull and antlers of a white-tailed deer. The deer-skull headdress had fallen from safekeeping during the eruption. The three-pronged antlers of a young adult buck were painted red, with a slight dab of blue on the right tine. Small bits of cordage around the base of the antlers indicate the deer skull and antlers were worn as a headdress.

Brown and Gerstle point out that for the Maya, the color red, the direction east, and the white-tailed-deer mask were conceptually linked. Various Maya communities connect the color red with the rising sun and link the white-tailed deer to the rain-god Chac. These ancient residents of this village on the banks of the Rio Sucio may have attended religious ceremonies at a nearby larger Classic Maya center, but they were also able "to intervene directly with the supernatural" in their own modest villages and in their own homes.

And this we know because of the tragedy more than fourteen centuries ago, when the fires of the earth erupted and the village of Cerén was frozen in ash.

. . .

Fire is a recurrent threat to city life, particularly in premodern urban centers. When London's Great Fire raged across the city in September 1666, Samuel Pepys climbed the Tower of London to view "an infinite great fire" as he called it, adding, "it made me weep to see it. The churches, houses, and all on fire and flaming at once; and a horrid noise the flames made, and the cracking of houses at their ruins." Tacitus, wrote of the Great Fire of Rome in A.D. 64, a wind-fanned inferno that swept across the imperial city, leveling three of its fourteen districts, reducing seven others "to a few scorched and mangled ruins," and leaving behind the enduring—although false—rumor that the emperor Nero had played his lyre as Rome burned.

Tacitus had also mentioned the fear of fire as a possible explanation for the isolated homesteads of Germanic tribes, suggesting that the distance between houses inhibited the risk of flames (as mentioned in chapter 1). In fact, the wattle-and-daub houses of temperate Europe were more difficult to burn than Tacitus assumed, which leads to an interesting problem of burning down the house.

Dating approximately 5500 to 4700 B.C., burned houses are found in a large area of Europe—from Romania across Serbia and Bulgaria to eastern Hungary and southeastern Ukraine, but not in the contemporary prehistoric communities of the Central European river valleys. Although there were variations, it is extremely common for archaeologists excavating the early agricultural communities to find charred evidence of burned houses: ashy layers, charred stumps of house-posts, and fire-reddened clay floors. These ancient conflagrations had the unintentional benefit of preserving architectural elements as well as other materials like carbonized seeds and animal bones. Neolithic dwellings were substantial buildings made from upright timbers that supported thatched roofs and wattle-and-daub walls, walls made from a wickerwork of saplings slathered with a thick coat of clay daub. Frequently the flames baked the clay daub into fire-hardened chunks scored by the imprints of saplings and posts. Somewhat uncritically, archaeologists thanked their luck at finding such well-preserved, charred remains of Neolithic lives, presumably the relicts of ancient accidental house fires.

At least that is what was thought until a couple of archaeologists set fire to such a dwelling.

In 1977 archaeologists working in northeastern Serbia purchased the abandoned hulk of a wattle-and-daub farm house. Similar in construction to the Neolithic dwellings, the house had been built in the early twentieth century. The walls, though still standing, sagged with time. In places, the roof thatch had fallen and clay daub had scaled off the walls, but the structure was still largely intact. The archaeologists photographed and mapped the house, and placed some additional items inside to simulate Neolithic house wares: a bed of reeds, a bowl of grain, some animal bones, potsherds, and flakes of flint.[11]

And then they torched the place.

What happened next was fascinating, and not just because of the latent fascination with arson. The fire sparked in the central hearth and spread to the reed bed. Flames licked up the walls. In less than six minutes, the dry thatch roared and blazed. Huge plumes of black smoked billowed from the house. In merely twenty minutes, the thatch was gone and the rafters collapsed.

But after this initial explosion of flame, the fire slackened. The fire ebbed sufficiently that it was actually possible to enter the house. At this point, Neolithic homeowners could have rushed in, tossed out the last burning thatch and rafters, smothered the rest of the fire, and saved their house.

But the archaeologists allowed it to burn.

Over the next thirty hours, the fire slowly smoldered. Secondary fires caught and flared, but died out again. The wattle-and-daub walls were charred but upright. The house stood.

Based on this experiment with fires, the archaeologists concluded "the durability of the structure through such a long-lasting fire has clear archaeological implications. Although the prehistoric thatched roofs might have caught fire with ease and probably some frequency, the houses themselves would have suffered little damage."

Given the thermal resiliency of this wattle-and-daub house, it is a surprise to learn how extensive burned houses are in the European Neolithic, especially in southeastern Europe from the beginnings of the Neolithic until the initial phases of the Bronze Age. Within southeastern Europe, the evidence for burned houses is pervasive. The archaeologist Mirjana Stevanović writes, "At virtually all the sites with preserved architecture we see the dramatic effect of a large-scale house fire and the massive accumulation of burned clay rubble of clay house floors and the daub of the superstructure. There has not yet been reported a single Later Neolithic site in the region with architecture remains that are completely unburned."[12]

A half-dozen alternative hypotheses were proposed to account for the burnings.[13] One possibility is that southeastern Europe homesteads were targeted by Kurgan raiders from the Pontic-Caspian steppes from north of the Black Sea, a hypothesis not supported by radiocarbon dating (the burned Neolithic houses are one to two thousand years older than the earliest Kurgan sites). A related idea is that the houses were torched during raids and skirmishes between local groups, a possible explanation but one that would probably produce less-consistent arson and more human victims.

Another possibility is that the fires were all accidental, a hypothesis not supported by the experimental burning of the Serbian farmhouse and requiring us to imagine uniquely absentminded and desperately accident-prone Neolithic communities.

Several other "pragmatic" explanations have been proposed: firing the house makes the clay daub more water proof, exterminates pests, or allows for reusing the fire-hardened daub for other purposes. Each of these hypotheses stumbles on a basic archaeological fact: the burned houses usually have offerings placed on the floors. It is unlikely that anyone would place bowls of food or, as in some cases, literally dozens of prized ceramic pots on a dwelling's floor before setting the house on fire just to exterminate termites or fix a leak.

In fact, the archaeological evidence points to a surprising conclusion: the Neolithic houses in southeastern Europe were burned by their inhabitants or the household's descendants as part of an intentional program of house destruction. As John Chapman has discussed, various clues that may indicate intentional burning—for example, evidence of high burning temperatures from stacks of firewood placed inside the dwellings—could also result from accidental causes. There is one line of evidence that seems unambiguously intentional: the placement of offerings before the house was torched.

In her detailed analysis of burned Neolithic houses in Opovo, Serbia, Stevanović used the patterns of fired daub and charcoal to reconstruct the paths of the spreading fire.[14] Applying the techniques of arson investigators to the archaeological site, Stevanović made two crucial discoveries: first, the fire had been ignited simultaneously at several different points, and second, the fires were set on the floor, not on the flammable roof. Further, the house fire burned at temperatures hotter than one would expect if the only fuels were the house itself; additional fuel was added to burn the house completely.

All of this points to the intentional burning of the house, but there is another interesting point about fire and place: each of the Opovo house plots were built on again. Rather than indicating burning and abandonment, the house fires in the Neolithic sites in southeastern Europe marked a particular stage in what the archaeologist Ruth Tringham has called "the use-life of houses."[15] "House burning," Stevanović writes, "may have been a ritualized act marking, for instance, the end of a house use-life or new beginning of a household head. In these circumstances, by housing the events of life and death of its inhabitants, houses are embedded in those events and as such they acquire their use-lives."[16]

It was not uncommon for ancient houses to burn. Although ritual house-burning has been most intensely studied in the Neolithic houses of southeastern Europe, other archaeologists working in other regions have observed the material traces of broadly analogous practices.

For example, Stuart Campbell has suggested that the site of Tell Arpachiyah, a small but extraordinarily rich site dating to 5800–5100 B.C. located near the northern Iraqi city of Mosul, was intentionally burned and abandoned in "a ritual destruction on a grand scale" that "marked the end of the role of the [Burnt Room] building and the individual or institution it may have housed" and "may also have been a key formal act in a conscious abandonment of the site." The floor of the Burnt Room was littered with elegant ceramics, many intentionally smashed in place, as well as stone bowls, valuable obsidian cores and blades, and other treasured items that were still useable after the structure burned down but were neither looted nor disturbed until Tell Arpachiyah was excavated in 1930.[17]

In northern Syria, the Late Neolithic/Early Halafian site of Tell Sabi Abyad was burned extensively sometime between 6000 and 5900 B.C., leaving behind "considerable in-situ deposits . . . [in] the houses of the Burnt Village, including ceramic and stone vessels, ground stone implements, flint and obsidian tools, human and animal figurines of unfired clay, labrets, axes, personal ornaments, tokens, and hundreds of clay sealings with stamp-seal impressions."[18] The excavators note that there was no evidence of violence or looting at the site, that some of the charred houses lacked domestic tools and artifacts, and no one disturbed the rich trove of objects buried under ash, suggesting that Tell Sabi Abyad was intentionally burned before being rebuilt and reoccupied.

Other intentional house fires occurred in other early farming communities across Europe. For example, the archaeologist Jessica Smyth has proposed that broadly analogous rituals connecting the end of a house cycle and the intentional burning of a dwelling may be present in Ireland at early Neolithic sites dating to 3800–3530/3520 B.C., although the evidence for this is more suggestive than convincing.[19] Even further afield, the archaeologist William H. Walker has suggested that evidence of fires at sites in the American Southwest may be products of intentional and ritual burnings rather than exclusively of raiding and arson. Ironically, even the ritual burnings may have intensified during violent times in the American Southwest as mourners burned the houses and possessions of those killed in warfare, a process that Walker suggests, resulted in a settlement pattern of death.[20]

Such far-flung examples of intentional burning imply neither historical connections between these societies nor some universal association between mortality and fire. Rather, they reflect the intersection of two fundamental themes around which humans organize their cultures: home and death. Of course, the ways humans think about and commemorate home and death are far from universal. However, it remains the case that people at different times and places burned down their homes in the past. That there should be both commonalities and variations in the human experience is one of the lessons that archaeology teaches.

. . .

The coast of Santa Barbara County, California, is a narrow plain wedged between the Pacific Ocean and the Santa Ynez Mountains, which crest at 4000 feet before crumbling into a chain of chaparral-covered ridges splintered by oak-lined streams and rivers. Today, most people live in a coastal strip about 20 miles long and less than 4 miles wide, a swath of urbanism that ranges from Oprah Winfrey's mansion in Montecito to the thin-walled studio apartments in the noisy student neighborhood of Isla Vista.

Originally, this region was occupied by the Chumash Indians, who at contact numbered between 18,000 and 20,000 people.[21] The Chumash established some of the largest and most densely settled communities anywhere in native North America, and did so as hunters and gatherers. The rich resources of the ocean and the diverse plant foods of the chaparral, mountain, and riparian communities meant that the Chumash had an abundant and relatively stable food supply. The largest precontact Chumash communities were located along the coastal plain, essentially in the same area where most people live today.

The names and locations of numerous Chumash villages were recorded by early Spanish explorers and by late nineteenth- and early twentieth-century anthropologists. The villages covered the Santa Barbara coastal plain, often on terraces flanking small seasonal creeks and streams. Some of the Chumash villages were quite large.[22] Baptism and marriage records in the archives of the Santa Barbara mission document villages and clusters of villages with upwards of 1000–2000 inhabitants. In 1792, the Spanish naturalist Longinos Martinez approvingly described the Chumash towns and houses (in marked contrasted to Spanish descriptions of native life in Baja California, as discussed in chapter 3):

> These Indians live in communities and have a fixed domicile. They arrange their houses in groups. The houses are well constructed, round like an oven, spacious and fairly comfortable; light enters from a hole in the roof. Their beds are made on frames and they cover themselves with skins and shawls. The beds have divisions between them like the cabins of a ship, so that if many people sleep in one house, they do not see one another. In the middle of the floor they make a fire for cooking seeds, fish, and other foods, for they eat everything boiled or roasted.[23]

The Chumash houses in the Santa Barbara Channel region, according to a 1786 Spanish observer, were:

> among all the huts which I saw in all the journey . . . the best. They are round in form, like a half orange, very spacious, large and high. In the middle of the

top, they have an aperture to afford light and to serve as a chimney, through which emerges the smoke of the fire which they make in the middle of the hut. Some of them also have two or three holes like little windows. The frames of all of them consist of arched and very strong poles, and the walls are of very thick grass interwoven. At the doors there is a mat which swings toward the inside like a screen, and another one toward the outside which they ordinarily bar with a whalebone or a stick.[24]

Archaeologist Lynn Gamble has made a thorough study of Chumash houses and village organization, in part with an eye to identifying Chumash houses in the archaeological record.[25] Based on explorers' accounts and ethnographers' interviews, Chumash houses were dome-shaped structures with elliptical plans. The houses apparently did not have central house posts, but rather were woven together from willow posts spaced along the base of the wall that were then bent over, interwoven with horizontal withes, and thatched with tule reeds. House varied from 4–16 meters in diameter, the largest houses found in the densely clustered villages of the Chumash coast.[26]

Driving today through the dense housing of the Santa Barbara coast, it is surprising to realize how many archaeological sites still dot the landscape. Despite the significant destruction of archaeological sites over the last 150 years, the prehistoric record of the Santa Barbara coast remains—plundered, battered, and far from pristine—but still there. And the sites still bring surprises.

In the mid-1980s, I directed a small excavation in a side canyon along the Santa Barbara coast on a narrow streamside terrace that was once a walnut orchard.[27] The project was part of an environmental impact assessment in advance of a development project slated to cover the site with a parking lot. The site had been discovered in an earlier survey and designated "SBA-1809," a rather sterile designation based on a system commonly used in California. Another phase in the environmental impact review had involved limited archaeological excavations that encountered a layer of fire-reddened earth about 70–100 centimeters below the surface. The burned soil may have been from something insignificant, such as a burned brush-pile from the old walnut orchard, but the presence of a few chipped stone flakes and other prehistoric objects hinted that additional investigation was required.

We placed our test pits in a cross-pattern, strategically located to intersect with the burned layer and find its edges. As we excavated the pits and screened the loosened soils, we found the scant traces of past lives.

There were a few large flakes made from quartzite, probably knocked off from cobbles found in the streambed, and small flakes of Monterrey chert, a distinctive stone found elsewhere along the Santa Barbara coast but not right at the site. So we knew that people had made stone tools, both from local stone and from raw materials carried to the site. The stone tools included a couple of small arrow points, the tip of a large knife or spear point, a flake scraper that had been used to work hides, and a pair of stone drill bits probably used to make shell beads (an activity also suggested by a small unfinished clam disk bead). So we knew that people hunted, worked hides, and made shell beads. We found a pair of hammer-stones, a couple of tarring pebbles, and a small fragment of asphaltum with the imprint of basketry, possibly from a woven water jug. We inferred that people used and possibly made tar-lined baskets at the site. Finally, a mix of animal bones hinted at centuries-old meals: bones of mule deer, cottontail rabbits, and jackrabbits in addition to bones from mackerel, sardines, surf perch, and other fish species. So we knew that the Chumash inhabitants hunted and fished.

But what was really surprising was the feature itself. As we exposed the surface of the burned layer, we could see that it was a rough oval 2.65 × 1.25 meters in area, its surface a slightly concave depression. The center of the feature had the thickest layer of ash, charcoal, and fire-reddened earth that thinned at the edges. A pair of glass trade beads sat on the burned surface, the glass fused by the fire's heat, which probably reached temperatures of over 500 degrees centigrade.

I concluded that we were looking at the remains of a small Chumash house. We obtained a radiocarbon sample that gave some contradictory dates when calibrated, alternatively pointing to an average age of A.D. 1680, 1750, or 1800. Based on the artifacts we discovered, I think SBA-1809 was occupied after first contact with Europeans (and thus the trade beads) but before the founding of Mission Santa Barbara in 1786, when many Chumash were forcibly resettled from their home villages to the mission.

In other words, we were glimpsing traces of Chumash culture just as their world was changing.

And yet it was puzzling that SBA-1809 did not fit the ethnohistoric and archaeological images of a Chumash house or other basic types of architecture. It was obviously not a large tule-covered house, as Longinos Martinez had described; the feature was simply too small to hold more than a single family. The feature was not a sweat lodge; despite having a burned surface—a trait that Gamble has noted is found in all excavated sweat lodges along the Santa Barbara coast—the SBA-1809 floor lacked the abundant fire-cracked rock used in sweat lodges or the large central posts required to support the weight of earth that covered sweat lodges.[28] Simply, the burned floor at SBA-1809 differed from the archaeological traces associated with other Chumash buildings, whether ramadas, windbreaks, smoke houses, menstrual huts, or male puberty huts.

The feature at SBA-1809 was a different type of structure; the site was a different kind of site. Unlike the large villages that lined the Santa Barbara coast, SBA-1809 apparently was occupied by a single family, perhaps even a single individual. Although the site was only a couple kilometers from the large Chumash towns on the coast, this house was removed and alone. Given that SBA-1809 was occupied during the uncertain years of transition between Chumash independence and Spanish colonialism, it is difficult to characterize the region's social landscape when this small house was built on the edge of a narrow creek. But it seems as if its occupants were separated from the vibrant humanity of a Chumash town. Perhaps they were outcasts or hermits or misanthropes, or perhaps simply people who longed for quiet. For reasons that we do not understand, this family created a different life in a distinctive home that was later abandoned and consumed by flames.

. . .

In the southeastern United States, the center of Cherokee towns held a large building known as a "townhouse." The Cherokee townhouse was essentially an everyday dwelling "writ large," using the same materials and incorporating the same plan and alignment, but averaging 13–15 meters square (45–50 feet), compared to the ordinary house of 4.5–8 meters square (15–25 feet).[29] Built from four upright posts that supported a bark roof and enclosed by wattle-and-daub walls, the townhouse represented the entire community. As the archaeologist Christopher Rodning writes, townhouses were "the hubs of public life in eighteenth-century Cherokee communities." Of the various types of Cherokee settlements—homesteads, hamlets, and villages—only those with a townhouse were considered a "town."

In Cherokee worldview, a powerful metaphoric parallel existed between the townhouse and individual houses. The townhouse sheltered the community. The individual house sheltered the household. The individual households became a community through the existence of the townhouse.

And the townhouse and the dwellings were linked by fire.

According to Cherokee myth, "in the beginning there was no fire and the world was cold," until Thunder deities hurled a lightening bolt into a hollow sycamore tree on a lonely, deserted island in the middle of a dark sea. All the animals saw the flickering light in the distance and craved its warmth. The animals who flew or swam volunteered to capture the fire.

Raven flew to the burning tree and landed on its branches, but an updraft singed and blackened his feathers; he panicked and fled the flames. The horned owl flew to the smoldering tree and landed safely, but a gust of wind blew acrid ashes into his eyes. Blinded by the cinders, he rubbed and rubbed his eyes, finally regaining his sight but leaving the blackened rings that still circle the horned owl's eyes. Different varieties of water snakes slid towards the island light only to be charred and blackened by the flames.

Finally, the water spider volunteered. She skated across the dark waves to the island's shore. Drawing fine threads from her body, she wove a silken bowl and placed a minute ember inside. Water spider carefully transported this elementary spark across the waters and brought fire to the world.[30]

This arachnid Prometheus gave humans a gift the Cherokees never forgot, and which they commemorated in an annual fire renewal ceremony. Each spring, every household doused its hearth fire and cleaned out the ashes and cold coals. New kindling was laid and fire was brought from the perpetual flame in the townhouse to relight each home's hearth. "Fires in domestic hearths," Rodning writes, "were connected directly to the fire kept in townhouse hearths."

A sacred and perpetual fire burned within the townhouse. While the Cherokees viewed the townhouse fire as a continuous flame, sometimes it was necessary to renew the hearth, for example if enemy raiders attacked and smothered its vital blaze. In such cases, a New Fire ceremony took place, and an example of this was observed by none other than John Howard Payne.

After authoring "Home, Sweet Home" and before his diplomatic appointment to Tunis (see chapter 2), Payne was an advocate against the forced relocation of the Cherokee from the southeastern United States to the Indian Territory. In 1835 Payne was in a Cherokee town in Georgia where he observed the New Fire ceremony. The townhouse hearth was cleaned, purified, and stacked with the "inner bark of seven different kinds of trees . . . carefully chosen from the east side of the trees," bark that "was clear and free from blemish." Using a fire-drill and goldenrod tinder, the official fire-starter and six assistants lit the townhouse fire. Burning wands were carried from the townhouse to every Cherokee dwelling where each cold hearth was rekindled.[31]

Rodning has analyzed the architecture and spatial patterns at the site of Coweeta Creek, a Cherokee town occupied from the fifteenth to early eighteenth centuries A.D. Located in southwestern North Carolina, the Coweeta Creek site exhibited a confusing pockmark of post-molds and other features that marked houses, ramadas, burials, and other activity areas surrounding a main plaza and a larger townhouse. Over time, a subtle difference occurred at the site. In the early centuries at Coweeta Creek, dwellings were rounded houses about 8–10 meters in diameter. When these houses were abandoned and reconstructed, the new structure was built in a nearby but new location—sometime shifting just a few meters—and generally retaining its relative position in the settlement. In these early centuries, Coweeta Creek lacked a townhouse.

But at approximately A.D. 1600 the first townhouse was built at Coweeta Creek, and its construction was accompanied by a change in the Cherokee houses. As in earlier centuries, the Coweeta Creek houses were rebuilt, but instead of shifting even a few meters away, the new houses were built exactly on the footprint of the earlier dwellings. In each construction phase the new dwelling pivoted around the hearth, slightly varying the positions of postholes but with the doorway in the same corner. As many as five dwellings were rebuilt, each on the same exact place.

This anchored reconstruction also characterized the townhouse. The Coweeta Creek townhouse was rebuilt at least six times. Each time the hearth was reconstructed in the same place and the four major roof timbers were spaced around the central fire, creating an unobstructed zone around the hearth. Although the townhouse doorway shifted slightly, it was always in the southeastern corner of the building, opening onto a covered ramada that fronted the town's plaza. The plaza was not merely an open space, but "an actively landscaped space and a setting for large public gatherings . . . covered with sand and clay."[32]

The tempo of rebuildings may have been associated with something as prosaic as the need to replace rotting timbers and bark roofs, but other traces suggest more powerful symbolic factors were involved. During the mid-1600s, select burials were placed in the townhouse floor and under the ramada. Some of the individuals were buried under the paths connecting the townhouse and plaza; others were interred in inside the townhouse around the hearth.

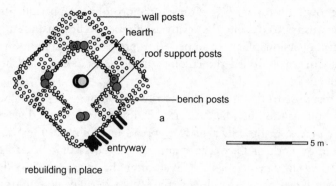

FIGURE 34. Rebuildings of Cherokee townhouses, Coweeta Creek, North Carolina. Courtesy of Christopher Rodning.

Why these select individuals were buried in the townhouse is unclear. The majority of the well-preserved skeletons are from adult men, although several children and one woman also were buried near the Coweeta Creek townhouse. Compared to people buried elsewhere at the site, the individuals interred within the townhouse and in the adjoining ramada were buried with more grave objects: shell beads, ornaments, clay pipes, and stone arrowheads.

The adult men in the graves may have been "the chief men" of a town, Rodning suggests, or the esteemed village elders known as "Beloved Men."[33] The early American ethnographer James Mooney wrote that "when they were ready to build a mound they began by laying a circle of stones on the surface of the ground. Next they made a fire in the center of the circle and put near it the body of some prominent chief or priest who had lately died."[34] According to Mooney's informants, a chief priest conducted rites over the burials and the grave goods, protecting them with a curse on any enemy who disturbed their remains. And thus, as Rodning observes, "these graves became part of the townhouse itself."[35]

And each time the Coweeta Creek townhouse was to be rebuilt, the old townhouse was burned. The graves were dug, the burials placed. The bark shingles were yanked down, the timbers were removed, and the entire townhouse was set ablaze. Once the flames died out and the embers cooled, a new townhouse was built precisely on the same spot.

Cherokee townhouses, Rodning writes, "were symbolic manifestations of Cherokee towns, they were architectural landmarks, and they were the settings for the practice of Cherokee public life."[36] The Coweeta

Creek townhouse was created during the protohistoric period, after the first Spanish entradas into the Southeast but before British and American military incursions. This was a period of progressive instability, as raids for Indian slaves roiled the colonial frontier, including the Cherokee homelands in Appalachia.

In response to this spreading chaos, townhouses were built, burned, and rebuilt as the Cherokee "asserted claims to and connections to particular places, in the midst of widespread instability in the Southeast in the aftermath of European contact," a process that Rodning calls "a strategy in emplacement."[37] Even after the individual dwellings at Coweeta Creek were abandoned, the local Cherokee community continued to use the townhouse. Although based on precontact architectural practices such as earlier mound building, the resolute placement of townhouse upon the exact site of earlier townhouse may have been a grimly determined, material gesture in which the Cherokee stated, "this is our home."

Thus, the Coweeta Creek townhouse—built from impermanent wood and bark, periodically burned, and then renewed—marked the presence of a community and the location of their home, until the descendents of Coweeta Creek and the other members of the Cherokee Nation were forced to march west from their homelands to the Indian Territory, driven along the Trail of Tears.

. . .

We often assume that permanent commemoration requires enduring materials: granite, marble, or steel. The British architect Edward Lutyen's Whitehall cenotaph, a memorial to the British and Commonwealth soldiers who died in World War I, was by popular demand translated from a temporary construction of plaster and wood into an understated obelisk of stone that honored "The Glorious Dead." The black-mirrored planes of jet granite exposed from the earth in Maya Lin's Vietnam Memorial remain a powerful evocation of loss. It is not surprising that the design for the memorial at the site of the September 11, 2001 attacks on the Twin Towers of the World Trade Center include two large sunken gardens excavated down to the permanent strata of Manhattan's bedrock.[38]

And yet Ozymandias challenges us: "Look on my works, ye Mighty, and despair!" the most permanent of monuments collapse into "that colossal wreck, boundless and bare / The lone and level sands stretch far away."

Commemoration depends on social action, not on building materials. The Shinto shrine of Ise originated as royal palaces and altars during the Yamato period of Japanese history. Located in an evergreen forest on the southern coast of Hokkaido, Ise contains two temple complexes. The most sacred is dedicated to Amaterasu-omikami, the Sun Goddess, and may be entered only by the Japanese emperor, his family, and priests. According to an ancient royal chronicle compiled in A.D. 720, Ise has been a pilgrimage center since it was determined that the Sun Goddess was too powerful a deity to be worshipped at palace shrines; a more distant temple was required. According to the chronicle, the Sun Goddess herself chose Ise, declaring it "a secluded and pleasant land. In this land I wish to dwell." The temples were built among the groves of Japanese cedar, where the Ise complex has stood since the third or fourth century A.D.

Yet, the shrine of Ise stands not because the building materials are impermeable to rot and time, but rather because the buildings are regularly demolished and rebuilt. With only a few lapses due to wars or other calamities, the Ise shrine has been torn down and reconstructed every twenty years since A.D. 690.[39] The example of Ise exemplifies Shakespeare's reminder that it is "not marble, nor the gilded monuments" that endure, things that become "unswept stone besmear'd with sluttish time," but it is rather "the living record of your memory."

Dwellings become monuments not through the permanence of construction materials, but because they are important symbols for human societies. Even when homes are torched, reduced by flames to ash and ember, their existence and the lives they sheltered may be remembered. And when those homes and their associated lives are forgotten, it is one of archaeology's tasks to recover and recall them.

Going Home

And I can't stay at home
In this world anymore.

—*Traditional hymn*

While Stonehenge and Machu Picchu are close rivals, arguably there is
no archaeological site on Earth more iconic than the Great Pyramids
of Egypt. The largest and first of the Great Pyramids was constructed
around 2560 B.C. for the pharaoh Khufu. For the next thirty-eight centuries, it was the tallest building in the world.

By the time Khufu's pyramid was completed, Egyptian society had
been transformed. Thousands of laborers had quarried limestone, shoved
the huge blocks up earthen ramps, levered the blocks into place, and
sheathed the construction with finished stone. Elaborate burial chambers were built inside and despite centuries of looting, enough fragments
and scraps remain to indicate the rich offerings of animals, servants, and
objects that accompanied the pharaoh into the parallel existence of the
dead.

This first great dynastic experiment along the Nile known as "the
Old Kingdom" marked a fundamental transformation in Egyptian society. The archaeologist Robert Wenke wrote: "[In predynastic Egypt] the
Nile Valley and Delta appear to have been occupied by people living
in small, functionally similar agricultural communities that were only
weakly interconnected politically and economically. By 2500 B.C., however, Egypt had become an integrated empire whose ruler's power, as
expressed through a complex hierarchical bureaucracy, touched every
citizen, and whose economic and military force was felt throughout the
eastern Mediterranean and North African world."[1]

The Great Pyramid, the most colossal funerary architecture ever created, had very humble conceptual foundations elaborated over those
two thousand years but that originated at home.

The Great Pyramid was preceded by funerary complexes consisting
of subterranean groups of rooms covered by brick and/or stone slab-
like constructions known as mastabas (*mastaba* being the Arabic word
for "bench"). The "bench" covered the subterranean chambers, forming a substantial superstructure. For example, some mastabas were over
50 meters long, covering multiple chambers filled with offerings and the
dead.

Yet, for all of these elaborations, the mastabas echoed even earlier,
more modest mortuary architecture where the dead were buried at home.
The Egyptologist Ann Macy Roth notes that "the large private tombs
of the Second and Third Dynasties . . . were viewed literally as houses
of the dead, and their substructures sometimes contained quintessen-
tially domestic features," including such homey furnishings as beds and
latrines.[2] The subterranean tomb complexes mirrored the spatial organization of early Egyptian homes, a pattern marked by tightly closed
spaces in which corridors were narrow and serpentine. Similar to elite
houses, elite tombs contained "service passages," permitting nobles and
servants to move through the building without encounter—much like
the Edwardian "great houses" depicted in the British television series
"Upstairs, Downstairs" or in the Robert Altman film "Gosford Park."

Just as the Edwardian great house sheltered more than a nuclear family, the ancient Egyptian house reflected in a mastaba was more than a
kin group. David Wengrow writes:

> The house that provided the prototype for the tomb was not the simple
> domestic unit. Rather, the mastaba complex constitutes a transformation
> of the extended household: a ritual space into which were crammed all the
> accoutrements and facilities of such an institution, from sumptuous living and
> entertainment quarters to granaries, boats, herds, store-houses, plantations
> and also many of the people who belonged to it. The mastaba tomb complex
> was, in short, a model estate for the dead, encompassing (on a reduced scale)
> many of the functions of a living estate that was not simply a productive unit,
> but a source of life for its dependants. As on a living estate, those functions
> were divided between a human collective comprising the estate-owner, close
> kin, officials and various levels of subordinates whose survival—in death as
> in life—was contingent upon membership in this wider unit.[3]

Even earlier in Egyptian prehistory, during the Predynastic Period and
before, the linkage between house and tomb was evident, although on a

reduced and modest scale. At Hierakonpolis a tomb complex (Locality 6) dating to 3600–3500 B.C. was an enclosure built from substantial posts of acacia timbers interspersed with smaller poles covered by reed and bulrush mats; the enclosure contained a tomb pit 5.5 × 3.1 meters in size.[4] While the enclosure and tomb were much simpler than later enclosures at Saqqara and royal tombs elsewhere, the size of the tomb and its associated offerings—including a sacrificed ten-year-old elephant and the earliest life-size stone statue of a human known from Egypt— have led excavators to contend that this was the tomb of an early king.[5]

In ancient Egypt, the connections between death and home had subtle origins. For example, during the Neolithic period, settlements were impermanent and shelters temporary. The dead were buried in grave pits and accompanied by personal objects, particularly combs, palettes, and pigments used for cosmetics. The emphasis was on the individual's body, but these grave goods suggest a belief in some form of existence after death. Wengrow writes that "there is . . . little indication that domestic practices played a formative role in restructuring human conceptions of the world" during the fifth millennium B.C. Mortuary rituals were not focused on the house, but upon "the bodies of people and animals," and Neolithic death rituals focused upon "incorporation" or "embodiment" rather than "domestication" and home.[6]

But along the Nile Valley, as in so many other regions of the ancient world, this changed with the development of agriculture and village life. This transformation was marked by the appearance of two key foods: bread and beer. Beginning at around 3800–3600 B.C., Egyptians made bread in thick-walled ceramic bowls that were preheated before the leavened dough was put inside and baked. Beer was made from partially baked loaves that were crumbled into water with yeast for fermentation and various fruits for flavoring.[7] By around 3300 B.C., bread and beer had become essential foods to honor the dead.

Burial practices also changed to incorporate mummification, especially among the elite. Carved stone slabs from tombs dating to the Second and Third Dynasties (ca. 2800–2600 B.C.) depict the deceased elite "owner of the tomb" seated in a chair in front of a table piled high with bread, fish, wine, meat, oils, and other foods. While the fundamental idea that the soul existed in another realm dates back to at least the Neolithic, the relationships between the living, the dead, and the gods had been redefined, ultimately reinforcing the pharaohs' royal power. The living provisioned the dead, the pharaoh channeled offerings to the gods, resulting in "ties of dependency that linked the king and the elite in life and death" and indirectly through the bonds of serfdom, servitude, and slavery humans who lived along the Nile.

Two final points about the domestic and the dead in ancient Egypt. First, the construction of the Old Kingdom pyramids translated a broad substrate of religious practice from one focused on the sustenance of the dead to one focused on the cult worship of the god-king. The Old Kingdom pyramids may have had architectural antecedents in the mastabas that covered house-like tombs, but those constructions implied a new religious conception focused on the royal mortuary cult.

And finally, there was a role for the dead within the domestic realm through most of the 6,500 years of Egyptian history. The newborn dead were buried in houses, ancestors were worshipped at household shrines—practices "that brought the deceased into the domestic realm."[8] Even in modest houses distant from the mortuary complexes of god-kings, the dead were at home.

. . .

I spent much of the 1980s investigating archaeological sites on the coastal desert of Peru. In 1981 I was introduced to Andean archaeology—and had my first experience with the archaeology of houses—as a graduate student on a research project excavating the site of Manchan in the Casma Valley, a provincial center that was part of the Chimú Empire.[9]

The Manchan research project explored how the Chimú Empire ruled its southern frontier, and my part of the project involved excavating ancient houses. The adobe structures with their elaborate ramps, niched walls, and storerooms had been the residences and plazas of provincial elites. Tucked between the elaborate adobe-walled compounds, there was a large barrio of modest dwellings covered by dune sands. The cane houses in the barrio contained the commoners' workshops and homes.

Manchan's barrio houses were built from river canes woven into a wickerwork—much like the rooms at Quebrada Santa Cristina (see chapter 6). Roofed with flat reed mats, the lattice walls of canes provided shade and some privacy in the densely occupied barrio.

My excavation team and I uncovered the prehistoric artifacts and features that marked a neighborhood bustling with life. Food was cooked over hardwood fires, and smoke drifted through the cane walls. Maize beer (chicha) was brewed in large clay pots stirred with carved wooden paddles. Cotton and llama wool were spun tightly into threads and yarns on twirling spindles. The fibers were woven into bolts of cloth on backstrap looms. Copper ore was crushed on stone slabs, smelted, and made into essential tools such as fishhooks, tweezers, and sewing needles. Children laughed and squalled. Mothers worried. Fathers returned from the fields, sat in the shade, and drank chicha from gourd bowls.

These were the working poor of Chimú society. The people dressed in homespun cotton. Food was simple but nourishing: fish and shellfish from the Pacific, the occasional treat of roasted guinea pig, maize and beans, avocados and yucca, with chilies and salt for flavoring. Fruits were prized for their juicy pulps, a sweet relief in the desert heat.

Life was unadorned in the Manchan barrio. So were the houses. I never found a single hint of architectural decoration: no fragments of painted daub or elaborately carved wood. Nothing about the barrio houses suggested anything other than the plain pragmatics of the working class.

In March 1982 we were excavating in one of the cane houses, and it contained the standard quotidian assemblages that we had come to expect. We were digging near an odd feature of eroded adobe blocks rimming a large storage jar buried in the ground. As we excavated an initial test pit, we noticed another small jar eroding out of the west sidewall. I decided to dig an adjacent pit and properly excavate the jar.

In fieldwork, as in life, one thing often leads to another.

We scraped away 10 to 15 centimeters of wind-blown sand before exposing a layer of household debris: shells, food remains, and lots of guinea pig dung. Typical barrio garbage. We dug through this layer, down into an earlier occupation where we noticed a small jumble of stones and adobe rubble. I thought it was the remains of a small cook-fire or hearth covered by a layer of household garbage.

And then I saw the skull. Amid the rubble and cobblestones, the smooth curve of a cranium dipped into the sand. The skull was the walnut hue of bone tarnished by flesh but unbleached by the sun.

As we brushed away the sand, I saw it was a child.

The child was probably between four and ten years old when it had died. The child's body was still too undeveloped to determine gender from the bones. There was no evidence of trauma, suggesting death from disease or perhaps an accident that left no mark.

The body had been placed in a small pit scooped into the house-floor. The sides of the burial pit were crusted by body fluids that had soaked into the sand.

The child sat facing north. The legs were drawn up on one side of the torso, the knees tucked close to the child's right ear. The child's crossed arms hugged the knees, as if against the cold of a centuries-old night.

We carefully documented the objects placed with this dead child. A simple necklace made from clay beads and fish vertebrae strung on a cotton cord dangled from the child's neck. A small copper pellet was in the child's mouth, reminiscent of the Greek custom of putting coins under a corpse's tongue to pay Charon, the ferryman who sculled the River Styx. At Manchan, it was common to find mandibles and maxilla emerald-stained by copper placed in the mouth of the deceased.

An arrangement of artifacts marked the gestures of closing the grave. An inverted gourd bowl covered the dead child's face, held in place by a swath of cloth that turbaned the child's head. A miniature pottery bottle, only eight centimeters tall, was placed just behind the right side of the child's head. Three large cobblestones were set in the mouth of the grave, in-filled with rubble, and sealed with a slurry of mud. A dark gray basalt hammer-stone had been pushed into the still-wet mud. A few pieces of meat and three cobs of corn were placed on the grave, as if in a last meal for the child.

And then the house was abandoned to the dead.

. . .

Far away in the Near East, the symbolic associations between home and death apparently became more articulated as agriculture between 13,000 and 9,500 years ago, and as Natufian food collectors gave way to Neolithic farmers (see chapter 4).[10]

The Natufians had buried their dead in various ways. Some of the interments were primary burials, although secondary burials increased over time. Burials were singular or sometimes in group graves in which the earlier burials were disturbed to make room for new corpses. The number of child burials during the Late Natufian period, with 5–7 year olds comprising nearly a third of the burials, is a silent index of difficult times, since even older children—who had survived the risks of infancy—were dying. All this points to the stresses faced by Natufians.

But, interestingly, the Natufians did not bury their dead in houses that were still occupied by the living. Natufian graves are found between buildings or in the floors of abandoned dwellings, but not in active homes. In contrast, later Early Neolithic houses were frequently built on top of burials, suggesting that the parcels were occupied by multiple generations of the same family who owned and inherited the building plot.[11]

Burials and houses changed during the Pre-Pottery Neolithic A (PPNA) period of 10,300–9,800 years ago. The dead were buried singly without grave goods in PPNA burial sites. For adults, the skulls were removed after the flesh and tendons had decayed; child burials were left intact. The adult skulls were then cached in groups, either in dwellings or in special structures, in a ceremony interpreted as emphasizing collective membership rather than individual status. During the ninth millennium B.C., skulls began to be placed in specific, nondomestic structures, a process that between 2950 and 2300 B.C. evolved into special charnel houses in which the skulls of village dwellers were stacked in what the archaeologist Meredith Chesson has called "libraries of the dead."[12]

A particularly clear prehistoric association between the house of the living and the house of the dead comes from early agricultural communities of central and northern Europe between 4000 and 3000 B.C.[13]

After approximately 7500 B.C., agricultural communities had appeared on the islands of the Aegean and the adjacent Hellenic peninsula of southern Europe.[14] As farming communities spread along the major river systems into central Europe, agrarian colonists originally from the Aegean or Anatolia came into contact with and intermarried among European populations. The introduction of agriculture, in turn, led to population growth and dispersal, furthering the diffusion and adoption of agricultural technology. By 4000 B.C. agriculturalists were settled in northwestern Germany, and farmers occupied a broad but lightly populated swath of central and western Europe.[15]

In the process, houses changed. Archaeologists excavating the site Olszanica B1, located near Krakow, Poland, exposed a set of ten massive longhouses.[16] Dating from the Early Neolithic (approximately 5415–4580/4100 B.C.), the long houses were built from large upright logs, 60–80 centimeters in diameter, covered in thick layers of mud daub, with interior posts that supported a sturdy roof that shed heavy winter snows. Similar Neolithic structures are known from throughout central and western Europe (as discussed in chapter 10).

The largest house at Olszanica (Longhouse 6) was 41.5 meters long and 6.5 meters wide; it may have housed 25–30 people, perhaps the entire community at that moment. Over centuries, these houses were rebuilt and new houses were erected over earlier ones. Many communities were surrounded by palisades or trenches. Some cemeteries were associated with single longhouses, while other cemeteries served several longhouse communities.[17]

In time another pattern emerged: people buried their dead in houses and subsequently tombs were built that represented houses. As the archaeologist Ian Hodder has argued, there are striking parallels between

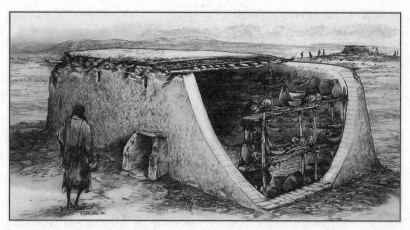

FIGURE 35. Reconstruction of Charnel House, Early Bronze Age II–III (ca. 2950–2300 B.C.), Babe dh-Dhra', Jordan. Courtesy M. Chesson and E. Carlson.

the longhouses of the European Neolithic and the architectural patterns of tombs known as long barrows.[18] Longhouses and long barrows have similar plans; they are long rectangular or trapezoidal forms divided into three major interior sectors. Their doorways were at the shorter end-walls, the entrances were marked by facades or offerings, and longhouses and long barrows overwhelmingly faced to the east and southeast. "The tombs signified houses," Hodder writes.

A shared notion links longhouses and long barrows: the constructions represent a "set of ideas and practices which focus on the house," what Hodder calls "the domus."[19] The domus represented not only the families living within longhouses, but the interlinked continuities of social life: the shared experiences of building the longhouse, the relationships between women and men, and ultimately the distinction between the cultural and domestic realm vs. the natural and external worlds.

As tombs were built in the form of houses, a symbolic transliteration occurred: tombs were houses of the dead, commemorations of the ancestral homes, and robust symbols of the stability of social forms. In the process, specific places were singled out and defined as special places, and then were refined through offerings, burials, and monuments.

Rather than emphasizing the achievements of a "great man" or the emergence of social elites, these early Neolithic mortuary practices may have been "bound up with particular histories and cycles of settlements and households. . . . Continuity and integration seem more important in the realm of the dead than differences between the living."[20]

What I find interesting is that the symbolic elaboration of the house occurs at other times and places in prehistory, and often involves the house being a special place for the dead. In turn, this is predicated on sedentism.

On the southwestern coast of Ecuador, the early Formative Valdivia tradition presents a parallel example of death and domus.[21] Valdivia is one of the earliest examples of settled village life known from South America, spanning the period from 4450 to 1450 B.C., and roughly overlapping with the otherwise unrelated Early Neolithic societies of Europe. Excavations at the Valdivia site of Real Alto uncovered evidence of an evolving pattern of how people built and symbolized their homes.

Between 4400 and 3300 B.C., Real Alto was a village of 50 to 60 people living in a dozen or more small elliptical houses that encircled a plaza. The Early Valdivia houses were relatively flimsy constructions, less than 2–4 meters across and made from slender, bent poles—only slightly more substantial than the temporary dwellings built by !Kung San hunters and gatherers in the Kalahari.

But at about 3000 B.C., Real Alto's inhabitants began building substantial oval dwellings from upright posts daubed in mud, significant constructions compared to the earlier, slight huts. As the houses grew in size, Real Alto also grew to about 600 to more than 1,000 people living in 90 to 100 houses. With this change in domestic architecture, the overall settlement plan evolved from a circle of houses around a plaza into a vast arrangement of houses around a central square.

And in the northern portion of the square stood two large mounds, counterpoised and in opposition.

These mounds each began as small wattle-and-daub structures, but over time the small mounds were enlarged and rebuilt upon. New and somewhat larger houses were constructed during the next couple of centuries. But at about 2700–2600 B.C., the pattern and purposes of buildings diverged.

The eastern mound was transformed into a place for feasts. The archaeologist Jorge Marcos suggested that feasts and other rituals took place in a mound-top building—possibly like men's houses in tribal societies in lowland Amazonia. During his excavations in the 1970s, Marcos uncovered garbage pits not filled with the everyday, domestic garbage found elsewhere at Real Alto, but with the remains of highly prized foods: bones of deer and sea turtle and shells of rock crab. In addition to the evidence of such delicacies, the pits contained smashed drinking bowls—the bowls broken in situ, with most of the fragments still present. Other pottery vessels and vases all pointed to recurrent feasts, and Marcos dubbed this mound the "Fiesta House Mound."

A different transformation occurred on the western mound at Real Alto, but one that was arguably less festive. Inside the remains of a mound-top structure was the grave of a woman, apparently 26–35 years old when she died. Her burial pit was lined with milling stones, broken metates, and manos. The care with which she was buried suggests a woman of high status, as do the various burials that surrounded her. Nearby was a scattering of seven bodies in a common grave, the skeletons partial and the burials secondary. The bodies were of a young adult male and a half-dozen prepubescent individuals of unknown gender. In addition, a man's body had been partially scraped of its flesh, the still-articulated portions of his corpse were placed in a grave, and then his loose bones were stacked on top along with a few chert knife-blades and a deer jawbone. This western mound was dubbed the "Charnel House."

Like so much in archaeology, the Charnel House discoveries were simultaneously concrete and ambiguous. Perhaps the individuals surrounding the high-status female were sacrificial victims or—in contrast—loved relatives. Possibly the dead were originally placed on the mound and then moved aside when the high-status female died, and the recovered bones were reburied. It is difficult to know.

Interestingly, during the excavations, people living near Real Alto told Marcos that they "understood these burials as those of protectors of the structures, and indicated that whenever possible they keep human bones, especially ancestor bones, in their homes as guardians against strangers."[22]

The Fiesta House Mound and the Charnel House stood only fifty meters apart, but occupied distinct conceptual poles. According to Marcos, the eastern Fiesta House Mound was associated with the living, the hidden power of men, and the libations and feasts that reflected and restated male power. In contrast, the western Charnel House was affiliated with death, the power of women, and it became a focal point for religious ceremony.

In spite of the universality of dying, human concepts of death are endlessly diverse. The dead are feared and avoided. The dead are loved and embraced. The dead are preserved for the next life. The dead are purified by flame for eternity. Mourners gash their own bodies as their blood flows in self-sacrifice. Mourners mark their loss by a calm letting-go. Death is a solo journey. Death must be accompanied by others. And so it goes, each conception of death marked by a mortuary variation unique and infinitely diverse.

Regardless of these variations, it appears that one of the first associations between the cosmos and the built environment is the symbolic connection between the house of the living and the house of the dead. This materialized metaphor seems to occur only after humans settle down and live in more substantial dwellings. At that point, the house becomes a template for multiple distinctions—between male and female, light and darkness, culture and nature, and so on. But the first such distinction that we can discern in the past is this polarity: the house and the living vs. the house and the dead.

. . .

Once sedentism was firmly established in the human experience, most people died at home. Not surprisingly, this is also true for most of American history. In part this reflected high mortality rates—particularly in cities—but also the fact that death was integrated into the domestic realm. Although precise census data are lacking and there are debates among historians about variations in U.S. historical mortality rates, average life expectancy varied between 35 to 45 years in the mid- and late nineteenth century.[23] Before the Civil War the crude death rate is estimated at approximately 15 deaths annually per thousand people living in rural areas and a significantly higher rate of 20 to 40 per thousand for city dwellers.[24] The "mortality penalty" from living in American cities had multiple causes, including the epidemics that repeatedly scythed through urban populations and the general unhealthy conditions brought about by overcrowding, poverty, and poor sanitation.

Life was shorter in low-lying cities. In a humid and swampy city like New Orleans, "mortality was truly virulent and peaks astonishing before the late 19th century. Yellow fever was especially severe in the marshy, swampy flat area near the delta of the Mississippi River, but cholera, typhoid fever, malaria, dysentery and other water- and insect-borne diseases were both endemic and epidemic."[25] During multiple epidemics between 1830 and 1860, New Orleans's crude mortality rates spiked to 100–145 deaths per thousand inhabitants, two or three times the death rates of other cities such as New York, Boston, or Baltimore. Even as late as 1960, New Orleans's death rate hovered around 50 deaths per 1000 occupants. It is no wonder that New Orleans jazz originated in funeral marches.

And it was even more likely for the young to die in nineteenth-century

America. Infant mortality was approximately 200 deaths per thousand births. Approximately 20–33 percent of children died before the age of ten. In American families and communities, such high mortality resulted in "the constant intrusion of death into the fabric of communal life."[26]

Whether in crowded tenements or rural farmhouses, people died at home and their families prepared the body for the grave. In his fascinating study of changing views about death in America, historian Gary Laderman writes that "death was integrated, through a series of rituals and symbols, into the life of the community." Laderman observes, "At the center of this network of practices and significations was the corpse, an irreducible object that evoked feelings of dread, fear and resignation, as well as reverence, respect, and hope. . . . From the place where death occurred, usually on a bed in the home, to the final destination of the body, in most cases a grave in the local burial ground, the treatment of the corpse generally depended on certain pre-established rituals."[27]

The body was laid out, washed, and wrapped in a burial shroud or sheeting. "Preparing the body was a duty for the close living relatives of the deceased, and they rarely hesitated to participate in these activities."[28] The body was placed in a coffin or laid out on a table to be watched over for the next one to three days. In part, this was done to eliminate the possibility of premature burial, apparently a prevalent fear; even closed caskets would have a small glass window so mourners could see if the deceased was not actually dead. The body was constantly accompanied by mourners, who consumed food and strong drink. This vigil or wake occurred in either a front room or the parlor of a house, the space designated by somber banners of black crepe and emptied of other furnishings. All mirrors were turned around or covered with cloth, and household clocks were stopped at the time of death in honor of the deceased. Once the wake concluded, the body was taken to the graveyard, borne by pallbearers or transported at a suitably somber pace in a horse-drawn carriage.

This fundamental trajectory of the dead from home to graveyard withstood significant changes in the way Protestant America thought about death, the body, and heaven. There is often a temptation to over-idealize changes in cultural values, especially in retrospect and from afar. Every human society—no matter how superficially homogeneous—holds various opinions about matters like the meaning of life and the nature of death. Antebellum America was anything but a homogeneous society, with significant immigrant populations, various religious traditions, and persistent (and sometimes hidden) practices relating to the dead.[29]

But there were marked changes among Protestant communities living in the northeastern United States, cultural trends felt elsewhere in the nation. Specifically, there was a well-documented shift in theological positions, "moving away from the stern, dogmatic, and oppressive sensibilities of the Puritan past and toward the Romantic, sentimental, and domestic characteristics of the nineteenth century."[30]

Puritan mortuary ritual was bare, ascetic, and unadorned, reflecting the view of the corruptible body and the nature of eternal judgment. "In the Puritan view," Laderman writes, "the corpse was a horrible sight that signified both human sin and the flight of the soul." Since divine judgment occurred at the moment of death and the details of the resurrection were beyond human understanding, "the lifeless body had no connection to the subsequent fate of the soul."[31] As the texts of funeral sermons make clear, "orthodox Puritans believed that both disease and death were punishments for the original sin of Adam. . . . With the corpse as proof, the funeral sermon was the ideal occasion to stress the theme of death's certainty."[32]

An alternative perspective on the dead developed in the course of the nineteenth century, one that cherished and domesticated the dead. Culminating in the "Victorian cult of memory," the developing concepts involved a reappraisal of

> how to make sense of death and the dead body. The new religious culture that was emerging contributed to the establishment of four trends in northern Protestant attitudes toward death: valorization of the affections of the survivors, memorialization of the dead, augmentation of the spiritual possibilities in the next world, and domestication of the corpse.
>
> In the first part of the nineteenth century, the death bed functioned as the location where all of these trends converged.[33]

These attitudes and rituals were severely tested by the American Civil War. The carnage of this first "modern" war is nearly beyond comprehension. With an estimated 625,000 Union and Confederate dead, more Americans lost their lives in the Civil War than in World War I and World War II combined. Over 61,000 troops died in May–June 1864 alone, more than in the eight years of the Vietnam War (1965–1973). On June 18, 1864 at Petersburg, Virginia, the First Maine Heavy Artillery lost 635 of its 900 men in seven minutes. The war was anything but civil.

Many dead soldiers were buried in unmarked graves, but some corpses made the journey home. The Civil War was transformative for embalming and mortuary practice as a profession. Previously used to preserve cadavers for medical school instruction, embalming became essential during the Civil War so the dead could be seen by their families once again.

Ten days after his assassination on April 15, 1865, the body of President Abraham Lincoln was placed on a funeral train that carried him from Washington, D.C., to Springfield, Illinois. During the thirteen-day journey, Lincoln's body lay in state a half-dozen times. Once in Springfield, the martyred president was still not allowed to rest in peace. Over the next three decades, Lincoln's corpse was moved seventeen times. It was the target of a robbery and ransom plot (fortunately thwarted), and a half-dozen partial openings of the casket. The last opening occurred in 1901, when Lincoln's features were described as perfectly recognizable despite the fact that clothing and an American flag interred with the former President had turned to dust. Lincoln's corpse had been embalmed repeatedly on the funeral train, effectively mummifying his body.[34]

Embalming changed undertaking into a profession. As Laderman observes, not only was embalming "the enduring signature of the nascent funeral industry," but it "transformed the rituals of disposal and the architectural space of death."[35] Undertakers traced their professional lineage back to ancient Egyptian mortuary arts, and the professionalization of funerals led to practices that Jessica Mitford famously dissected in "The American Way of Death." But in the mid-nineteenth century, the central advantage of embalming was that the dead could go home.

As the Puritanical views of the corpse as corrupt and of death as divine punishment for humanity's sin gave way to the sentimental embrace of the dead, this change in attitudes was reflected in various aspects of American culture, including in the archaeology of graveyards. In their classic paper "Death's Heads, Cherubs and Willow Trees: Experimental Archaeology in Colonial Cemeteries," the historical archaeologists Edwin Dethlefsen and James Deetz analyzed changing tombstone styles and motifs found in New England cemeteries. The earliest gravestones were inscribed with skeletal death heads that conveyed the Puritan notions of death, in which, as Dethlefsen and Deetz write:

> Mortality is stressed, little or no mention being made of an afterlife or resurrection of the dead, as shown by the following example:
>
>> Remember me as you pass by
>> As you are now so once was I
>> As I am now you soon must be
>> Prepare for death and follow me.
>
> Other epitaphs mention moldering dust, worms, and decay.[36]

Subsequently, winged cherubs replaced the death heads that had been universal, a change that took place in 1740–1760, which Dethlefsen and Deetz associate with "the progressive reduction in intensity of the Puritan ethic." By the early 1800s, cherubs were replaced with the willow-and-urn motif, which became one of the most enduring of all American symbols and "the hallmark of Victorian gravemarkers." This shift from death heads and cherubs to willow-and-urn led Dethlefsen and Deetz to conclude that "certainly funeral customs in the period preceding 1800 belong to another age and another set of values."[37]

The new values visible in New England cemeteries also travelled west, as I discovered in a research project at the historic Sunset Cemetery in Manhattan, Kansas. In the course of teaching an archaeological methods class at Kansas State University in 1988–1989, my students and I studied changes in gravestones at Sunset Cemetery.[38] Located on a knoll on the westernmost edge of the original town site and thus bathed in the last light of the setting sun, the first burial was laid to rest in Sunset Cemetery in 1860.

The original sector of the cemetery was set out on a rigid grid, but later incorporated meandering pathways as the rural cemetery movement gained in popularity. A columned mausoleum associated with a leading family was focal monument, as was a cannon incorporated into a monument to the Kansans who had fought with the Grand Army of the Republic.

Our sample examined tombstones dating from 1860 to 1980. Our study identified multiple themes, but two illuminate ideas of death and home in nineteenth-century Kansas.

First, the nineteenth-century grave markers for children were as tall and elaborate as those for adults. This contrasts with late twentieth-century practice in the Sunset Cemetery. More recent burials of infants and children are marked by relatively low tombstones; since the 1960s one sector of the cemetery has been reserved for infant burials (a part of the knoll where the bedrock is too shallow to allow for an adult's grave six feet deep). These graves are marked by rectangular metal plaques, some actually flush with the ground surface, inscribed with the child's name, dates of birth and death, and often some other motif, such as a lamb. According to a cemetery foreman, this part of the Sunset Cemetery is known to the groundskeepers as "Babyland."

Such treatment would have been incomprehensible in the United States during the Victorian era. Not only was the death of a child or infant marked by substantial gravestones, the markers were sculpted with motifs of innocence, such as rosebuds or lambs, and inscribed by heart-rending epitaphs. The grave markers in this Kansas cemetery reflected broader American values and practices of bereavement, a cult of memory also reflected in nineteenth-century "consolation literature," which Ann Douglas has defined as "openly fictionalized and avowedly factual accounts of deathbed scenes and celestial communications," which was "an important phenomenon in 19th century American culture . . . [that] incessantly stressed the importance of dying and the dead: it encouraged elaborate funerary practices, conspicuous methods of burial and commemoration, and microscopic viewings of a much inflated afterlife."[39]

Consolation literature was linked to another change in Protestant America: Heaven became Home.

This concept of a "domestic heaven" literally shaped historic burial practices in Manhattan, Kansas, as well as elsewhere in the United States. The common motifs on nineteenth-century gravestones included a finger pointing upward (a clear and relatively positive symbol about eternal judgment), a motif showing a handshake (sometimes accompanied by the word "Farewell"), and the "Gate of Heaven" symbol. This last symbol takes the form of either a pair of columns capped with an arch that has been sculpted in the round or as a two-dimensional engraving on a tombstone.[40]

Heaven had become home, and the graveyard became a resting place between earthly existence and everlasting life. For the Kansas pioneers buried in Sunset Cemetery, the notion of pilgrimage was a powerful theme, and it was captured in a poem written by a Manhattan resident in 1866, a local bookseller Simon Foy; the first stanza is:

To Sunset Hill the weary pilgrims go.
With folded hands and patient lips grown still.
Up from the shadows of the vale below,
They make their way beyond to Sunset Hill.

Despite its treacly sentiments, this poem and the tombstones of Sunset Cemetery display a concept of death that is distant from Puritan's view of the body as destined to "worms and corruption." The concept of death as pilgrimage and heaven as home remains a trope in American culture, but one now rivaled by other visions of death.

Fundamental to that change was the role of the funeral director and the funeral home in twentieth-century America. As embalming transformed undertaking into a profession, the process also separated the corpse from home. Although undertakers could prepare the body on site, by the early twentieth century it became increasingly common to transport the dead to the funeral home.

Concurrently, changes in American domestic architecture resulted in the elimination of the parlor—a space reserved for special purposes such as entertaining guests or housing a wake. Domestic architecture also changed, particularly as the bungalow became a common house type. Bungalow design eliminated the parlor in lieu of a combined living room and dining room area found in the front of the house. So the dead were taken from the home, and the house no longer had space for the dead.[41]

As Laderman notes, funeral establishments had multiple spaces: not only an embalming room, a stock room, and office, but increasingly a chapel and parlor where living relatives could "be 'at home' with their dead—if only for a short period of contemplation and release." Embalming served to restore a lifelike appearance to the corpse, and the highest accolade of the mortuary arts was that the dead "looked good." So while the social custom of viewing the body was retained, the setting and process had changed fundamentally. These "new ritual patterns for disposing of the dead," Laderman writes, "relieved living relatives of traditional duties. Dead bodies, in effect, disappeared from the everyday world of twentieth-century Americans."[42]

And with increasing frequency, the dead even disappeared from the graveyard. The first modern cremation in American history occurred on December 6, 1876, in the small town of Washington, Pennsylvania, an event "hailed . . . as a harbinger of a new age of scientific progress and ritual simplicity" and alternately "denounced . . . as Satan's errand."[43] Advocates presented cremation as a swift and sanitary alternative to the slow decay of burial, simultaneously "a relief to the mind" and a way "to make the dead harmless to the living."[44] Instead of being burned outdoors on a funeral pyre, the deceased would be incinerated indoors in a modern, scientific furnace, thus sparing loved ones gruesome visions and noxious fumes. Unlike the primitive pyres in which the body was scorched by uneven flames, but not completely destroyed, modern cremation furnaces reduced the corpse by heat alone, reducing it to its constituent elements unmixed with ash, dirt, or other "foreign matter."[45]

By the late 1800s cremation was no longer a stigmatized practice in the United States, but one with little following. At no point in the nineteenth century were more than one percent of the dead cremated, Stephen Prothero estimates, and even as late as the early 1960s the ratio was no more than 3.7 percent. Only recently have cremations increased to about 25 percent of all American deaths.

The major factors that resulted in the increased popularity of cremations were changing American cultural views of body, spirit, and eternity. While most Americans still preferred the rituals of burial that retained the human body—a broad cross section that included white conservative and African-American Protestants, American Muslims, and Hispanic Catholics—more and more Americans embraced a fluid set of religious notions that Prothero calls "spiritual," its touchstone being the phrase, "I have a body, but I am a soul." These individuals, Prothero notes, "wanted their exits from the world of bodies to reflect their alternative spiritualities."[46] These exits could be marked by having their ashes spread at sea or in favorite landscapes, enclosed in custom-made urns or in safe-deposit boxes, or even launched into outer space, as in the cases of Gene Rodenberry, the creator of *Star Trek,* and Timothy Leary, the psychedelic pioneer and '6os icon, whose partial ashes pass overhead every ninety minutes in two small cartridges the size of lipstick tubes in low-altitude orbit encircling the Earth.

Unlike the Victorian cult of memory in which the presence of the dead was lingered over, commemorated, and enshrined in the United States, in the early decades of the twenty-first century it is more common to hear cultural metaphors surrounding the "acceptance" of death and the search for "closure." And regardless of how one might react to the sentiments and logics encoded in such phrases, one point is obvious: these concepts are not domestic. For more and more Americans, the afterlife is not viewed as a homey existence paralleling this world. While there is little evidence of a return to Puritanical concerns with evil and the corrupt corpse, neither is there a tendency to envision the afterlife as a version of this world, a domestic heaven as described in nineteenth-century consolation literature, let alone that envisioned in ancient Egypt.

Rather, there is a strong current in American culture that views death as an utterly different transformation, a release of spirit in which the human remains, reduced by fire to their essential elements, may be placed in a cartridge orbiting in space far away from home.

The dead leave their bodies. The dead leave home.

CHAPTER 12

Conclusion

An object [is] the sum of its complications.

—Wallace Stevens

On the western edge of Ireland on the coast just south of Doolin, County Clare, an abandoned road leads towards the wave-hammered Cliffs of Moher. The sea is an indistinct grey. The cliffs are black, undercut, and crumbling, the eroded edge of the Burren, a nearly treeless region of carboniferous limestone, Clare shale, and sandstones scraped by glacial ice and rainwater. *Burren* comes from the Irish *boireann*, "a place of rocks."[1]

The old road crosses pastures and bogs before passing an abandoned village from the starving times. Although the Great Famine is usually blamed on a potato blight that struck between 1845 and 1849, it was—as with all human affairs—more complicated. The natural disaster of the mid-nineteenth century was made worse by population increase and injustice. Ireland's population had tripled in the previous sixty years, but the economy stagnated under the rule of English and Anglo-Irish landlords. For most Irish, life offered only three options: squalid poverty, emigration to America or Australia, or enlistment in the British Army. As the Duke of Wellington stated, "Ireland was an inexhaustible nursery for the finest soldiers," and Irish soldiers extended the reach of the British Empire at the same time that British soldiers evicted peasants and destroyed their houses back home in Ireland.[2]

The potato, first cultivated in the prehispanic Andes, had readily adapted to the relatively warm winters and damp soils of Ireland, providing subsistence for Irish peasants as the grains and wool they raised were sold to pay rent or were delivered to their landlords.

FIGURE 36. Ruins of a potato famine village, near Doolin, Ireland, 2009. Photo by author.

The first crop failure of 1845 was followed by another blighted harvest in 1848. Rents continued to be demanded, peasants in arrears were evicted, and their houses were "tumbled," or razed. An estimated one million people died during these famine years, and corpses lay stinking in infertile fields. Relief efforts organized by the British government forced starving people to labor for their handouts, working at road-building and stone-hauling to get a daily dish of boiled cornmeal mush. Not surprisingly, the local authorities who administered the relief efforts often used the works project to improve their own field-walls and farm roads.[3]

Here along the Irish coast, the chances of survival were slightly better than inland. Fish could be caught, mussels and periwinkles gathered. Boys were lowered on long ropes over the cliff edges to rob eggs from nests of herring gulls, auks, and puffins.

Nonetheless, life was brutal in this thin-soiled landscape. In his classic documentary film, *The Man of Aran*, Robert Flaherty depicts a farmer and his wife living on the largest island, Arrain. The wife collects loads of seaweed on the shore, heaping the kelp into baskets and loading them onto her donkey. Meanwhile, the man works to widen a narrow seam of soil, using a sledge hammer to crush the flanking limestone. The wife arrives with the seaweed, and the couple spread the kelp over the limestone as mulch. Before these people can plant, they must first make the soil.

My family and I walk along the abandoned road south of Doolin and look at the famine houses. Each settlement is a small cluster of four to six houses and stone-walled corrals. The houses are rectangular dwellings with low gabled roofs. Built from irregular slabs of shale, the walls lack mortar, although they may have been daubed and whitewashed in the past. A hearth was built at one end, and the peat smoke must have filled the small house, as there are no traces of a chimney. The house is fully exposed on this cliff to the rage of Atlantic storms. The stones tumble, and cattle graze among the rubble.

As the potato blight spread, Irish families fled. Starving and wretched, they walked to the ports and took passage for America, many dying before the emigrant ships landed in New York, Boston, or Montreal. The potato famines of 1845 and 1848 were followed by decades of wet summers when the crops failed, a relentless cycle of decline that continued for the balance of the nineteenth century. By the end of these desperate times, a million Irish had died. Another million had left home.

. . .

This book is my attempt to introduce a general reader to archaeology, but a kind of archaeology that is less focused on spectacular temples or fabulous tombs and rather is more reflective of what archaeology actually is and what archaeologists actually do. At its most fundamental, archaeology is an attempt to use material evidence to document and understand the human experience. Most of our efforts are focused on past societies, but many archaeologists are also interested in recent or modern cases. What is common to our endeavors is the effort to understand human actions based on the material record of sites, features, and artifacts. Of course, we turn to historic documents and ethnographic accounts as aids in understanding the human experience, but ultimately we archaeologists are interested in the irreducible materiality of objects and their implications.`

This book has focused on one domain of the material record: human homes. I have written about home because so many dimensions of the human experience intersect there. Our houses allow us to physically adapt to the environment and to conceptually order the cosmos. Human dwellings enclose social groups of diverse forms—from nuclear families to entire clans, from hundreds of people to solitary hermits. Our houses solve problems of social life—for example, serving as architectural templates for appropriate behaviors—and our dwellings create social problems when we create environments of "social irritation." Our houses stand as symbols of equality or proclaim the social divides between people. We seek safety in our homes, not only from the elements, but increasingly from inchoate fear, or we may invite the supernatural into our homes for dangerous encounters. Much of what we humans do occurs at home.

And, as noted throughout this book, we have been doing this for literally hundreds of thousands of years, even—at least in some limited manner—before we were human. Although the earliest evidence of shelter remains a matter of debate and controversy, the archaeological evidence suggests that our hominid ancestors used fire and built simple constructions by circa 1.4 to 0.5 million years ago.

By at least 60,000 years ago, our hominid cousins, the Neanderthals, were organizing the spaces they occupied: burying their dead in the rear of Kebara Cave, making tools in other areas, casting out garbage in yet another place. This spatial organization is a characteristic of humans, even in open-air sites. It is a process that becomes pronounced, however, when we begin to build and occupy homes. The trend towards sedentism has its origins in the Upper Paleolithic, such as in the massive winter huts made from mammoth bones at Mezhrich. Sedentism developed independently of agriculture, but was usually triggered when our foods were stored and/or the tools needed to process those foods were too heavy to be readily carried.

Depending on the region, our homes began to be associated with complex meanings after we became sedentary or after we began using the same structure repeatedly (as exemplified by the Saami tent). The investiture of complex meanings into our homes is a subset of a larger and much older domain, the use of symbols. The best evidence I know of for using our homes as templates of the cosmos all date after the development of relatively sedentary life, expressed by sites usually dating to the last 10–15,000 years.

Once this threshold was crossed, our homes became rich frameworks for the construction of meaning. We use them to order the differences between Life and Death, Female and Male, Nature and Culture, and on and on and on, anchoring such bipolar conceptions in our homes. We make our houses sacred; we build houses for our gods. We bring the dead into our homes or we expel the ghosts from our homes, casting them into the disorder of the otherworld. We may even imbue our homes with a vital force of their own, burning them at the end of their lives so we can rebuild and thus remember.

I have written about the prehistory of home because the human home is the place where so much culture occurs, and it has had a recurrent place in human cultures over vast distances of time and space. But beyond that somewhat academic justification, *The Prehistory of Home* is my effort to engage the reader with an archaeology of human experience by connecting events and sites that are ancient and distant to lives and places that are current and near.

. . .

Lancaster, California, sprawls between the Mohave Desert and the San Andreas Fault, and the first decade of the twenty-first century has been difficult. Lancaster and its neighbor, Palmdale, are in the Antelope Valley, roughly seventy miles north of Los Angeles. Originally a whistle-stop on the Southern Pacific Railroad, Lancaster was a small town supported by gold and borax mining until the 1930s, when the U.S. military established large bases in the region. The enormous Edwards Air Force Base, in turn, attracted major aerospace companies to establish manufacturing plants in the region.

Lancaster boomed.

In 1977 Lancaster had about 37,000 citizens; by 2009 over 145,000 people lived there. As the aviation industry experienced one of its periodic downturns in the 1990s, people were forced to commute further from home to find work. Frequently commuters drove 70–100 miles to jobs in the Los Angeles basin, a rush-hour drive of 2–4 hours each way depending on traffic. Every morning. Every evening. And yet, to many people the commute was worth it because housing cost much less in Lancaster than in Los Angeles, which meant that one could seize a key part of the American dream: owning your own home.

And then the recession hit.

In the fall of 2010 Lancaster's 93535 zip code had the dubious distinction of having one of the highest foreclosure rates in the United States. It had the highest foreclosure rate of anywhere in Southern California, second in the state only to the 95206 zip code in my boyhood hometown of Stockton, California.

When you drive through the streets of Lancaster, the economic collapse is obvious. Clearly, the highest impact has been on commercial properties. Entire shopping malls, brand new and shiny, stand empty and dark.

New housing tracts are similarly hard-hit. A dusty field has a weathered sign announcing a public hearing for a new housing development; the public hearing was held in June 2008, but the field is still empty. Even worse are the houses that were actually built and now are worth much less. A large development of one- and two-story homes—the two-car garage doors the dominant feature of the front elevation—contains houses that were originally built to be sold in the range of $375,000–$400,000; they are now worth $160,000–$200,000. The developer is trying to sell some of the new homes at the lower price. Yellow and white balloons on the front fences of the model homes signal a festivity that few people really feel.

Perhaps the most depressed and depressing neighborhoods are the older tracts far away from the balloons and brochures, ranch houses built in the 1970s and 1980s. It is generally easy to spot the abandoned homes: the front lawns are dead. On streets with names that range from sterile coordinates ("Avenue J-8") to floral fantasies ("Fern Street"), the withered plots of grass-straw stand out from the neighboring lawns of occupied houses that their owners determinedly keep green.

But the clearest evidence of foreclosure is the garbage strewn in front of the house. A broken chair sits in the driveway. A drift of clothing, busted toys, and other abandoned possessions are the material evidence of the lost homes of Lancaster.

And yet on the same day I saw all this evidence of lives unraveling, I drove by the Springdale Elementary School. It was a Saturday, so I was surprised to see the schoolyard swarming with people working on the buildings.

Men were sanding the outside walls of classrooms. Small packs of children with garbage bags foraged across the playground clearing trash. Women covered windows with plastic sheeting and masking tape as a team of men started a paint compressor.

I spoke to a woman who was one of the coordinators of the event. She clicked off her cell phone. About one hundred volunteers were at Springdale Elementary School, she told me, to paint and repair the buildings. "It really needed it," she said. I asked if this was organized by the school district or the PTA.

"No, not really," she answered, "although folks from the PTA are here." She looked at me and said:

"You see—we are a community here."

Notes

1. THE PREHISTORY OF HOME

1. T. Ingold, "Building, Dwelling, Living: How Animals and People Make Themselves at Home in the World," in *Shifting Contexts*, ed. M. Strathern (London: Routledge, 1995), 57–80.

2. J. Rykwert, "House and Home," *Social Research* 58, no. 1 (1991): 51–62.

3. C. Geertz, *The Interpretation of Cultures* (New York: Basic Books, 1973), 5.

4. Not his real name.

5. S. Mallet, "Understanding Home: A Critical Review of the Literature," *The Sociological Review* 52, no. 1 (2004): 62–89.

6. S. Brink, "Home: The Term and Concept from a Linguistic and Settlement-Historical Viewpoint," in *The Home: Words, Interpretations, Meanings and Environments*, ed. D. Benjamin and D. Stea (Aldershot, UK: Avebury, 1995), 17–24.

7. Tacitus, *Germania*, trans. W. Peterson (London: William Heinmann, 1998 [1914]), 287.

8. Rykwert, "House and Home," 51–62.

9. M. Rodríguez Martínez, P. Ortíz Ceballos, M. Coe, R. Diehl, S. Houston, K. Taube, and A. Delgado Calderón, "Oldest Writing in the New World," *Science* 313 (2006): 1610–14.

10. C. Runnels and T. van Andel, "The Lower and Middle Paleolithic of Thessaly, Greece," *Journal of Field Archaeology* 20, no. 3 (1993): 299–317; T. Jacobsen, "Franchthi Cave and the Beginning of Settled Village Life in Greece" *Hesperia* 50, no. 4 (1981), 303–19.

11. S. Weiner, Q. Xu, and P. Goldberg, "Evidence for the Use of Fire at Zhoukoudian, China," *Science* 281 (1998): 251–53.

12. In addition to the numerous articles and books cited in the following pages, there is an enormous archaeological literature concerning with human dwellings and the creation of home. This literature, not unexpectedly, approaches

dwellings and home from a variety of vantage points, and the results are of varying interest to the general reader. For overviews of archaeological approaches to domestic architecture, see S. Steadman, "Recent Research in the Archaeology of Architecture: Beyond the Foundations" *Journal of Archaeological Research* 4, no. 1 (1996): 51–93; and the provocative article and excellent bibliography provided by M. Cutting in her 2006 article "More Than One Way to Study a Building: Approaches to Prehistoric Household and Settlement Space," *Oxford Journal of Archaeology* 25, no. 93: 225–46. The reader will gain a sense of the broad contours of the field from three edited volumes from the early 1990s: S. Kent, ed., *Domestic Architecture and the Use of Space: An Interdisciplinary Cross-Cultural Study* (Cambridge: Cambridge University Press, 1993); R. Samson, ed., *The Social Archaeology of Houses*, (Edinburgh: Edinburgh University Press, 1990); and M. Parker Pearson and C. Richard, eds., *Architecture and Order: Approaches to Social Space*, (London: Routledge, 1994).

Another current in the archaeological literature discusses how houses are also considered as social entities. On the one hand there is an enormous literature concerning the relationships between houses and households. A classic text is R. Wilk and W. Rathje's article, "Household Archaeology," *American Behavioral Scientist* 25, no. 6 (1982): 617–39. A cross-cultural survey is found in R. Blanton's *Houses and Households: A Comparative Study* (New York: Plenum, 1994). Review articles summarizing major trends in the literature on household archaeology include: J. Hendon, "Archaeological Approaches to the Organization of Domestic Labor: Household Practice and Domestic Relations," *Annual Review of Anthropology* 25 (1996): 45–61; C. Robin, "New Directions in Classic Maya Household Archaeology," *Journal of Archaeological Research* 11, no. 4 (2003): 307–56; D. Nash, "Household Archaeology in the Andes," *Journal of Anthropological Research* 17, no. 3 (2009): 205–61, and in the introductory chapters of S. Souvatzi, *A Social Archaeology of Households in Neolithic Greece: An Anthropological Approach* (Cambridge: Cambridge University Press, 2008). Some valuable edited collections include E. Sobel, D. Gahr, and K. Ames, eds., *Household Archaeology on the Northwest Coast* (Ann Arbor, MI: International Monographs in Prehistory, 2006); R. Wilk and W. Ashmore, eds., *Household and Community in the Mesoamerican Past* (Albuquerque: University of New Mexico Press, 1988); P. Allison, ed., *The Archaeology of Household Activities*, (London: Routledge, 1999); R. Santley and K. Hirth, eds., *Prehispanic Domestic Units in Western Mesoamerica: Studies of the Household, Compound, and Residence* (Boca Raton: CRC Press, 1992); and M. Aldenderfer, ed., *Domestic Architecture, Ethnicity and Complementarity in the South-Central Andes* (Iowa City: University of Iowa Press, 1993).

A different line of literature concerns the "social house" in which "the house" designates an enduring social entity—such as in the House of Tudor or the House of Stuart. This idea originates in the works of the social anthropologist Claude Lévi-Strauss, but has been applied and amplified by archaeologists; see for example, articles in R. Joyce and S. Gillespie, eds., *Beyond Kinship: Social and Material Reproduction in House Societies* (Philadelphia: University of Pennsylvania Press, 2000) and R. Beck, Jr., ed., *The Durable House: House Society Models in Archaeology,* Center for Archaeological Investigations, Occasional Paper 35 (Carbondale: Southern Illinois University, 2007).

Relationships between gender and the domestic realm are discussed by R. Tringham, "Households with Faces: the Challenge of Gender in Prehistoric Architectural Remains," in *Engendering Archaeology: Women and Prehistory* ed. J. Gero and M. Conkey, (Malden, MA: Blackwell, 1991), 93–131; J. Hendon, "The Engendered Household" in *The Handbook of Gender in Archaeology,* ed. S. Nelson, (Lanham, MD: Altamira Press/Rowman and Littlefield, 2006), 171–98; and C. Antonaccio, "Architecture and Behavior: Building Gender into Greek Houses" *The Classical World* 93, no. 5 (2000): 517–33; and in L. Nevett, *House and Society in the Ancient Greek World,* (Cambridge: Cambridge University Press, 2001).

Given the pivotal role of houses and households in human life, these references are simply a starting-point to a vast archaeological literature.

13. D. Frankfurther, *Religion in Roman Egypt: Assimilation and Resistance* (Princeton: Princeton University Press, 2000), 139.

2. STARTER HOMES

1. D. Scott, *The Singing Bourgeois: Songs of the Victorian Drawing Room and Parlour* (Aldershot, UK: Ashgate, 2001).

2. C.H. Brainard, *John Howard Payne: A Biographical Sketch of the Author of "Home Sweet Home"; with a Narrative of the Removal of His Remains from Tunis to Washington.* (Washington, DC: George A. Coolidge, 1885), 27.

3. Quoted in J.L. McDonough, *Stones River—Bloody Winter in Tennessee.* (Knoxville: University of Tennessee Press, 1980), 78.

4. "Local Miscellany—John Howard Payne—The Unveiling of A Bronze Bust at Prospect Park," *New York Times,* September 27, 1873.

5. *New York Times,* March 23, 1883; Brainard, *John Howard Payne,* 99–144.

6. K. von Frisch, *Animal Architecture* (New York: Harcourt Brace, Jovanovich, 1974), 22. Von Frisch won the Nobel Prize for his research in animal ethology, a co-recipient with Konrad Lorenz.

7. For additional sources on animal architecture, see M. Hansell, *Animal Architecture and Building Behavior* (London: Longman, 1984); M. Hansell, *Bird Nests and Construction Behaviour* (Cambridge: Cambridge University Press, 2000); J. Gould and C. Gould, *Animal Architects: Building and the Evolution of Intelligence* (New York: Basic Books, 2007); J. Turner, *The Extended Organism: The Physiology of Animal-Built Structure* (Cambridge, MA: Harvard University Press, 2000).

8. R. Dawkins, *The Extended Phenotype: The Long Reach of the Gene* (Oxford: Oxford University Press, 1999).

9. Gould and Gould, *Animal Architects,* 1–2; Hansell, *Animal Architecture and Building Behavior,* 2.

10. Hansell, *Animal Architecture and Building Behavior,* 12.

11. J. Anderson, E. Williamson, and J. Carter, "Chimpanzees of Sapo Forest, Liberia: Density, Nests, Tools and Meat-eating," *Primates* 24, no. 4 (1983): 594–601; J. Baldwin, J. Sabater Pi, W. McGrew, and C. Tutin, "Comparisons of

Nests Made by Different Populations of Chimpanzees *(Pan troglodytes)*," *Primates* 22, no. 4 (1981): 474–86; D. Doran, "Influence of Seasonality on Activity Patterns, Feeding Behavior, Ranging, and Grouping Patterns in Tai Chimpanzees," *International Journal of Primatology*, 18, no. 2 (1997): 183–206; B. Fruth and G. Hohman, "Comparative Analyses of Nest-Building Behavior in Bonobos and Chimpanzees," in *Chimpanzee Cultures*, ed. R. Wrangham, W. McGrew, F. de Waal, and P. Heltne (Chicago: University of Chicago Press, 1996), 109–28; B. Fruth and G. Hohman, "Nest Building Behavior in the Great Apes: The Great Leap Forward?" in *Great Ape Societies*, ed. W. McGrew, L. Marchant, and T. Nishida (Cambridge: Cambridge University Press, 1996), 225–40; J. Goodall, "Nest Building Behavior in the Free Ranging Chimpanzee," *Annals of the New York Academy of Sciences* 102 (1962): 455–67; J. Goodall, *The Chimpanzees of Gombe: Patterns of Behavior* (Cambridge, MA: Harvard University Press, 1986); W. McGrew, *The Cultured Chimpanzee: Reflections on Cultural Primatology* (Cambridge: Cambridge University Press, 2004).

    12. McGrew, *The Cultured Chimpanzee*, 108.

    13. G. Schaller, *The Mountain Gorilla: Ecology and Behavior* (Chicago: University of Chicago Press, 1963); C. Tutin, R. Parnell, L. White, and M. Fernandez, "Nest Building by Lowland Gorillas in the Lope Reserve, Gabon: Environmental Influences and Implications for Censusing," *International Journal of Primatology* 16, no. 1 (1995): 53–76; P. Mehlman and D. Doran, "Influencing Western Gorilla Nest Construction at Mondika Research Center," *International Journal of Primatology* 23, no. 6 (2002): 1257–87; M. Remis, "Nesting Behavior of Lowland Gorillas in the Dzanga-Sangha Reserve, Central African Republic: Implications for Population Estimates and Understandings of Group Dynamics," *Tropics* 2, no. 4 (1993): 245–55.

    14. D. Fossey, *Gorillas in the Mist* (Boston: Houghton Mifflin, 1983), 47.

    15. Schaller, *The Mountain Gorilla*, 187.

    16. Y. Iwata and C. Ando, "Bed and Bed-site Reuse by Western Lowland Gorillas (Gorilla g. gorilla) in Moukalaba-Doudou National Park, Gabon," *Primates* 48 (2007): 77–80.

    17. Schaller, *The Mountain Gorilla*, 191–92, 194.

    18. See McGrew, *The Cultured Chimpanzee*, 109–11 for a summary and critique.

    19. Mehlman and Donan, "Influencing Western Gorilla Nest Construction," 1282.

    20. J. Sept, "Was There No Place Like Home? A New Perspective on Early Hominid Archaeological Sites from the Mapping of Chimpanzee Nests," *Current Anthropology* 33, no. 2 (1992): 187–207.

    21. A detailed account of this hypothesis is articulated by C. Owen Lovejoy, "The Origin of Man," *Science* 211, no. 4480 (1981), 341–50.

    22. P. Stuart-Macadam, "Breastfeeding in Prehistory," in *Breastfeeding: Biocultural Perspectives*, ed. P. Stuart-Macadam and K. Dettwyler (New York: Aldine de Gruyter, 1995), 75–99.

    23. A sample of this large literature includes R. Lee and I. DeVore, eds., *Man the Hunter*, (Chicago: Aldine Publishing, 1968); K. Hawkes, J. O'Connell, and N. Jones, "Hunting and Nuclear Families: Some Lessons from the Hadza about

Men's Work," *Current Anthropology* 42, no. 5 (2001): 681–709. For an extensive review from a behavioral ecology perspective, see M. Gurven, "To Give and To Give Not: The Behavioral Ecology of Human Food Transfers," *Brain and Behavioral Sciences* 27 (2004): 543–48.

24. M. Leakey, *Olduvai Gorge*, vol. 3, *Excavations in Beds I and II, 1960–1963* (Cambridge: Cambridge University Press, 1971).

25. M. Leakey, *Olduvai Gorge: My Search for Early Man.* (London: Collins, 1979), 55.

26. B. Isaac, ed., *The Archaeology of Human Origins: Papers by Glynn Isaac* (Cambridge: Cambridge University Press, 1989), 234–57.

27. L. Binford, *Bones: Ancient Men and Modern Myths,* (New York: Academic Press, 1981), and "Human Ancestors: Changing Views of Their Behavior," *Journal of Anthropological Archaeology* 4 (1985): 292–327; R. Potts, *Early Hominid Activities at Olduvai* (New York: Aldine de Gruyter, 1988); L. Rose and F. Marshall, "Meat Eating, Hominid Sociality, and Home Bases Revisited," *Current Anthropology* 37, no. 2 (1996): 307–38. For alternative views, see T. Plummer, "Flaked Stones and Old Bones: Biological and Cultural Evolution at the Dawn of Technology," *Yearbook of Physical Anthropology* 47 (2004): 118–64.

28. For reviews, see the articles by T. Plummer, "Discord after Discard: Reconstructing Aspects of Oldowan Hominin Behavior," and by C. Marean and Z. Assefa, "The Middle and Upper Pleistocene African Record for the Biological and Behavioral Origins of Modern Humans," both in *African Archaeology: A Critical Introduction,* ed. A. Stahl, (Malden, MA: Blackwell, 2005) 55–92 and 93–129 (respectively); and J. Sept, "Shadows on a Changing Landscape: Comparing Nesting Patterns of Hominids and Chimpanzees Since Their Last Common Ancestor," *American Journal of Primatology* 46 (1998): 85–101.

29. J. Yellen, "Behavioural and Taphonomic Patterning at Katanda 9: A Middle Stone Age Site, Kivu Province, Zaire," *Journal of Archaeological Sciences* 23 (1996): 915–32.

30. H. de Lumley, "A Paleolithic Camp at Nice," *Scientific American* 220 (1969): 42–50; and "Cultural Evolution in France in Its Paleoecological Setting During the Middle Pleistocene," in *After the Australopithecines: Stratigraphy, Ecology, and Culture Change in the Middle Pleistocene,* ed. K. Butzer and G. Isaac (The Hague: Mouton, 1975) 745–808.

31. For example, the reports of de Lumley's excavations consist of a short article written at the time of excavation, an eight-page article in *Scientific American,* and a brief discussion of Terra Amata within a review article on Middle Pleistocene cultural evolution in France.

32. P. Villa, *Terra Amata and the Middle Pleistocene archaeological record of southern France* (Berkeley: University of California Press, 1983), 72.

33. D. Mania, "The Zonal Division of the Lower Paleolithic Open-air Site Bilzingsleben," *Anthropologie* 29 (1991): 17–24; H. Schwarz, R. Grün, A. Latham, D. Mania, K. Brunnacker, "The Bilzingsleben Archaeological Site: New Dating Evidence," *Archaeometry* 30, no. 1 (2007), 5–17; D. Mania and U. Mania, "The Natural and Sociocultural Environment of Homo Erectus at Bilzingsleben, Germany," in *The Hominid Individual in Context: Archaeological Investigations of*

Lower and Middle Paleolithic Landscapes, Locales, and Artefacts, ed. C. Gamble and M. Porr (London: Routledge, 2005), 98–115.

34. C. Gamble, *The Paleolithic Societies of Europe* (Cambridge: Cambridge University Press, 1999), 153–73; Mania and Mania, "The Natural and Socio-cultural Environment," 102.

35. R. Wrangham, *Catching Fire: How Cooking Made Us Human* (New York: Basic Books, 2009); R. Wrangham, J. Jones, G. Laden, D. Pilbeam, N. Conklin-Brittain, "The Raw and the Stolen: Cooking and the Ecology of Human Origins," *Current Anthropology* 40, no. 5 (1999): 567–77.

36. As I write this in September 2009, an enormous arson-caused fire 32 miles north of my office has burned more that 250 square miles in the mountains north of Los Angeles, and fire season is just beginning.

37. S. James, "Hominid Use of Fire in the Lower and Middle Pleistocene: A Review of the Evidence," *Current Anthropology* 30 (1989): 1–26; for an alternative view, see J. Gowlett, "The Early Settlement of Northern Europe: Fire History in the Context of Climate Change and the Social Brain," *Comptes Rendus Paleovol* 5 (2006): 299–310.

38. S. Weiner, Q. Xu, P. Goldberg, J. Liu, O. Bar-Yosef, "Evidence for the Use of Fire at Zhoukoudian, China," *Science* 281 (1998): 251–53.

39. J. Clark and J. Harris, "Fire and Its Roles in Early Hominid Lifeways," *The African Archaeological Review* 3 (1985): 3–27.

40. N. Goren-Inbar, N. Alperson, K. Nira, E. Mordechai, O. Simchoni, Y. Melamed, A. Ben-Nun, and E. Werker, "Evidence of Hominin Control of Fire at Gesher Benot Ya'aqov, Israel," *Science* 304, no. 5671 (2004): 725–27; N. Goren-Inbar, C. Feibel, K. Verosub, Y. Melamed, M. Kislev, E. Tchernov, and I. Saragusti, "Pleistocene Milestones on the Out-of-Africa Corridor at Gesher Benot Ya'aqov, Israel," *Science* 289, no. 5481 (2000): 944–47.

3. MOBILE HOMES

1. The portaledge was redesigned by John Middendorf, a climber and designer, to provide a structure that would survive rigorous conditions during big wall ascents. For more information, see http://www.johnmiddendorf.com/indexfiles/portfolio.pdf. Figure 3 is reproduced with Mr. Middendorf's permission; all rights reserved.

2. L. Binford, "Mobility, Housing and Environment: A Comparative Study," *Journal of Anthropological Research* 46, no. 2 (1990): 119–52.

3. G. Vico, *The New Science of Giambattista Vico,* trans. T. Bergin and M. Fisch (Ithaca, NY: Cornell University Press, 1984 [1774]), 78.

4. Vico, *The New Science,* 72.

5. Vitruvius, *On Architecture,* trans. and ed. F. Granger (London: William Heinemann, 1931) 2.1, p. 79.

6. W. Chambers, *A Treatise on the Decorative Part of Civil Architecture* (London: Lockwood, 1862 [1791]), 77.

7. Baegert's statement is quoted in Z. Engelhardt, *The Missions and Missionaries of California,* vol. 1, *Lower California* (San Francisco: James Barry, 1908), 154.

8. M. del Barco, *Historia Natural y Crónica de la Antigua California* (Mexico City: Universidad Nacional Autónoma de México, 1988 [1770–1780]), 188. Translation mine.

9. L. Sales, *Observations on California*, trans. C. Rudkin (Los Angeles: Dawson's Book Store, 1956 [1772–1790]), 29.

10. J. Moore, "The San Quintín—El Rosario Region," in *The Prehistory of Baja California: Advances in the Archaeology of the Forgotten Peninsula*, ed. D. Laylander and J. Moore (Gainesville: University Press of Florida 2006), 179–95.

11. M. Jackson, *At Home in the World* (Durham, NC: Duke University Press 1995).

12. O. Bar-Yosef, B. Vandermeersch, B. Arensburg, A. Belfer-Cohen, P. Goldberg, H. Laville, L. Meignen, Y. Rak, J.D. Speth, E. Tchernov, A.-M. Tillier, and S. Weiner, "The Excavations in Kebara Cave, Mt. Carmel," *Current Anthropology* 33 (1992): 497–550. For additional discussions of Middle Paleolithic burial practices, see A. Belfer-Cohen and E. Hovers, "In the Eye of the Beholder: Mousterian and Natufian Burials in the Levant," *Current Anthropology* 33 (1992): 463–71. For a skeptical review of the Kebara 2 burial, see R. Gargett, "Middle Paleolithic Burial is Not a Dead Issue: The View from Qafzeh, Saint-Césaire, Kebara, Amud, and Dederiyeh," *Journal of Human Evolution* 37 (1999): 27–90.

13. A. Leroi-Gourhan and M. Brézillon, *Fouilles de Pincevent: Essai d'analyse ethnographique d'un habitat magdalénien (La Section 36)*, Gallia Préhistoire, Supp. 7 (Paris: Centre National de la Recherche Scientifique, 1972); J. Enloe and F. David, "Food Sharing in the Paleolithic: Carcass Refitting at Pincevent," in *Piecing Together the Past: Applications of Refitting Studies in Archaeology*, ed. J. Hofman and J. Enloe, British Archaeological Reports International Series 578 (1992): 296–315; J. Enloe, "Geological Processes and Site Integrity at a Late Paleolithic Open-Air Site in Northern France," *Geoarchaeology* 21, no. 6 (2006): 523–40.

14. J.F. O'Connell, "Alyawara Site Structure and Its Archaeological Implications," *American Antiquity* 52, no. 1 (1987): 74–108.

15. D. Seymour, "Distinctive Places, Suitable Spaces: Conceptualizing Mobile Group Occupational Duration and Landscape Use," *International Journal of Historical Archaeology* 12 (2009): 255–81, and "Nineteenth-century Apache Wickiups: Historically Documented Models for Archaeological Signatures of the Dwellings of Mobile People," *Antiquity* 83 (2009): 157–64.

16. H. Wilkins, "An Investigation of the Adaptive Opportunity of Rudimentary Structures Based on Field Experiments," *Building and Environment* 42 (2007): 3883–93.

17. A. Velichko, E. Kurenkova, and P. Dolukhanov, "Human Socio-economic Adaptation to Environment in Late Paleolithic, Mesolithic and Neolithic Eastern Europe," *Quaternary International* 203 (2009): 1–9.

18. J. Hoffecker, "Innovation and Technological Knowledge in the Upper Paleolithic of Northern Eurasia," *Evolutionary Anthropology* 14 (2005): 186–98.

19. C. Gamble, W. Davies, P. Pettit and M. Richards, "Climate Change and Evolving Human Diversity in Europe during the Last Glacial," *Philosophical*

Transactions of the Royal Society 359 (2004): 243–54, esp. 247; Velichko et al., "Human Socio-economic Adaptation," 2.

20. Hoffecker, "Innovation and Technological Knowledge," 191–92.

21. M. Gladikh, N. Korniez, and O. Soffer, "Mammoth-bone Dwelling on the Russian Plain," *Scientific American* 251, no. 5 (1984): 164–75; L. Iakovleva and F. Djindjian, "New Data on Mammoth Bone Settlements of Eastern Europe in the Light of the New Excavations of the Gontsy Site (Ukraine)," *Quaternary International* 126–128 (2005): 195–207; O. Soffer, *The Upper Paleolithic of the Central Russian Plain*, (Orlando, FL: Academic Press, 1985).

4. DURABLE GOODS

1. J. Millar, *Observations Concerning the Distinction of Ranks in Society* (London: John Murray, 1771), 2.

2. Montesquieu [Charles de Secondat, Baron de la Brède et de Montesquieu], *The Spirit of Laws*, trans. T. Nugent (Cincinnati: Robert Clarke, 1873 [1748]), 319.

3. J.-J. Rousseau, *A Discourse Upon the Origin and Foundation of the Inequality Among Mankind* (New York: Burt Franklin, 1971 [1761]), 107.

4. Rousseau, *Discourse Upon the Origin of and Foundation of Inequality*, 112.

5. Rousseau, *Discourse Upon the Origin of and Foundation of Inequality*, 112–13.

6. V. Childe, *Man Makes Himself* (New York: New American Library, 1983 [1936]), 55.

7. Agriculture is usually defined as an economic system based on domesticated plants and animals, modified species genetically distinct from their wild relatives. Cultivation refers to human actions that encourage plant growth, whether the plants are wild or domesticates.

8. D. Cohn and R. Morin, "American Mobility: Who Moves? Who Stays Put? Where's Home?" *Pew Research Center* (2008), http://pewresearch.org/pubs/1058/american-mobility-moversstayers-places-and-reasons.pdf.

9. A. Janiak and E. Wasmer, "Mobility in Europe—Why It Is Low, the Bottlenecks, and the Policy Solutions," *European Union Economic Papers 340* (2008), http://ec.europa.eu/economy_finance/publications/publication13173_en.

10. J. Habu, *Ancient Jomon of Japan* (Cambridge: Cambridge University Press, 2004); R. Pearson, "Jomon Hot Spot: Increasing Sedentism in Southwestern Japan in the Incipient Jomon (14,000–9250 cal. BC) and Earliest Jomon (9250–5300 cal. BC) Periods," *World Archaeology* 38, no. 2 (2006): 239–58, and "Debating Jomon Complexity," *Asian Perspectives* 46, no. 2 (2007): 361–88.

11. M. Tsukada, "Vegetation in Prehistoric Japan: The Last 20,000 Years," in *Windows on the Japanese Past*, ed. R. Pearson, G. Barnes, and K. Hutterer (Ann Arbor: Center for Japanese Studies, University of Michigan, 1986), 11–56. See also T. Sakaguchi, "Storage Adaptations among Hunter-Gatherers: A Quantitative Approach to the Jomon Period," *Journal of Anthropological Archaeology* 28 (2009): 290–303.

12. J. Habu, "Growth and Decline in Complex Hunter-Gatherer Societies:

A Case Study from the Jomon Period Sannai Maruyama Site, Japan," *Antiquity* 82, no. 3 (2008): 571–84; Habu, *Ancient Jomon of Japan*, 108–32.

13. W. Hitoshi, "Community Habitation and Food Gathering in Prehistoric Japan: An Ethnographic Interpretation of the Archaeological Evidence," in *Windows on the Japanese Past*, ed. R. Pearson, G. Barnes, and K. Hutterer (Ann Arbor: Center for Japanese Studies, University of Michigan, 1991), 229–54.

14. J. Schor, *The Overworked American: The Unexpected Decline of Leisure* (New York: Basic Books, 1991).

15. Based on the online cost calculator, of Global Mobility Solutions, http://tools.gmsrelo.com/ToolsFas/Tool_MovingQuoteState.asp.

16. http://www.rvtravel.com/rvforum/viewtopic.php?t = 2216.

17. According to its professional organization, the Self Storage Association.

18. J. Arnold and U. Lang, "Changing American Home Life: Trends in Domestic Leisure and Storage among Middle-class Families," *Journal of Family and Economic Issues* 28 (2007): 23–48. For additional information on the Center on Everyday Lives of Families, see the webpage at www.celf.ucla.edu.

19. J.B. Jackson, "The Domestication of the Garage," in *Landscape in Sight: Looking at America*, ed. H.L. Horowitz (New Haven: Yale, 1997), 118–25, esp. 123.

20. Arnold and Lang, "Changing American Home Life," 41. Two points of personal interest. First, I have been a friend and colleague of Dr. Arnold since our graduate school days at the University of California, Santa Barbara. Second, I wrote the above during my Christmas holiday when one of my many chores was cleaning out our garage.

21. J. Davies, S. Sandström, A. Shorrocks, and E. Wolff, "The Level and Distribution of Global Household Wealth," NBER Working Paper 15508 (2009), http://www.nber.org/papers/w15508.

22. P. Menzel, *Material World: A Global Family Portrait.* (San Francisco: Sierra Club Books, 1994).

23. Menzel, *Material World*, 255.

24. For a history of archaeological research, see C. Maisels, *The Near East: Archaeology in the Cradle of Civilization* (London: Routledge, 1993).

25. Garrod's life and career are summarized by her colleague, the archaeologist Gertrude Caton-Thompson, "Dorothy Ann Elizabeth Garrod, 1892–1968," *Proceedings of the British Academy* 55 (1969): 339–61; and in the excellent dissertation by P.J. Smith, *A Splendid Idiosyncrasy: Prehistory at Cambridge 1915–1950* (PhD diss., Cavendish College, Cambridge University, 2004).

26. Quoted in Smith, *A Splendid Idiosyncrasy*, 179.

27. D. Garrod, "A New Mesolithic Industry: The Natufian of Palestine," *The Journal of the Royal Anthropological Institute of Great Britain and Ireland* 62 (1932): 257–69, esp. 261.

28. Garrod, "A New Mesolithic Industry," 268.

29. For overviews, see O. Bar-Yosef, "The Natufian Culture in the Levant, Threshold to the Origins of Agriculture," *Evolutionary Anthropology* 6, no. 5 (1998): 159–77; and O. Bar-Yosef and A. Belfer-Cohen, "The Origins of Sedentism and Farming Communities in the Levant," *Journal of World Prehistory* 3, no. 4 (1989): 447–98. For reviews of paleoclimate models, see D.O. Henry's

dated but extremely useful 1986 article, "The Prehistory and Paleoenvironments of Jordan : An Overview," *Paléorient* 12, no. 2: 5–26; for a more recent review, see S. Robinson, S. Black, B. Sellwood, and P. Valdes, "A Review of Paleoclimates and Paleoenvironments in the Levant and Eastern Mediterranean from 25,000–5000 Years BP: Setting the Environmental Background to the Evolution of Human Civilization," *Quaternary Science Review* 25 (2006):1517–41. For additional overviews of the Natufian, see A. Belfer-Cohen, "The Natufian in the Levant," *Annual Review of Anthropology*, 20 (1991): 167–86, and a critical response by B. Boyd, "On 'sedentism' in the Later Epipalaeolithic (Natufian) Levant" *World Archaeology* 38, no. 2 (2006): 164–78. On transformations in houses, see A. Goring-Morris and A. Belfer-Cohen, "A Roof Over One's Head: Developments in Near Eastern Residential Architecture Across the Epipaleolithic-Neolithic Transition," in *The Neolithic Demographic Transition and Its Consequences*, ed. J.-P. Boquet-Appel and O. Bar-Yosef (New York: Springer, 2008), 239–86.

30. Bar-Yosef, "The Natufian Culture in the Levant."

31. D. Lieberman refers to this as a "radiating" strategy; see his 1993 article, "The Rise and Fall of Seasonal Mobility among Hunter-Gatherers: The Case of the Southern Levant," *Current Anthropology*, 34, no. 5: 599–631.

32. D. Lieberman, "Seasonality and Gazelle Hunting at Hayonim Cave: New ·Evidence for "Sedentism" during the Natufian," *Paléorient* 17, no. 1 (1991): 47–57.

33. For recent literature on cultivation before domestication, see E. Weiss, M. Kislev, and A. Hartmann, "Autonomous Cultivation before Domestication," *Science* 312 (2006): 1608–10; G. Willcox, S. Fornite, L. Herveux, "Early Holocene Cultivation before Domestication in Northern Syria," *Vegetation History and Archaeobotany* 17, no. 3 (2008): 313–25.

34. I. Kuijt and B. Finlayson, "Evidence for Food Storage and Predomestication Granaries 11,000 Years Ago in the Jordan Valley," *Proceedings of the National Academy of Sciences*, (2009), www.pnas.org_cgi_doi_10.1073_pnas .0812764106.

35. Kuijt and Finlayson, "Evidence for Food Storage," 4.

36. R.P. Harrison, *The Dominion of the Dead*. (Chicago: University of Chicago Press, 2003), 3 and 19.

37. Harrison, *The Dominion of the Dead*, 39.

38. See Conklin's nuanced and outstanding book, *Consuming Grief: Compassionate Cannibalism in an Amazonian Society* (Austin: University of Texas Press, 2001).

39. J. Littleton, "From the Perspective of Time: Hunter-gatherer Burials in South-eastern Australia," *Antiquity* 81, no. 4 (2007): 1013–28; Littleton draws on the ethnographic observations regarding landscape made by H. Morphy, "Landscape and the Reproduction of the Ancestral Past," in *The Anthropology of Landscape*, ed. E. Hirsch and M. O'Hanlon (Oxford: Clarendon Press, 1995), 184–209.

40. Y. Okada, "Jomon Culture of Northeastern Japan and the Sannai Maruyama Site," *Senri Ethnological Studies* 63 (2003): 173–86.

41. I. Kuijt, "Negotiating Equality through Ritual: A Consideration of Late

Natufian and Prepottery Neolithic A Mortuary Practices," *Journal of Anthropological Archaeology* 15 (1996): 313–36.

42. T. Watkins, "The Origins of House and Home?" *World Archaeology* 21, no. 3 (1990): 336–47, esp. 344. See also T. Watkins, "Architecture and the Symbolic Construction of New Worlds," in *Domesticating Space: Construction, Community, and Cosmology in the Late Prehistoric Near East*, ed. E. J. Banning and M. Chazan, Studies in Early Near Eastern Production, Subsistence, and Environment 6 (Berlin: Ex Oriente, 2006), 15–24.

5. MODEL HOMES

1. P. Bourdieu, "The Kabyle House or the World Reversed," in *Rules and Meanings*, ed. M. Douglas (Harmondsworth, UK: Penguin, 1972), 98–110.

2. T. Plummer, "Discord after Discard: Reconstructing Aspects of Oldowan Homin Behavior," in *African Archaeology: A Critical Introduction*, ed. A. Stahl (Malden, MA: Blackwell, 2005), 55–92.

3. C. Marean and Z. Assefa, "The Middle and Upper Pleistocene African Record for the Biological and Behavioral Origins of Modern Humans," in *African Archaeology: A Critical Introduction*, ed. A. Stahl (Malden, MA: Blackwell, 2005), 93–129.

4. C. Henshilwood, F. d'Errico, R. Yates, Z. Jacobs, C. Tribolo, G. Duller, N. Mercier, J. Sealy, H. Valladas, I. Watts, and A. Wintle, "Emergence of Modern Human Behavior: Middle Stone Age Engravings from South Africa," *Science* 295, no. 5558 (2002), 1278–81; C. Henshilwood, F. d'Errico, M. Vanhaeren, K. Van Niekerk, and Z. Jacobs, "Middle Stone Age Shell Beads from South Africa," *Science*, 304, no. 5669 (2004), 404.

5. A. Bouzouggar, N. Bartonb, M. Vanhaeren, F. d'Errico, S. Collcutt, T. Higham, E. Hodge, S. Parfittk, E. Rhodes, J. Schwenninger, C. Stringer, E. Turner, S. Ward, A. Moutmir, and A. Stambouli, "82,000-year-old Shell Beads from North Africa and Implications for the Origins of Modern Human Behavior," *Proceedings of the National Academy of Sciences* 104, no. 24 (2007): 9964–69.

6. Z. Hebert, *Barbarian in the Garden*, trans. M. Marsh and J. Anders (Manchester, UK: Carcanet, 1985), 11.

7. On interpretations of Upper Paleolithic cave art, see R. Guthrie, *The Nature of Paleolithic Art* (Chicago: University of Chicago Press, 2006); D. Lewis-Williams, *The Mind in the Cave: Consciousness and the Origins of Art* (London: Thames and Hudson, 2004); J. Clottes, *Return to Chauvet Cave: Excavating the Birthplace of Art—The First Full Report* (London: Thames and Hudson, 2003); P. Bahn, *Cave Art: A Guide to the Decorated Ice Age Caves of Europe*, 3rd ed. (London: Frances Lincoln, 2007); S. Mithen, *The Prehistory of Mind: A Search for the Origins of Art, Religion and Science*, (London: Thames and Hudson, 1996); O. Bar-Yosef, "The Upper Paleolithic Revolution," *Annual Review of Anthropology* 31 (2002): 336–39; L. Malafouris, "Beyond and Before Representation: Towards an Enactive Conception of the Paleolithic Image," in *Image and Imagination: A Global Prehistory of Figurative Representation*, ed. C. Renfrew and I. Morley (Cambridge, UK: MacDonald Institute of Archaeology, 2007), 289–302.

8. R. White, "Beyond Art: Towards an Understanding of the Origins of Material Representation in Europe," *Annual Review of Anthropology* 21 (1992): 537–64.

9. R. Bednarik, "A Taphonomy of Palaeoart," *Antiquity* 68 (1994): 258–75. For a broader review of Australian rock art, see J. Mulvaney and J. Kamminga, *Prehistory of Australia* (Washington, DC: Smithsonian Institution Press, 1999), 357–406. For an outstanding inquiry into contemporary traditional Yolngu art and society, see H. Morphy, *Ancestral Connections: Art and an Aboriginal System of Knowledge* (Chicago: University of Chicago Press, 1991).

10. R. Bednarik, G. Aslin, and E. Bedarnik, "The Cave Petroglyphs of Australia," *Cave Art Research* 3 (2003): 1–7.

11. R. Bradley, *An Archaeology of Natural Places* (London: Routledge, 2000), 98–103.

12. On !Kung San rock art, see J. Lewis-Williams, *The Rock Art of Southern Africa* (Cambridge: Cambridge University Press, 1983), and relevant sections of *The Mind in the Cave: Consciousness and the Origins of Art* (London: Thames and Hudson, 2002). P. Taçon and S. Ousman discuss interesting parallels between hunter-gatherer rock arts in southern Africa and northern Australia in "Worlds Within Stone: the Inner and Outer Rock-art Landscapes of Northern Australia and Southern Africa," in *Pictures in Place: The Figured Landscapes of Rock-Art,* ed. C. Chippindale and G. Nash (Cambridge: Cambridge University Press, 2004), 39–68. On !Kung San houses, see J. Yellen, *Archaeological Approaches to the Present: Models for Reconstructing the Past* (New York: Academic Press, 1977).

13. F. Boas, *The Central Eskimo,* Smithsonian Institution, *Bureau of American Ethnology,* 6th Annual Report (1884–85) 539–46, 600–606. Cf. P. Nabokov and R. Easton, *Native American Architecture* (New York: Oxford University Press, 1989), 196, who assert that the raised platform bed "is associated with women, their soapstone lamps and gear, and the land," while the lower forechamber "is associated with men, their tools, and the sea." Although Nabokov and Easton reproduce Boas's illustration from Davis Strait, Boas does not record those symbolic associations.

14. J. Reser, "Mythic: Aboriginal (Yolugu)," *Encyclopedia of Vernacular Architecture,* ed. P. Oliver (Cambridge: Cambridge University Press, 1997), 602–3.

15. This discussion is based on T. Yates's intriguing article, "Habitus and Social Space: Some Suggestions about Meaning in the Saami (Lapp) Tent, ca. 1700–1900," in *The Meaning of Things: Material Culture and Social Expression,* ed. I. Hodder (London: Unwin Hyman, 1989), 249–62.

16. S. Jett and V. Spencer, *Navaho Architecture: Forms, History, Distribution* (Tucson: University of Arizona Press, 1981); Nabokov and Easton, *Native American Architecture;* S. Jett, "Navajo: Kayenta," in *Encyclopedia of Vernacular Architecture,* ed. P. Oliver (Cambridge: Cambridge University Press, 1997), 1934; S. Kent, "Navajo: Hogan Symbolism," in *Encyclopedia of Vernacular Architecture,* ed. P. Oliver (Cambridge: Cambridge University Press, 1997), 1935–36.

17. Kent, "Navajo: Hogan Symbolism," 1935.

18. L. Lamphere, "Symbolic Elements in Navaho Ritual," *Southwestern Journal of Anthropology* 25 (1969): 279–305.

19. K. Starr, *The Dream Endures: California Enters the 1940s* (Oxford: Oxford University Press, 1997), 158.

20. The phrase "existential insider" is from E. Relph's 1976 book, *Place and Placelessness* (London: Pion Limited).

21. S. Mintz and S. Kellogg, *Domestic Revolutions: A Social History of American Family Life* (New York: Free Press, 1989).

22. J. Vollmer, P. Schulz, and J.M. Chebra, "The American Master Bedroom: Its Changing Location and Significance to the Family," *Journal of Interior Design* 31, no. 1 (2005): 1–13.

23. Accessed electronically on January 5, 2009, at http://www.npr.org/templates/story/story.php?storyId = 5525283.

24. W. Wedel, "An Introduction to Pawnee Archeology," *Bureau of American Ethnology*, Bulletin No. 112 (1936); W. Wedel, "Prehistory and Environment in the Central Great Plains," *Transactions of the Kansas Academy of Science* 50, no. 1 (1947): 1–18; and W. Wedel, "An Introduction to Kansas Archeology," *Bureau of American Ethnology*, Bulletin No. 174 (1959).

25. A. Fletcher, "Pawnee Star Lore," *Journal of American Folklore* 16, no.60 (1903): 10–15. See also A. Fletcher, "Star Cult among the Pawnee—A Preliminary Report," *American Anthropologist* 4, no.4 (1902): 730–36; A. Fletcher with J. Murie, "The Hako: A Pawnee Ceremony," *Bureau of American Ethnology*, 22nd Annual Report, Part 2 (1900–1901). On Fletcher's remarkable life as early anthropologist and Indian rights advocate, see J. Mark, *A Stranger in Her Native Land: Alice Fletcher and the American Indian* (Lincoln: University of Nebraska Press, 1988).

26. Fletcher, "Star Cult among the Pawnee," 735.

27. Following quotations from Fletcher, *The Hako*, 24, 33–34.

28. The excavations at the C.C. Witt site are discussed by P. O'Brien in "Prehistoric Evidence for Pawnee Cosmology," *American Anthropologist* 88, no. 4 (1986): 939–46, and in "Evidence for the Antiquity of Gender Roles in the Central Plains Tradition," *Archaeological Papers of the American Anthropological Association* 2, no. 1 (1990): 61–72.

29. For additional examples of bird symbols among historic Plains groups, D. Ubelaker and W. Wedel, "Bird Bones, Burials, and Bundles in Plains Archaeology," *American Antiquity* 40, no. 4 (1975): 444–52.

30. S. Schama, *The Embarrassment of Riches: An Interpretation of Dutch Culture in the Golden Age* (New York: Alfred A. Knopf, 1987), 581.

31. Schama, *The Embarrassment of Riches*, 389, 391.

6. APARTMENT LIVING

1. N. Biddle, ed., *The Journals of the Expedition under the Command of Capt^s. Lewis and Clark, to the Sources of the Missouri, thence across the Rocky Mountains, and down to the River Columbia to the Pacific Ocean, Performed during the years 1804-5-6, by Order of the Government of the United States*, 2 vols. (New York: Heritage Press, 1962), 455.

2. L. Marshall, "Sharing, Talking and Giving: Relief of Social Tensions among !Kung Bushmen," *Africa* 31, no. 3 (1961): 231–49.

3. There is a vast literature on Çatalhöyük, including technical reports and popular syntheses. For a lavishly illustrated summary of James Mellaart's 1961–1965 excavations see his *Çatal Hüyük: A Neolithic Town in Anatolia* (London: Thames and Hudson, 1967); for Mellaart's annual excavation reports, see the annual *Anatolian Studies* from 1962–1966 (volumes 12–16). For an excellent overview of the more recent excavations directed by Ian Hodder, see his *The Leopard's Tale: Revealing the Mysteries of Çatalhöyük* (London: Thames and Hudson, 2006). For more technical discussions, see I. Hodder, "Çatalhöyük in the Context of the Middle Eastern Neolithic," *Annual Review of Anthropology* 36 (2007): 105–20; I. Hodder and C. Cessford, "Daily Practice and Social Memory at Çatalhöyük," *American Antiquity* 69, no. 1 (2004): 17–40, and a wealth of technical reports and data sets on the research project's at http://www.catalhoyuk.com.

4. Hodder, *The Leopard's Tale*, 98.

5. R. Waterson, *The Living House: An Anthropology of Architecture in South-East Asia* (London: Thames and Hudson, 1997).

6. G. Coupland and E. Banning, "Introduction: The Archaeology of Big Houses," in *People Who Lived in Big Houses: Archaeological Perspectives on Large Domestic Structures*, ed. G. Coupland and E. Banning, Monographs in World Archaeology 27 (Madison, WI: Prehistory Press, 1996), 1–9, esp. 1.

7. S. de Champlain, *Voyages of Samuel de Champlain 1604–1618*, ed. W. Grant (New York: Charles Scribner's Sons, 1907), 313–14; accessed March 11, 2010 via Google Books. See also D. Snow, *The Iroquois* (Malden, MA: Blackwell, 1994), 40–41, for an insightful analysis of this passage.

8. L.H. Morgan, *League of the Ho-dé-no-sau-nee or Iroquois* (New York: Burt Franklin, 1966 [1851]), 307.

9. The following is based on G. Warrick, "Evolution of the Iroquoian Longhouse," in *People Who Lived in Big Houses: Archaeological Perspectives on Large Domestic Structures*, ed. G. Coupland and E. Banning, Monographs in World Archaeology 27 (Madison, WI: Prehistory Press, 1996), 11–26.

10. G. Warrick, "The Precontact Iroquoian Occupation of Southern Ontario," in *Archaeology of the Iroquois: Selected Readings and Research Sources*, ed. J. Kerber (Syracuse, NY: Syracuse University Press, 2007), 124–63, esp. 127.

11. L. Morgan, *Houses and House-Life of the American Aborigines* (Chicago: University of Chicago Press, 1965 [1881]), 128–29.

12. For a discussion, see J. Birch, "Rethinking the Archaeological Application of Iroquoian Kinship," *Canadian Journal of Archaeology* 32 (2008): 194–213.

13. For an introduction to the extensive literature on matrilocal residence, see D. Levinson and M. Malone, *Toward Explaining Human Culture: A Critical Review of the Findings of Worldwide Cross-Cultural Research* (New Haven, CT: HRAF Press, 1980); M. Ember and C. Ember, "The Conditions Favoring Matrilocal vs. Patrilocal Residence," *American Anthropologist* 73, no. 3 (1971): 571–94; M. Helms, "Matrilocality, Social Solidarity and Culture Contact: Three Case Histories," *Southwestern Journal of Anthropology* 26 (1970): 197–212.

14. B. Trigger, *The Children of Aataentsic: A History of the Huron People to 1660;* (Kingston and Montreal: McGill-Queen's University Press, 1987), 45.

15. Trigger, *The Children of Aataentsic,* 115–17, 135–37; Snow, *The Iro-*

quois, 38–46; R. Williamson, "What Will Be Has Always Been: The Past and Present of Northern Iroquoians," in *Handbook of North American Archaeology,* ed. T Pauketat (Oxford: Oxford University Press, forthcoming).

16. M. Kapches, "The Iroquoian Longhouse: Architectural and Cultural Identity," in *Archaeology of the Iroquois: Selected Readings and Research Sources,* ed. J. Kerber (Syracuse, NY: Syracuse University Press, 2007), 174–88, esp. 176, and her "The Spatial Dynamics of Ontario Iroquoian Longhouses," *American Antiquity* 55, no.1 (1990): 49–67.

17. Morgan, *Houses and House-Life,* 66–67.

18. Warrick, "Evolution of the Iroquoian Longhouse," 12.

19. This discussion is based on E. Tooker, "Northern Iroquoian Sociopolitical Organization," *American Anthropologist* 72, no. 1 (1970): 90–97; Trigger, *The Children of Aataentsic,* 54–59; Morgan, *League of the Ho-dé-no-sau-nee or Iroquois,* 74–89; Snow, *The Iroquois,* 52–66. Note that Morgan uses the term "tribes" to refer to "clans."

20. Trigger, *The Children of Aataentsic,* 45.

21. W. Engelbrecht, "New York Iroquois Political Development," in *Archaeology of the Iroquois: Selected Readings and Research Sources,* ed. J. Kerber (Syracuse, NY: Syracuse University Press, 2007), 219–32.

22. For a fascinating description of a 1636 ceremony by the Jesuit Fr. Jean de Brebeuf, see K. Kidd, "The Excavation and Historical Identification of a Huron Ossuary," *American Antiquity,* 18, no. 4 (1953), 359–79.

23. Snow, *The Iroquois,* 111.

24. I discuss our findings at Quebrada Santa Cristina in two articles: "Cultural Responses to Environmental Catastrophes: Post–El Niño Subsistence on the Prehistoric North Coast of Peru," *Latin American Antiquity* 2 (1991): 27–47, and "Prehispanic Raised Field Agriculture in the Casma Valley: Recent Data, New Hypotheses," *Journal of Field Archaeology* 15 (1988): 265–76.

25. L. Wells, *Holocene Fluvial and Shoreline History as a Function of Human and Geologic Factors in Arid Northern Peru* (PhD diss., Stanford University, 1988).

26. An enormous archaeological literature exists for the North American Southwest, a canon of writings sufficiently diverse and deep to require its own historiography, for example: J. Snead, *Ruins and Rivals: The Making of Southwest Archaeology* (Tucson: University of Arizona Press, 2004); and L. Cordell and G. Gumerman, eds., *Dynamics of Southwest Prehistory* (Birmingham: University of Alabama Press, 2006). An excellent single-volume overview of the region's prehistory is L. Cordell, *Archaeology of the Southwest* (Walnut Creek: Left Coast Press, 1997); while S. Lekson's *A History of the Ancient Southwest* (Santa Fe, NM: School of Advanced Research Press, 2008) is a bold, multidimensional study of the prehistoric Southwest and the history of southwestern archaeology. For a review of the literature on abandonment, see M. Nelson and G. Schachner, "Understanding Abandonments in the North American Southwest," *Journal of Archaeological Research* 10, no. 2 (2002): 167–206.

27. Excellent overviews for the Hohokam have been provided by P. Crown, "The Hohokam of the American Southwest," *Journal of World Prehistory* 4, no. 2 (1990): 223–55; J. Bayman, "The Hohokam of Southwest North America,"

Journal of World Prehistory 15, no. 3 (2001): 257–310; and S. Fish and P. Fish, eds., *The Hohokam Millenium* (Santa Fe, NM: School for Advanced Research Press, 2008); each source has an extensive bibliography. Other studies referred to above include P. Crown, "Classic Period Hohokam Settlement and Land Use in the Casa Grande Ruins Area, Arizona," *Journal of Field Archaeology* 14, no. 2 (1987): 147–62. For the Mogollon region, see M. Blake, S. LeBlanc, and P. Minnis, "Changing Settlement and Population in the Mimbres Valley, SW New Mexico," *Journal of Field Archaeology* 13, no. 4 (1986): 439–64.

28. Chaco Canyon and the "Chaco Phenomena" have a vast archaeological literature; recent overviews include S. Lekson, "Chaco and Paquimé: Complexity, History, and Landscape," in *North American Archaeology*, ed. T. Pauketat and D. Loren, (Malden, MA: Blackwell, 2005), 235–72; and the articles in J. Kantner and N. Mahoney, *Great House Communities Across the Chacoan Landscape*, Anthropological Papers of the University of Arizona 64 (Tucson: University of Arizona Press, 2000). On Chaco's influence on other communities, see R. Van Dyke, "The Chaco Connection: Evaluating Bonito Style Architecture in Outlier Communities," *Journal of Anthropological Archaeology* 18, no. 4 (1999): 461–73, and "Chaco Reloaded: Discursive Social Memory on the Post-Chacoan Landscape," *Journal of Social Archaeology* 9, no. 2 (2009): 220–48. Also see Lekson's *Great Pueblo Architecture of Chaco Canyon*, Publications in Archaeology 18B, National Park Service (Albuquerque, 1984) and his provocative *Chaco Meridian: Centers of Political Power in the Ancient Southwest* (Walnut Creek, CA: Altamira Press, 1999).

29. S. Lekson, "Chaco and Paquimé," 241.

30. S. Lekson and C. Cameron, "The Abandonment of Chaco Canyon, the Mesa Verde Migrations, and the Reorganization of the Pueblo World," *Journal of Anthropological Archaeology* 14 (1995): 184–202.

31. W. Lipe, "Notes from the North," in *The Archaeology of Chaco Canyon: An Eleventh-Century Pueblo Regional Center*, ed. S. Lekson (Santa Fe, NM: SAR Press, 2006), 261–313; W. Lipe, "The Depopulation of the Northern San Juan: Conditions in the Turbulent 1200s," *Journal of Anthropological Archaeology* 14 (1995): 143–69.

32. T. Kohler, M. Varien, A. Wright, and K. Kuckleman, "Mesa Verde Migrations," *American Scientist* 96, no. 2 (2008): 146–53; W. Lipe and M. Varien, "Pueblo III (A.D. 1150–1300)" in *Colorado Prehistory: A Context for the Southern Colorado River Basin*, ed. W. Lipe, M. Varien, and R. Wilshusen (Cortez, CO: Colorado Council of Professional Archaeologists, 1999), 290–352. See also Lekson and Cameron, "The Abandonment of Chaco Canyon."

33. E. Morris, "The House of the Great Kiva at Aztec Ruins," *Anthropological Papers* 26, American Museum of Natural History (1921), 5; R. Lister and F. Lister, *Aztec Ruins on the Animas: Excavated, Preserved and Interpreted* (Santa Fe: University of New Mexico Press, 1987).

34. Kohler et al., "Mesa Verde Migrations," 153.

35. Lipe, "The Depopulation of the Northern San Juan," 163.

36. F. Ellis, "An Outline of Laguna Pueblo History and Social Organization," *Southwestern Journal of Anthropology* 15, no. 4 (1959): 325–47; L. White, "The

Acoma Indians," *Bureau of American Ethnology,* 47th Annual Report, Washington, DC (1929–30).

37. F. Ellis, "Where Did the People Come From?" *El Palacio* 74, no. 3 (1967): 35–43; L. Cordell, "Tracing Migration Pathways from the Receiving End," *Journal of Anthropological Archaeology* 14 (1995): 203–11.

38. M. Graves, W. Longacre, S. Holbrook, "Aggregation and Abandonment at Grasshopper Pueblo, Arizona," *Journal of Field Archaeology* 9, no. 2 (1982): 193–206.

39. W. Walker, V. Lamotta, E. Charles Adams, "Katsinas and Kiva Abandonment at Homol'ovi: A Deposit-Oriented Perspective on Religion in Southwest Prehistory," in *The Archaeology of Regional Interaction: Religion, Warfare, and Exchange Across the American Southwest and Beyond,* ed. M. Hegemon (Boulder, CO: University Press of Colorado, 2000), 341–60, esp. 342.

40. T. Ferguson, *Historic Zuni Architecture and Society: An Archaeological Application of Space Syntax,* Anthropological Papers of the University of Arizona 60 (1996), 145. Also see D. Triadan, "Dancing Gods: Performance and Political Organization in the Prehistoric Southwest," in *Archaeology of Performance: Theaters of Power, Community, and Politics,* ed. T. Inomata and L. Coben, (Lanham, MD: Altamira Press, 2006) 159–86; and Lekson and Cameron, "The Abandonment of Chaco Canyon," 191–94.

41. R. Rappaport, *Pigs for the Ancestors: Ritual in the Ecology of a New Guinea People* (New Haven, CT: Yale University Press, 1968). This discussion draws on the following articles, M. Bandy, "Fissioning, Scalar Stress, and Social Evolution in Early Village Societies," *American Anthropologist* 106, no. 2 (2004): 322–33; M. Friesen, "Resource Structure, Scalar Stress, and the Development of Inuit Social Organization," *World Archaeology* 31, no. 1 (1999): 21–37; and M. Adler and R. Wilshusen, "Large-Scale Integrative Facilities in Tribal Societies: Cross-Cultural and Southwestern US Examples," *World Archaeology,* 22, no. 2 (1990): 133–46.

42. For a discussion of utopian experiments, see C. Erasmus, *In Search of the Common Good: Utopian Experiments Past and Future* (New York: Free Press, 1977).

43. J. Levy, *Orayvi Revisited: Social Stratification in an "Egalitarian" Society.* (Santa Fe, NM: SAR Press, 1992); and C. Cameron, "Room Size, Organization of Construction, and Archaeological Interpretation in the Puebloan Southwest," *Journal of Anthropological Archaeology* 18 (1999): 201–39.

7. GATED COMMUNITIES

Epigraph: D. Hare, "Wall: A Monologue," *New York Review of Books* 56, no. 7 (2009): 8.

1. Herodotus, *The Histories,* trans. A. de Sélincourt (Harmondsworth, UK: Penguin, 1975), 81–83.

2. A. Layard, *Early Adventures in Persia, Susiana, and Babylonia, Including a Residence among the Bakhtiyari and Other Wild Tribes Before the Discovery of Nineveh* (London: John Murray, 1887).

3. M. Van De Mieroop, *The Ancient Mesopotamian City* (Oxford: Oxford University Press, 1999); S. Pollock, *Ancient Mesopotamia: The Eden that Never Was* (Cambridge: Cambridge University Press, 1999).

4. Pollock, *Ancient Mesopotamia*, 47.

5. A.R. George, trans., *The Epic of Gilgamesh: the Babylonian Epic Poem and Other Texts in Akkadian and Sumerian* (London: Penguin, 1999).

6. S. Dyson, *Rome: A Living Portrait of an Ancient City* (Baltimore, MD: Johns Hopkins University Press, 2010), 18, 342.

7. N. Davis, *Europe: A Brief History,* (New York: Harper Perennial, 1996), 306, 335.

8. http://bldgblog.blogspot.com/2008/03/trenches-of-approach.html.

9. W.G. Sebald, *Austerlitz,* trans. A. Bell (New York: Modern Library, 2001), 16.

10. Sebald, *Austerlitz,* 19.

11. D. Breeze and B. Dobson, "Hadrian's Wall: Some Problems," *Britannia* 3 (1972): 182–208; D. Breeze and B. Dobson, "The Development of the Mural Frontier in Britain from Hadrian to Caracalla," *Proceedings of the Society of Antiquaries of Scotland* 102 (1969–70), 107–21; D. Breeze, "Roman Forces and Native Populations," *Proceedings of the Society of Antiquaries of Scotland* 115 (1985), 223–28.

12. R. Shippee, "The 'Great Wall of Peru' and Other Aerial Photographic Studies by the Shippee-Johnson Peruvian Expedition," *Geographical Review,* 22, no. 1 (1932): 1–29; see also C. Roosevelt, "Ancient Civilizations of the Santa Valley and Chavin," *Geographical Review,* 25, no. 1 (1935): 21–42; and W. Denevan, "The 1931 Shippee-Johnson Aerial Photography Expedition to Peru," *Geographical Review,* 83, no. 3 (1993): 238–51.

13. D. Wilson, *Prehispanic Settlement Patterns in the Lower Santa Valley: A Regional Perspective on the Origins and Development of Complex North Coast Society* (Washington, DC: Smithsonian Institution Press, 1988), 251–55, 258–59.

14. A.N. Waldron, "The Problem of the Great Wall of China," *Harvard Journal of Asiatic Studies* 43, no. 2 (1983): 643–63. N. Hines, "China Finds Another 1,000 Miles of the Great Wall," *Times* (London), April 20, 2009, accessed May 6, 2009 at http://www.timesonline.co.uk/tol/news/world/asia/article6134158.ece.

15. W. Harmless, *Desert Christians: An Introduction to the Literature of Early Monasticism* (Oxford: Oxford University Press, 2004), 85. See also J. Gribomant, "Monasticism and Asceticism: I Eastern Christianity," in *Christian Spirituality: Origins to the Twelfth Century,* ed. B. McGinn, J. Leclerq, and J. Meyerdoff, (London: Routledge, 1985), 89–112.

16. Athanasius, *Life of St. Antony,* quoted in Harmless, *Desert Christians,* 65.

17. Harmless, *Desert Christians,* 86.

18. On Kellia, see A. Guillaumont's brief 1964 note, "Le site de 'Cellia' (Basse Égypte)," *Revue archéologique* (July–September): 43–50; P. Miquel, A. Guillaumont, M. Rassart-Debergh, Ph. Bridel, and A. de Vogue, *Déserts Chrétiens d'Égypte* (Nice: Culture Sud, 1993); and for an overview of the Coptic architectural traditions, see A. Badawy, *Coptic Art and Archaeology* (Cambridge, MA: MIT Press, 1978).

19. V. Turner, *The Ritual Process: Structure and Anti-Structure* (New York: Aldine, 1969), 95.

20. G. Barnes, "An Introduction to Buddhist Archaeology," *World Archaeology* 27, no. 2 (1995): 165–82. In the same volume of *World Archaeology*, see also, D. Chakrabarti, "Buddhist Sites across South Asia as Influenced by Political Economic Forces," 185–202, and R. Coningham, "Monks, Caves and Kings: A Reassessment of the Nature of Early Buddhism in Sri Lanka," 222–42. See also Coningham's excellent overview, "The Archaeology of Buddhism," in *Archaeology and World Religions*, ed. T. Insoll (London: Routledge, 2001), 61–95.

21. For overviews to Chan Chan and the Chimú Empire, see: M. Moseley and K. Day, eds., *Chan Chan: Andean Desert City* (Santa Fe: University of New Mexico Press, 1982); M. Moseley and A. Cordy-Collins, eds., *The Northern Dynasties: Kingship and Statecraft in Chimor* (Washington, DC: Dumbarton Oaks, 1990); J. Moore and C. Mackey, "The Chimú Empire," in *The Handbook of South American Archaeology*, ed. H. Silverman and W. Isbell (New York: Springer, 2008), 783–807. On Chan Chan's royal compounds, see J. Pillsbury and B. Leonard, "Identifying Chimú Palaces: Elite Residential Architecture in the Late Intermediate Period," in *Palaces of the Ancient New World*, ed. S. Evans and J. Pillsbury (Washington, DC: Dumbarton Oaks, 2004), 247–98.

22. S. Uceda, "Esculturas en miniatura y una maqueta en Madera: El Culto a los Muertos y a los Ancestros en la época Chimú," *Beiträge zur Allgemeinen und Vergleichenden Archäogie* 19 (1999): 259–311.

23. C. Lévi-Strauss, *The Savage Mind* (Chicago: University of Chicago Press, 1966), 23. For a discussion of the archaeology of such dedicated objects, see R. Osborne, "Hoards, Votives, Offerings: The Archaeology of the Dedicated Object," *World Archaeology* 36, no. 1 (2004): 1–10.

24. W. Horn and E. Born, *The Plan of St. Gall: A Study of the Architecture and Economy of and Life in a Paradigmatic Carolingian Monastery*, 3 vols. (Berkeley: University of California Press, 1979), 1:328.

25. Horn and Born, *The Plan of St. Gall*, 1:241.

26. R. Gilchrist, *Gender and Material Culture: The Archaeology of Religious Women* (New York: Routledge, 1997), 40–42.

27. R. Gilchrist, *Gender and Material Culture*, 19.

28. R. Gilchrist, "Unsexing the Body: The Interior Sexuality of Medieval Religious Women" in *Archaeologies of Sexuality*, ed. R. Schmidt and B. Voss (London: Routledge, 2000), 89–103, esp. 89.

29. Gilchrist, *Gender and Material Culture*, 139.

30. Gilchrist, *Gender and Material Culture*, 144.

31. Gilchrist, *Gender and Material Culture*, 144.

32. Quoted in Gilchrist, *Gender and Material Culture*, 144.

33. See, for example, L. Nevett, "Separation or Seclusion? Towards an Archaeological Approach to Investigating Women in the Greek Household in the Fifth to Third Centuries B.C.," in *Architecture and Order: Approaches to Social Space*, ed. M. Pearson and C. Richards, (London: Routledge, 1994), 98–112; D. Small, "Initial Study of the Structure of Women's Seclusion in the Archaeological Past," in *The Archaeology of Gender: Proceedings of the 22ⁿᵈ Annual Chacmool Con-*

ference, ed. D. Walde and N. Willows (Calgary: Department of Anthropology, University of Calgary, 1991), 336–42.

34. The term *Swahili* is broadly applied to occupants of the East African coast, derived from the Arabic word for "coast," *sahil*. For introductions to the fascinating archaeology of this region, see M. Horton, "Swahili Architecture, Space, and Social Structure," in *Architecture and Order: Approaches to Social Space,* ed. M. Pearson and C. Richards (London: Routledge, 1994), 147–69; M. Horton and J. Middleton, *The Swahili: Social Landscape of a Mercantile Society* (Malden, MA: Wiley-Blackwell, 2000); L. Donley-Reid, "House Power: Swahili Space and Symbolic Markers," in *Symbolic and Structural Archaeology,* ed. I. Hodder (Cambridge: Cambridge University Press, 1982), 63–73; and L. Donley-Reid, "Life in the Swahili Town House Reveals the Symbolic Meaning of Spaces and Artefact Assemblages," *African Archaeological Review* 5 (1987): 181–92; A. LaViolette, "Swahili Cosmopolitanism in Africa and the Indian Ocean World, A.D. 600–1500," *Archaeologies: Journal of the World Archaeological Congress* 4, no. 1 (2008): 24–49.

35. Donley-Reid, "House Power," 63.

36. Donley-Reid, "House Power," 65.

37. A marriage between patrilateral parallel cousins, in ethnographic jargon.

38. The 1997 estimate cited by S. Low, "Incorporation and Gated Communities in the Greater Metro–Los Angeles Region as a Model of Privatization of Residential Communities" *Home Cultures* 5, no. 1 (2008): 85–108; additional data from biennial American Housing Survey accessed online at www.census .gov/hhes/www/housing/ahs/ nationaldata.html.

39. For a history of the founding of Chiefland Astronomy Village, see https:// www.tomclarkbooks.com/tomclarkbooks.com/Chiefland_EX_I.html.

40. S. Low, "The Edge and the Center: Gated Communities and the Discourse of Urban Fear," *American Anthropologist* 103, no. 1 (2001): 45–58; and S. Low, "Urban Fear: Building Fortress America," *City and Society* (Annual Review) (1997): 52–72.

41. E. Vesselinov, *Journal of Urban Affairs* 29, no. 2 (2007): 109–27.

42. B. Ehrenreich, "Hell is a Gated Community," *The Progressive* 72, no. 2 (2008): 12–13. For additional discussions, see E. Blakely and M. Snyder, *Fortress America: Gated Communities in the United States* (Washington, DC: Brookings Institute Press, 1997); M. Davis, "Fortress LA," in *City of Quartz: Excavating the Future in Los Angeles* (London: Verso, 1990).

43. T. Sanchez, R. Lang, and D. Dhavale, "Security versus Status? A First Look at the Census's Gated Community Data," *Journal of Planning Education and Research* 24 (2005): 281–91.

8. NOBLE HOUSES

1. Possibly a reference to a previous Inca king, Huaynacapac. A. Hocquenghem, *Para Vencer la Muerte,* Travaux de l'Institut d'Études Andines 109 (1998): 236.

2. A. del Solar y Taboada, "Relación de los servicios de Indias de don Juan

Ruiz de Arce, conquistador del Perú," *Boletín de la Académica de la Historia* 102 (1933): 358.

3. A. Zarate, *The Discovery and Conquest of Peru,* trans. J. Cohen (London: The Folio Society, 1981 [1555]), 71.

4. P. Pizarro, *Relation of the Discovery and Conquest of the Kingdoms of Peru,* trans. P. Means (New York: The Cortes Society, 1921 [1571]), 164.

5. A. Enriquez de Guzman, *The Life and Acts of Don Alonzo Enriquez de Guzman, 1518–1543,* trans. C. Markham (London: The Hakluyt Society, 1862 [1543]), 95.

6. J. Quilter, preface to *Palace of the Ancient New World,* ed. S. Evans and J. Pillsbury (Washington, DC: Dumbarton Oaks, 1998), vii–viii.

7. More than a century since his death, Schliemann continues to fascinate and enrage. See his classic accounts, *Troy and Its Remains: A Narrative of Researches and Discoveries Made on the Side of Ilium and in the Trojan Plain* (London: John Murray, 1875) and *Mycenae: A Narrative of Researches and Discoveries at Mycenae and Tiryns* (New York: Scribner Armstrong, 1880). On the discovery of "Priam's Treasure," see D. Traill, "Schliemann's Discovery of 'Priam's Treasure': A Re-Examination of the Evidence," *The Journal of Hellenic Studies* 104 (1984): 96–115, esp. 99. For the debates about Schliemann's self-mythologizing and exaggerations, see W. M. Calder, III and D. A. Traill, eds., *Myth, Scandal, and History: The Heinrich Schliemann Controversy* (Detroit: Wayne State University Press, 1986). For alternative perspectives, see O. Dickinson, "The 'Face of Agamemnon,'" *Hesperia* 74, no. 3 (2005): 299–308; and D. Easton, "Heinrich Schliemann: Hero or Fraud?" *The Classical World* 91, no. 5 (1998): 335–43.

8. Easton, "Heinrich Schliemann ," 341.

9. Cited by J. Driessen, *An Early Destruction in the Mycenaean Palace at Knossos: A New Interpretation of the Excavation Field Notes of the South-East Area of the West Wing,* Acta Archaeological Lovaniensia Monographie 2 (Leuven: Leuven Unviersity Press, 1990), 5.

10. A. Evans, "Summary Report of the Excavations in 1900: I. The Palace," *The Annual of the British School at Athens,* 6 (1899/1900): 3–70, esp. 12–14.

11. S. Alcock and J. Cherry, "The Mediterranean World," in *The Human Past,* ed. C. Scarre (London: Thames and Hudson, 2009), 472–517, esp. 480.

12. H. Bingham, *Lost City of the Incas: The Story of Machu Picchu and Its Builders.* (New York: Atheneum, 1965 [1948]), 152–53.

13. Alcock and Cherry, "The Mediterranean World," 480.

14. The following discussion of Lerna and the House of Tiles is based on the excavations directed by J. Caskey. For a brief "touristic" overview to the site, see J. Caskey and E. T. Blackburn, *Lerna in the Argolid: A Short Guide* (Princeton, NJ: American School of Classical Studies at Athens, 1997). Annual site reports for the 1952–1958 field seasons were published between 1954 and 1960 in *Hesperia* (volumes 23–29), these are cited and summarized by Caskey in "The Early Helladic Period in the Argolid," *Hesperia* 29, no. 3 (1960): 285–303; and in "Lerna in the Early Bronze Age," *American Journal of Archaeology* 72, no. 4 (1968): 313–16. For studies of the clay seals from Lerna, see M. Heath Wiencke, "Early Helladic Clay Sealings from the House of the Tiles at Lerna," *Hespe-*

ria 27, no. 2 (1958): 81–121, and "Further Seals and Sealings from Lerna," *Hesperia* 38, no. 4 (1969): 500–21. For an interesting discussion of craft specialization as it relates to the chipped stone industry at Lerna, see B. Hartenberger and C. Runnels, "The Organization of Flaked Stone Production at Bronze Age Lerna," *Hesperia* 70, no. 3 (2001): 255–83.

15. Caskey, "The Early Helladic Period in the Argolid," 289.

16. J. Shaw, "The Early Helladic II Corridor House: Development and Form." *American Journal of Archaeology* 91, no. 1 (1987): 59–79, esp. 78.

17. M. Heath Wiencke, "Change in Early Helladic II," *American Journal of Archaeology* 93, no. 4 (1989): 495–509.

18. C. Renfrew, *The Emergence of Civilisation: The Cyclades and the Aegean in the Third Millennium B.C.* (London: Methuen, 1972).

19. J. Cherry, "Polities and Palaces: Some Problems in Minoan State Formation," in *Peer Polity Interaction and Socio-Political Change,* ed. C. Renfrew and J. Cherry (Cambridge: Cambridge University Press, 1986), 19–46; B. Cunliffe, *Europe Between the Oceans, 9000 BC–AD 1000,* (New Haven, CT: Yale University Press, 2008), 188–95. On Minoan palaces, see L. Hitchcock, *Minoan Architecture: A Contextual Analysis,* Studies in Mediterranean Archaeology and Literature 15, (Jonsered: Paul Åströms Förlag, 2000); and J. McEnroe, *Architecture of Minoan Crete: Constructing Identity in the Aegean Bronze Age* (Austin: University of Texas Press, 2010). For a critical review of assumptions about Minoan palaces, see I. Schoep, "Assessing the Role of Architecture in Conspicuous Consumption in the Middle Minoan I–II Periods," *Oxford Journal of Archaeology* 23, no. 3 (2004): 243–69.

20. McEnroe, *Architecture of Minoan Crete,* 69.

21. D. Preziosi and L. Hitchcock, *Aegean Art and Architecture* (Oxford: Oxford University Press, 1999), 64–65.

22. B. Bowser, "From Pottery to Politics: An Ethnoarchaeological Study of Political Factionalism, Ethnicity and Domestic Pottery Style in the Ecuadorian Amazon," *Journal of Archaeological Method and Theory* 7, no. 3 (2000): 219–40; and "The Amazonian House," *Expedition* 46, no. 2 (2004): 18–23; B. Bowser and J. Patton, "Domestic Spaces as Public Places: An Ethnoarchaeological Case Study of Houses, Gender, and Politics in the Ecuadorian Amazon," *Journal of Archaeological Method and Theory* 11, no.2 (2004): 157–81; and "Learning and Transmission of Pottery Style: Women's Life Histories and Communities of Practice in the Ecuadorian Amazon," in *Cultural Transmission and Material Culture: Breaking Down the Boundaries,* ed. M. Stark, B. Bowser, and L. Horne (Tucson: University of Arizona Press, 2008), 105–29; and "Women's Leadership: Political Alliance, Economic Resources, and Reproductive Success in the Ecuadorian Amazon," in *The Emergence of Leadership: Transitions in Decision Making from Small-Scale to Middle-Range Societies,* ed. K. Vaughn, J. Kantner, and J. Eerkens (Santa Fe, NM: School of Advanced Research Press, 2009), 51–71; J. Patton, "Meat Sharing for Coalitional Support," *Evolution and Human Behavior* 26 (2005): 137–57.

23. Bowser, "From Pottery to Politics," 229.

24. "Ancient Cult of the Viking Kings," *Copenhagen Post,* October 12, 2009, accessed on June 7, 2010 at http://www.cphpost.dk/culture/denmark-through

-the-looking-glass/47182-ancient-cult-of-the-viking-kings.html; see J. Niles, ed., *Beowulf and Lejre,* Arizona Center for Medieval and Renaissance Studies (Phoenix: Arizona State University, 2007).

25. P. Nabokov and R. Easton, *Native American Architecture* (Oxford: Oxford University Press, 1989), 227–84.

26. J. Cook, *A Voyage to the Pacific Ocean Undertaken by the Command of His Majesty* (Dublin: Lord Commissioners of the Admiralty, 1784), 2:314–17. Note: "train-oil" refers to oil made from whale blubber.

27. See footnotes in Cook, *A Voyage to the Pacific Ocean,* 317–18.

28. The following discussion is based on the extensive writings of Kenneth Ames. For overviews see his "The Archaeology of the Longue Durée: Temporal and Spatial Scale in the Evolution of Social Complexity on the Southern Northwest Coast," *Antiquity* 65 (1991): 935–45; "The Northwest Coast: Complex Hunter-Gatherers, Ecology and Social Evolution," *Annual Reviews of Anthropology* 23 (1994): 209–29; and "The Northwest Coast," *Evolutionary Anthropology* 12 (2003): 19–33. On the development of Northwest Coast plank houses, see "Life in the Big House: Household Labor and Dwelling Size on the Northwest Coast," in *People Who Lived in Big Houses, Archaeological Perspectives on Large Domestic Structures,* ed. C. Coupland and E. Banning (Madison, WI: Prehistory Press, 1996), 178–200. On household economy and chiefly power, see "Chiefly Power and Household Production on the Northwest Coast," in *Foundations of Social Inequality,* ed. T. Price and G. Feinman (New York: Plenum, 1995), 155–87; and "Thinking about Household Archaeology on the Northwest Coast," in *Household Archaeology on the Northwest Coast,* ed. E. Sobal, D. Trieu Gahr, and K. Ames (Ann Arbor, MI: International Monographs in Prehistory, 2006), 16–36.

29. Ames, "Chiefly Power and Household Production," 163–69.

30. L. Donald, *Aboriginal Slavery on the Northwest Coast of North America* (Berkeley: University of California Press, 1997), 34.

31. Aristotle, *Politics,* book 1, section 1253b.

32. Ames, "Chiefly Power and Household Production," 171.

33. F. Boas and G. Hunt, "The Social Organization and Secret Societies of the Kwakiutl Indians," *Report of the National Museum for 1895* (Washington, DC: Government Printing Office, 1895), 311–737.

34. Boas and Hunt, "The Social Organization and Secret Societies of the Kwakiutl Indians," 346.

35. C. Lévi-Strauss, *The Way of the Masks,* trans. S. Modeleski (Vancouver: Douglas and McIntyre Limited, 1983); see also R. Joyce and S. Gillespie, eds., *Beyond Kinship: Social and Material Reproduction in House Societies* (Philadelphia: University of Pennsylvania Press, 2000); and R. Beck, Jr., ed., *The Durable House: House Society Models in Archaeology,* Center for Archaeological Investigations, Occasional Paper 35 (Carbondale: Southern Illinois University, 2007).

36. Ames, "Chiefly Power and Household Production," 180.

37. D. Vigil, "Anatomy of a Man Room, Where Men Can Be Men," *SFGate,* February 1, 2009, accessed June 10, 2010 at http://www.sfgate.com/cgi-bin/article.cgi?f = /c/a/2009/02/01/HO6F15F905.DTL#ixzzoqSt8rU6W.

9. SACRED HOMES

1. Lord Raglan, *The Temple and the House* (London: Routledge and Kegan Paul, 1964). A sense of Raglan's eccentricities is given in the first paragraph: "The theory put forward in this book is that houses were originally neither shelters nor dwellings but temples, that is to say buildings erected for ritual purposes. To those who would reject this theory out of hand I suggest a comparison with men's hats," ix. For a contemporary review of Raglan's study, see E. Leach, "Testament of an English Eccentric," *New York Review of Books,* Sept. 16, 1965, accessed at http://www.nybooks.com/articles/archives/1965/sep/16/testament-of-an-english-eccentric.

2. E. Leach, "The Gatekeepers of Heaven: Anthropological Aspects of Grandiose Architecture," *Journal of Anthropological Research* 39, no. 3 (1983): 243–64, esp. 243–44.

3. R. Bradley, "A Life Less Ordinary: The Ritualization of the Domestic Sphere in Later Prehistoric Europe," *Cambridge Archaeological Journal* 13, no. 1 (2003): 5–23.

4. For discussion, see C. Tilley, *An Ethnography of the Neolithic: Early Prehistoric Societies in Southern Scandinavia* (Cambridge: Cambridge University Press, 1996), 62–66.

5. M. Mixco, *Kiliwa Texts: "When I Have Donned My Crest of Stars,"* University of Utah Anthropological Papers 107 (1983), 48 and 47.

6. One notable exception is the large prehistoric village described by Matthew DesLauriers on Isla Cedros just off the central Pacific Coast of Baja California, where DesLauriers has mapped some 481 house pits at a single site.

7. J. Baegert, *The Letters of Jacob Baegert, 1749–1761: Jesuit Missionary in Baja California,* trans. E. Schulz-Bischof and ed. D.B. Nunis, Jr. (Los Angeles: Dawson's Book Shop, 1982), 92

8. P. Meigs, "The Kiliwa Indians of Lower California," *Ibero-Americana* 15 (Berkeley: University of California Press, 1939).

9. M. Beard, *The Fires of Vesuvius: Pompeii Lost and Found* (Cambridge, MA: Harvard University Press, 2009) 279, 285. For an overview of the spatial order of Roman houses, see A. Wallace-Hadrill, *Houses and Society in Pompeii and Herculaneum* (Princeton: Princeton University Press, 1994), especially his discussion of the allusions between domestic and public architecture, 17–37. For a provocative phenomenological discussion of the Roman house, see C. Knight's "The Spatiality of the Roman Domestic Setting: An Interpretation of Symbolic Content," in *Architecture and Order: Approaches to Social Space,* ed. M. Pearson and C. Richards (London: Routledge, 1994), 113–46. For the archaeobotanical analysis of Pompeian domestic offerings, see M. Robinson, "Domestic Burnt Offerings and Sacrifices at Roman and Pre-Roman Pompeii, Italy," *Vegetation History and Archaeobotany* 11 (2002): 93–99.

10. "Mana" as the early twentieth-century French anthropologists Hubert and Mauss defined it, is "not only a force, a being; it is also an action, a quality and a state. In other words, the term is at once a noun, an adjective and a verb." M. Mauss and H. Hubert, *A General Theory of Magic,* trans. R. Brain (London: Routledge, 2001 [1902]), 133. Given the complexity of the concept and the elusiveness of its definition, not surprisingly a large theoretical literature exists;

a critical introduction is found in R. Keesing's "Rethinking 'Mana,'" *Journal of Anthropological Research*, 40, no. 1 (1984): 137–56. For recent discussions of the distribution of the word and concept of mana in Austronesian and Malayo-Polynesian languages, see R. Blust, "Proto-Oceanic *mana Revisited." *Oceanic Linguistics* 46 (2007): 404–23; J. Blevins, "Some Comparative Notes on Proto-Oceanic *mana: Inside and Outside the Austronesian Family," *Oceanic Linguistics*, 47, no. 2 (2008): 253–74. For the discussion of semangat and cognates in Malay and Indonesian languages, see R. Waterson's overview in *The Living House: An Anthropology of Architecture in South-East Asia* (London: Thames and Hudson, 1997), 115–18.

11. Waterson, *Living House*, 116.

12. D. Oliver, *The Pacific Islands* (New York: Natural History Library, American Museum of Natural History, 1961), 72–73.

13. P. Kirch and R. Green, *Hawaiki, Ancestral Polynesia: An Essay in Historical Anthropology* (Cambridge: Cambridge University Press, 2001), 239–41.

14. For overviews to the prehistoric settlement of the Pacific, see P. Kirch, *On the Road of the Winds: An Archaeological History of the Pacific Islands before the European Contact* (Berkeley: University of California Press, 2000); and P. Bellwood, *Man's Conquest of the Pacific: the Prehistory of Southeast Asia and Oceania* (Oxford: Oxford University Press, 1979), and *Prehistory of the Indo-Malaysian Archipelago* (Canberra: Australia National University Press, 2007).

15. R. Blust, "Austronesian Culture History: Some Linguistic Inferences and Their Relations to the Archaeological Record," *World Archaeology* 8, no. 1 (1976): 119–43, and "The Prehistory of the Austronesian-Speaking Peoples: A View from Language, " *Journal of World Prehistory* 9, no. 4 (1995): 453–510.

16. For a brief and lucid overview, see P. Kirch, "Lapita and Its Aftermath: The Austronesian Settlement of Oceania," *Transactions of the American Philosophical Society* 86, no. 5 (1996): 57–70.

17. Waterson, *Living House*, 118. Examples also from Waterson, pp. 89, 118.

18. T. Henry, *Ancient Tahiti*, Bernice P. Bishop Museum, Bulletin 48, (Honolulu, 1928), 342–43.

19. Henry, *Ancient Tahiti*, 426.

20. Kirch and Green, *Hawaiki, Ancestral Polynesia*, 249–54.

21. J. Davies journal quoted in *The History of the Tahitian Mission, 1799–1830 Written by John Davies*, ed. C. Newbury (London: Hakluyt Society; Cambridge: Cambridge University Press, 1961), 127–28, n. 2.

22. Cf. T. Henry, *Ancient Tahiti*, 135.

23. J. Kahn and J. Coil, "What House Posts Tell Us about Status Differences in Prehistoric Tahitian Society: An Interpretation of Charcoal Analysis, Sacred Woods, and Inter-site Variability," *Journal of the Polynesian Society*, 115, no. 4 (2006): 319–52, esp. 342.

24. For a brief critical review of issues of origins, see A. Kehoe, "Eliade and Hultkrantz: The European Primitivism Tradition," *American Indian Quarterly* 20, no. 3/4 (1996): 377–92.

25. E. Devlet, "Rock Art and Material Culture of Siberian and Central Asian

Shamanism," in *The Archaeology of Shamanism*, ed. N. Price (London: Routledge, 2001), 54.

26. R. Flannery, "The Shaking-Tent Rite among the Montagnais of James Bay," *Primitive Man* 12, no.1 (1939): 11–16.

27. See, for example, D. Collier, "Conjuring among the Kiowa," *Primitive Man* 17, no. 3/4 (1944): 45–49; J. Cooper, "The Shaking Tent Rite among Plains and Forest Algonquians," *Primitive Man* 17, no. 3/4 (1944): 60–84; R Flannery, "The Gros Ventre Shaking Tent," *Primitive Man* 17, no. 3/4 (1944): 54–59; A. Hallowell, "The Spirits of the Dead in Saulteaux Life and Thought," *Journal of the Royal Anthropological Institute of Great Britain and Ireland* 70, no. 1 (1940): 29–51.

28. D. Anderson, "Dwellings, Storage and Summer Site Structure among Siberian Orochen Evenkis: Hunter-Gatherer Vernacular Architecture under Post-Socialist Conditions," *Norwegian Archaeological Review* 39, no. 1 (2006): 1–26. For an excellent historical overview of twentieth-century perspectives on Siberian groups, see A. Sirina, "Soviet Traditions in the Study of Siberian Hunter-Gatherer Society" in *Hunter-Gatherers in History, Archaeology and Anthropology*, ed. A. Barnard (Oxford: Berg, 2004), 89–101.

29. A. Anisimov, "The Shaman's Tent of the Evenks and the Origin of the Shamanistic Rite," in *Studies in Siberian Shamanism*, ed. H. Michael (Toronto: University of Toronto Press, 1963), 84–123.

10. HOME FIRES

1. An extensive body of archaeological literature regarding Pompeii and Herculaneum is introduced to the general reader in Mary Beard's *The Fires of Vesuvius: Pompeii Lost and Found* (Cambridge, MA: Harvard University Press, 2008) and in Roger Ling's *Pompeii: History, Life and Afterlife* (Stroud, UK: Tempus, 2005); Paul Zanker's *Pompeii: Public and Private Life* (Cambridge, MA: Harvard University Press, 1998). For a brief introduction to the history of archaeological investigations, see Lale Özgenel, "A Tale of Two Cities: In Search for Ancient Pompeii and Herculaneum," Middle East Technical University (Ankara)—Journal of the Faculty of Architecture (METU-JFA) 25, no. 1 (2008): 1–25. For Pompeii houses, see A. Wallace-Hadrill, *House and Society in Pompeii and Herculaneum* (Princeton: Princeton University Press, 1994), and for Pompeii's households, see P.M. Allison's *Pompeian Households, An Analysis of the Material Culture*, Cotsen Institute of Archaeology, Monograph 42, University of California, Los Angeles (2004). For a fascinating overview of the significance of Pompeii and Herculaneum on western scholarship in the Renaissance, Enlightenment, and since, see the articles in the beautiful volume edited by V. Coates and J. Seydl, *Antiquity Recovered: The Legacy of Pompeii and Herculaneum* (Los Angeles: J. Paul Getty Museum, 2007), and the article by Penelope Allison, "Recurring Tremors: the Continuing Impact of the AD 79 Eruption of Mt. Vesuvius" in *Natural Disasters and Cultural Change*, ed. R. Torrence and J. Grattan (London: Routledge, 2002), 107–25.

2. H. Sigurdsson, S. Cashdollar, and S. Sparks, "The Eruption of Vesuvius in

A.D. 79: Reconstruction from Historical and Volcanological Evidence," *American Journal of Archaeology* 86, no.1 (1982): 39–51, esp. 40–41.

3. Sigurdsson et al., "The Eruption of Vesuvius," 49.

4. Ling, *Pompeii*, 13.

5. W.D. Howells, *Italian Journeys* (2004 [1867]), 67. Accessed online http://www.gutenberg.org/cache/epub/14276/pg14276.html

6. Beard, *The Fires of Vesuvius*, 7.

7. J.W. von Goethe, *Italian Journey*, trans. W.H. Auden and E. Mayer (Harmondsworth, UK: Penguin Classics, 1970 [1786–1788]), 203.

8. E.g., D. Thomas and R. Kelly, *Archaeology* (Belmont, CA: Thompson/Wadsworth, 2006), 117–18. The following discussion regarding Cerén is based on the long-term excavations directed by Payson Sheets. See the outstanding chapters in the volume edited by Sheets, *Before the Volcano Erupted: The Ancient Cerén Village in Central America* (Austin: University of Texas Press, 2002) and the associated webpage at ceren.colorado.edu. For additional discussions, see P. Sheets, H. Beaubien, M. Beaudry, A. Gerstle, B. McKee, C. Miller, H. Spetzler, and D. Tucker, "Household Archaeology at Cerén, El Salvador," *Ancient Mesoamerica* 1 (1990): 81–90; P. Sheets, "Provisioning the Cerén Household: The Vertical Economy, Village Economy and Household Economy in the Southeastern Maya Periphery," *Ancient Mesoamerica* 11 (2000): 217–30; and R. Dull, J. Southon, and P. Sheets, "Volcanism, Ecology and Culture: A Reassessment of the Volcán Ilopango Tbj eruption in the Southern Maya Realm," *Latin American Antiquity*, 12, no.1 (2001): 25–44.

9. Dull et al., "Volcanism, Ecology and Culture," 27.

10. L. Brown and A. Gerstle, "Structure 10: Feasting and Village Festivals," in *Before the Volcano Erupted: The Ancient Cerén Village in Central America*, ed. P. Sheets (Austin: University of Texas Press, 2002), 97–103, esp. 100. Although not cited above, Brown has done fascinating ethnoarchaeological research on ancient and modern ritual practices; see her articles "From Discard to Divination: Demarcating the Sacred Through the Collection and Curation of Discarded Objects," *Latin American Antiquity* 11, no. 4 (2000): 319–33; "Dangerous Places and Wild Spaces: Creating Meaning with Materials and Space at Contemporary Maya Shrines on El Duende," *Journal of Archaeological Method and Theory* 11, no. 1 (2004): 31–58; the article coauthored with K. Emery, "Negotiations with the Animate Forest: Hunting Shrines in the Guatemalan Highlands," *Journal of Archaeological Method and Theory* 15 (2008): 300–37; and the article coauthored with Sheets "Distinguishing Domestic from Ceremonial Structures in Southern Mesoamerica: Suggestions from Cerén, El Salvador," *Mayab* 13 (2000): 11–21.

11. H. Bankoff and F. Winter, "A House Burning in Serbia—What Do Burned Remains Tell an Archaeologist?" *Archaeology* 32 (1979): 8–14, esp. 14.

12. M. Stevanović, "The Age of Clay: The Social Dynamics of House Destruction," *Journal of Anthropological Archaeology* 16 (1997): 334–95, esp. 337.

13. Summarized in J. Chapman, "Deliberate House-Burning in the Prehistory of Central and Eastern Europe," in *Glyfer och arkeologiska rum: En vänbok till Jarl Nordbladh*, ed. A. Gustafsson and H. Karlsson (Göteborg: University of Göteborg Press, 1999), 113–26, esp. 115–18.

14. Stevanović, "The Age of Clay," 381, 387.

15. R. Tringham, "Engendered Places in Prehistory," *Gender, Place and Culture* 1 (1994): 169–203.

16. Stevanović, "The Age of Clay," 387.

17. Tell Arpachiyah was excavated in 1933 by the British archaeologist Max Mallowan. An overview of the excavations, a detailed discussion of the artifacts, and the hypothesis of ritual burning are presented by S. Campbell, "The Burnt House at Arpachiyah: A Reexamination," *Bulletin of the American Schools of Oriental Research* 318 (2000): 1–40

18. P. Akkermans and M. Verhoeven, "An Image of Complexity: The Burnt Village at Late Neolithic Sabi Abyad," *American Journal of Archaeology* 99, no. 1 (1995): 5–32. M. Verhoeven, "Death, Fire, and Abandonment: Ritual Practice at Late Neolithic Tell Sabi Abyad, Syria," *Archaeological Dialogues* 7, no. 1 (2000): 46–83.

19. J. Smyth, "The Role of the House in Early Neolithic Ireland," *European Journal of Archaeology* 9 (2006): 229–57.

20. W. Walker, "Stratigraphy and Practical Reason," *American Anthropologist* 104, no. 1 (2002): 169–77. The intentional burning of war victims' homes was observed historically in the aftermath of nineteenth-century battles between American Indian groups from the Lower Colorado River delta, who raided Maricopa settlements along the Salt and Gila rivers.

21. The most comprehensive recent overview of the mainland Chumash is Lynn Gamble's *The Chumash World At European Contact: Power, Trade and Feasting Among Complex Hunters and Gatherers* (Berkeley: University of California Press, 2008). For major overviews of archaeology and prehistory of adjacent Chumash territories, see J. Arnold, ed., *Origins of a Pacific Coast Chiefdom: The Chumash of the Channel Islands* (Salt Lake City: University of Utah Press, 2001) and *Foundations of Chumash Complexity* (Los Angeles: Cotsen Institute of Archaeology, University of California, Los Angeles, 2004); M. Glassow, *Purisimeño Chumash Prehistory: Maritime Adaptations along the Southern California Coast* (Orlando: Harcourt Brace, 1996); D. Kennet, *The Island Chumash: Behavioral Ecology of a Maritime Society* (Berkeley: University of California Press, 2005).

22. Reconstructions of Chumash village locations and populations are found in A. Brown, "The Aboriginal Population of the Santa Barbara Channel," *University of California Archaeological Survey Reports* 69 (1967); C. King, "Chumash Inter-village Economic Exchange," in *Native Californians: A Theoretical Retrospective,* ed. L. Bean and T. Blackburn (Ramona, CA: Ballena Press, 1976), 289–318; and Gamble, *The Chumash World,* 65–112.

23. J. Longinos Martinez, *Journal: Notes and Observations of the Naturalist of the Botanical Expedition in Old and New California and the South Coast, 1791–1702,* ed. and trans. L. Simpson (San Francisco: John Howell Publishers, 1961), 51.

24. H. Bolton, *Font's Complete Diary: A Chronicle of the Founding of San Francisco* (Berkeley: University of California Press, 1931), 251–52.

25. For overviews of Chumash architecture, see Gamble, *The Chumash World,* 113–49; T. Hudson and T. Blackburn, *The Material Culture of the Chu-*

mash Interaction Sphere, Vol. 11: Food Preparation and Shelter, Ballena Press Anthropological Papers 27 (1983); and L. Gamble, "Chumash Architecture: Sweatlodges and Houses," *Journal of California and Great Basin Anthropology,* 17, no. 1 (1995): 54–92.

26. Gamble, "Chumash Architecture," 56.

27. J. Moore, "A Late Prehistoric Homestead on the Santa Barbara Coast," in *Journal of California and Great Basin Anthropology* 9, no. 1 (1987): 100–109.

28. Gamble, "Chumash Architecture," 57.

29. C. Rodning, "Building and Rebuilding Cherokee Houses and Townhouses in Southwestern North Carolina," in *The Durable House: House Society Models in Archaeology,* ed. R. Beck, Jr., Center for Archaeological Investigations, Occasional Paper 35 (2007): 464–84; C. Rodning, "Domestic Houses at Coweeta Creek," *Southeastern Archaeology* 28 (2009): 1–26.

30. J. Mooney, "Myths of the Cherokee," *Bureau of American Ethnology, 19th Annual Report* (1900): 240–42.

31. Mooney, "Myths of the Cherokee," 502–3.

32. Rodning, "Building and Rebuilding Cherokee Houses," 474.

33. C. Rodning, "Mounds, Myths, and Cherokee Townhouses in Southwestern North Carolina," *American Antiquity* 74 (2009): 627–63; esp. 642.

34. Mooney, "Myths of the Cherokee," 396.

35. Rodning, "Building and Rebuilding Cherokee Houses," 476.

36. Rodning, "Mounds, Myths, and Cherokee Townhouses," 627.

37. Rodning, "Mounds, Myths, and Cherokee Townhouses," 654.

38. See A. Greenberg, "Lutyens's Cenotaph," *Journal of the Society of Architectural Historians* 48, no. 1 (1989): 5–23; M. Lin, "Making the Memorial," *New York Review of Books,* November 2, 2000; "WTC Memorial Jury Statement for Winning Design," January 13, 2004, at http://www.wtcsitememorial.org.

39. The Ise shrine is discussed in C. Humphrey and P. Vitebsky, *Sacred Architecture* (Boston: Little, Brown, 1997); J. Reynolds, "Ise Shrine and a Modernist Construction of Japanese Tradition," *The Art Bulletin,* 83, no. 2 (2001): 316–41; and F. Bock, "The Rites of Renewal at Ise," *Monumenta Nipponica,* 29, no. 1 (1974): 55–68.

11. GOING HOME

1. R. Wenke, "Egypt: Origins of Complex Society," *Annual Review of Anthropology* 18 (1989): 129–55, esp. 129.

2. A. Roth, "Social Change in the Fourth Dynasty: The Spatial Organization of Pyramids, Tombs, and Cemeteries," *Journal of the American Research Center in Egypt* 30 (1993): 33–55, esp. 40.

3. R. Wengrow, *The Archaeology of Early Egypt: Social Transformations in North-East Africa, 10,000 to 2650 BC.* (Cambridge: Cambridge University Press, 2006), 244.

4. B. Adams, "Locality 6 in 2000: Amazing Revelations," *Nekhen News* 13, no. 2 (2001): 4–7.

5. R. Friedman, "Excavating Egypt's Early Kings," *Nekhen News* 17 (2005): 4–6.

6. Wengrow, *The Archaeology of Early Egypt*, 71.

7. Wengrow, *The Archaeology of Early Egypt*, 94–98. For an outstanding overview of beer brewing in ancient Egypt and traditional Africa, see P. McGovern, *Uncorking the Past: The Quest for Wine, Beer and Other Alcoholic Beverages* (Berkeley: University of California Press, 2009), 241–65.

8. A. Stevens, "Domestic Religious Practices," in *UCLA Encyclopedia of Egyptology*, ed. W. Wendrich and J. Dieleman (Los Angeles: University of California, Los Angeles, 2009). Retrieved from: http://escholarship.org/uc/item/7s07628w p. 11.

9. The Proyecto Chimú Sur (1981–1986) was directed by Dr. Carol Mackey and Dr. Alexandra U. Klymyshyn and funded by the National Science Foundation, the Earthwatch Foundation, and other agencies. I am eternally grateful for the opportunity to participate in this project that, literally, changed my life.

10. For overviews, see O. Bar-Yosef, "Natufian Culture in the Levant, Threshold to the Origins of Agriculture," *Evolutionary Anthropology* 6 (1998): 159–77; D. Henry, *From Foraging to Agriculture: The Levant at the End of the Ice Age* (Philadelphia; University of Pennsylvania, 1989); A. Moore, "The Development of Neolithic Societies in the Near East," in *Advances in World Archaeology*, ed. F. Wendorf and A. Close (New York: Academic Press, 1985), 4:1–69. On architecture and ritual, see J. Cauvin, *The Birth of the Gods and the Origins of Agriculture* (Cambridge, Cambridge University Press, 2000); G. Rollefson, "Neolithic 'Ain Ghazal (Jordan): Ritual and Ceremony II" *Paléorient* 12, no. 1 (1986): 45–52; I. Kuijt, "Negotiating Equality through Ritual: A Consideration of Late Natufian and Prepottery Neolithic Period A Mortuary Practices," *Journal of Anthropological Archaeology* 15 (1996): 313–36; I. Kujit and M. Chesson, "Lumps of Clay and Pieces of Stone: Ambiguity, Bodies, and Identity as Portrayed in Neolithic Figurines," in *Archaeologies of the Middle East: Critical Perspectives*, ed. S. Pollack and R. Bernbeck (Malden, MA: Blackwell, 2005), 152–83.

11. B. Byrd, "Public and Private, Domestic and Corporate: The Emergence of the Southwest Asian Village," *American Antiquity* 59 (1994): 639–66, esp. 660.

12. M. Chesson, "Libraries of the Dead: Early Bronze Age Charnel Houses and Social Identity at Urban Bab edh-Dhra', Jordan," *Journal of Anthropological Archaeology* 18 (1999): 137–64.

13. For a synopsis of the genetic evidence for the spread of agriculture into Europe see C. Renfrew, "From Molecular Genetics to Archaeogenetics" *Proceedings of the National Academy of Sciences* 98, no. 9 (2001): 4830–32; accessed electronically at www.pnas.org/ogi/doi/10.1073/pnas.091084198. On the Kückhoven well and early Neolithic in temperate Europe, see P. Bahn, "The Great Wooden Well of Kückhoven," *Nature* 354 (1991): 269.

14. For an example, see E. Peltenburg and S. Colledge, "Agro-pastoralist Colonization of Cyprus in the 10th Millennium BP: Initial Assessments," *Antiquity* 74, no. 286 (2000), 844–53.

15. A. Whittle, *Europe in the Neolithic: The Creation of New Worlds* (Cambridge: Cambridge University Press, 1996), 144–74.

16. S. Milisauskas, "An Analysis of Linear Culture Longhouses at Olszanica B1, Poland," *World Archaeology* 4, no. 1 (1972), 57–74; S. Milisauskas and

J. Kruk, "Neolithic Economy in Central Europe," *Journal of World Prehistory* 3 (1989): 403–46.

17. Whittle, *Europe in the Neolithic*, 168.

18. I. Hodder, "Burials, Houses, Women and Men in the European Neolithic," in *Ideology, Power and Prehistory*, ed. D. Miller and C. Tilley (Cambridge: Cambridge University Press, 1984), 51–68; and "Architecture and Meaning: The Example of Neolithic Houses and Tombs," in *Architecture and Order: Approaches to Social Space*, ed. M. Parker Pearson and C. Richards (London: Routledge, 1994), 73–86.

19. Hodder, "Architecture and Meaning," 80.

20. Whittle, *Europe in the Neolithic*, 169.

21. D. Lathrap, J. Marcos, and J. Zeidler, "Real Alto: An Ancient Ceremonial Center," *Archaeology* 30 (1977): 2–13; J. Marcos, *The Ceremonial Precinct at Real Alto: Organization of Time and Space in Valdivia Society* (PhD diss., University of Illinois, Urbana-Champaign, 1978); J. Marcos, "A Reassessment of the Ecuadorian Formative," in *The Archaeology of Formative Ecuador*, ed. J. Raymond and R. Burger (Washington, DC: Dumbarton Oaks, 2003), 7–32; J. Zeidler, *Social Space in Valdivia Society: Community Patterning and Domestic Structure at Real Alto, 3000–2000 BC* (PhD diss., University of Illinois, Urbana-Champaign, 1984); J. Zeidler, "The Ecuadorian Formative," in *Handbook of South American Archaeology*, ed. H. Silverman and W. Isbell (New York: Springer, (2008), 459–88.

22. Marcos, *The Ceremonial Precinct at Real Alto*, 42.

23. M. Haines and R. Avery, "The American Life Table of 1830–1860: An Evaluation," *Journal of Interdisciplinary History* 11, no. 1 (1980): 73–95, esp. 84.

24. G. Laderman, *The Sacred Remains: American Attitudes Toward Death, 1799–1883*. (New Haven, CT: Yale University Press, 1996), 24.

25. M. Haines, "The Urban Mortality Transition in the United States," *National Bureau of Economic Research* (2001): 5; for a valuable review, see S. Preston, "Mortality Trends," *Annual Review of Sociology* 3 (1977): 163–78.

26. Laderman, *The Sacred Remains*, 25.

27. Laderman, *The Sacred Remains*, 26.

28. Laderman, *The Sacred Remains*, 29.

29. Just to cite one robust line of archaeological research, there is a large literature on the religious practices of African-American slaves in the antebellum American South and in the Caribbean; for overviews, see C. Orser, "The Archaeology of African-American Slave Religion in the Antebellum South," *Cambridge Archaeological Journal* 4, no. 1 (1994): 33–45; and C. Fennell, "Early African America: Archaeological Studies of Significance and Diversity," *Journal of Archaeological Research*, (2010) Springer, published online 15 July 2010, accessed http://o-www.springerlink.com.torofind.csudh.edu/content/ 5g1q344n 152071m8/fulltext.pdf; and for two case studies, P. Stamford, "The Archaeology of African-American Slavery and Material Culture," *The William and Mary Quarterly* 53, no. 1 (1996): 87–114; and P. Stamford, "'Strong is the Bond of Kinship': West African–Style Ancestor Shrines and Subfloor Pits on African-American Quarters," in *Historical Archaeology, Identity Formation, and the Interpretation of Ethnicity,*

ed. M. Franklin and G. Fessler (Colonial Williamsburg Research Publications, Colonial Williamsburg Foundation, Virginia, 1999), 71–91.

30. Laderman, *The Sacred Remains*, 55.

31. Laderman, *The Sacred Remains*, 52.

32. D. Smith and J. Hacker, "Cultural Demography: New England Deaths and the Puritan Perception of Risk," *Journal of Interdisciplinary History*, 26, no. 3 (1996): 367–92, esp. 375.

33. Laderman, *The Sacred Remains*, 55.

34. Details of the funeral procession to Illinois are in R. Newman, "'In This Sad World of Ours, Sorrow Comes to All': A Timetable for the Lincoln Funeral Train," *Journal of the Illinois State Historical Society* 58, no. 1 (1965): 5–20. On the plot to steal Lincoln's corpse, see T. Craughwell, *Stealing Lincoln's Body* (Cambridge, MA: Harvard University Press, 2007). For an excellent online resource, see the "Abraham Lincoln Research Site" at http://rogerjnorton.com/Lincoln.html (accessed September 23, 2010). For a fascinating study of the reburial tradition in American history, see M. Kammen, *Digging up the Dead: A History of Notable American Reburials* (Chicago: University of Chicago Press, 2010).

35. G. Laderman, *Rest in Peace: A Cultural History of the Death and the Funeral Home in Twentieth-Century America* (Oxford: Oxford University Press, 2003), 6–7.

36. E. Dethlefsen and J. Deetz, "Death's Heads, Cherubs and Willow Trees: Experimental Archaeology in Colonial Cemeteries," *American Antiquity* 31, no. 4 (1966): 502–10, esp. 506.

37. Dethlefsen and Deetz, "Death's Heads," 508.

38. J. Moore, C. Blaker, and G. Smith, "Cherished Are the Dead: Changing Social Dimensions in a Kansas Cemetery," *Plains Anthropologist* 36 (1991): 67–78.

39. A. Douglas, "Heaven Our Home: Consolation Literature in the Northern United States, 1830–1880," *American Quarterly* 26, no. 5 (1974): 496–515.

40. This idea of an open and beckoning heavenly portal is captured in the phrase, "The Gates Ajar," which was both the title of a best-selling fictional guide to mourning published by Elizabeth Stuart Phelps in 1868 and a hymnal written by one Lydia Barter in 1871, whose opening stanza is: *There is a gate that stands ajar, / And through its portals gleaming, / A radiance from the Cross afar, / The Saviour's love revealing.*

41. For changes in American domestic architecture, see. C. Clark, *The American Family Home, 1800–1960* (Chapel Hill: University of North Carolina Press, 1986); for discussions of Victorian domestic architecture and the parlor in Great Britain, see T. Logan, *The Victorian Parlour* (Cambridge: Cambridge University Press, 2001), especially 5–14.

42. Laderman, *Rest in Peace*, 20, 22.

43. S. Prothero, *Purified by Fire: A History of Cremation in America*. (Berkeley: University of California Press, 2001), 15.

44. Prothero, *Purified by Fire*, 17, 19.

45. Prothero, *Purified by Fire*, 24.

46. Prothero, *Purified by Fire*, 187.

12. CONCLUSION

1. J. Feehan, "The Rocks and Landforms of the Burren," in *The Book of the Burren*, ed., J. O'Connell and A. Korff (Newtownlynch Doorus, Ireland: Tír Eolas, 2001), 14.

2. Quoted in N. Davis, *Europe: A History* (New York: HarperPerennial, 1996), 832.

3. T. Robinson, *Stones Of Arran: Pilgrimage* (London: Faber and Faber, 2008), 42.

Illustration Credits

1. Photo by author.
2. Reproduced courtesy of Cambridge University Press.
3. Copyright John Middendorf. Used by permission.
4. Original by Eugéne-Emanuel Viollet-le-Duc (1876), *The Habitations of Man in All Ages,* trans. B. Bucknell (London: Sampson, Low, Marston, and Rivington). Not in copyright.
5. Scene in Geronimo's camp . . . before surrender to General Crook, March 27, 1886: group in Natches's camp; boys with rifles, Library of Congress; LC-USZ62–46636; accessed at http://hdl.loc.gov/loc.pnp/cph.3a46801.
6. Photographer : Perezoso. "Reconstruction d'une habitation en tipi au Site de Sannai Maruyama." Accessed at http://commons.wikimedia.org/wiki/File:SannaiTipi.jpg. Public domain.
7. Redrawn with modifications from P. Bourdieu (1970), "The Berber House or the World Reversed" in *Exhanges et communications: Mélange offerts à Claude Lévi-Strauss àl'occasion de son 6oe anniversaire* (The Hague: Mouton).
8. Redrawn with modifications from T. Yates (1989), "Habitus and social space: some suggestions about meaning in the Saami (Lapp) tent, ca. 1700—1900" in *The Meaning of Things: Material Culture and Social Expression,* edited by Ian Hodder.
9. Photo by author.
10. Original drawing by author.
11. Redrawn with modifications from P. O'Brien (1986), "Prehistoric Evidence for Pawnee Cosmology," *American Anthropologist* 88, no. 4: 939–46.

12. Jacob Ochtervelt (1634–1682), *Street Musicians at the Door,* 1665. Oil on Canvas (27 × 22 ½ in) Saint Louis Museum of Art, Gift of Mrs. Eugene A. Perry, in memory of her mother, Mrs. Claude Kilpatrick, 163:1928. Image copyright © The St. Louis Museum of Art. Used by permission.

13. Jan Steen (1626–1679) *The Dissolute Household,* ca. 1663–64. Oil on canvas (42 ½ × 35 ½ in) The Jack and Belle Linsky Collection, The Metropolitan Museum of Art, New York, NY (1982.60.31). Image copyright © The Metropolitan Museum of Art/Art Resource, NY. Used by permission.

14. Redrawn with modifications from J. Mellaart (1967), *Çatal Hüyük: A Neolithic Town in Anatolia* (London: Thames and Hudson).

15. L. Morgan (1881), *Houses and House-Life of the American Aborigines.* Bureau of American Ethnology, Smithsonian Institution. Public domain.

16. Photo by author.

17. Photo by author.

18. Photo courtesy of Stephanie Hawkins.

19. Cliff Palace Ruins Before Excavations, unknown photographer; National Anthropological Archives, Smithsonian Institution, Ms. 2420–05. Used by permission.

20. California Division of Corrections and Rehabilitation; State of California. Accessed at http://www.cdcr.ca.gov/News/images/overcrowding/CIM1_081006v1.jpg. Public domain.

21. Modified from *The Encyclopaedia,* 1728. Public domain.

22. View of Great Wall of Santa, Shippee-Johnson Expedition; AMNH Image 334611. American Museum of Natural History Library. Used by permission.

23. Redrawn with modifications from A. Badawy (1978), *Coptic Art and Archaeology* (Cambridge, MA: MIT Press).

24. View of Chan Chan, Shippee-Johnson Expedition; AMNH Image 334876. American Museum of Natural History Library. Used by permission.

25. Photo courtesy of Santiago Uceda.

26. From J. Rudolf Rahn, *Geschichte der Bildenden Künste in der Schweiz. Von den Ältesten Zeiten bis zum Schlusse des Mittelalters.* (Zürich, 1876). Accessed at http://upload.wikimedia.org/wikipedia/commons/5/58/Rahn_Kloster_Sanct_Gallen_nach_Lasius.jpg. Public domain.

27. Redrawn with modifications from B. Bowser and J. Patton (2004), "Domestic Spaces as Public Places: An Ethnoarchaeological Case Study of Houses, Gender, and Politics in the Ecuadorian Amazon," *Journal of Archaeological Method and Theory* 11, no. 2: 157–81.

28. J. Webber (1778), "Interior of a Nootka House." Archives of the State of New South Wales, Australia. Used by permission. Not for further reproduction.

29. Redrawn with modifications from R. Bradley (2003), "A Life Less Ordinary: the Ritualization of the Domestic Sphere in Later Prehistoric Europe." *Cambridge Archaeological Journal* 13, no. 1: 5–23.

30. Casa dei Vettii a Pompei: Larario. Photographer: Patricio Lorente. September 2005. Licensed under Creative Commons Attribution-Share Alike 2.5 Generic License. Accessed at http://commons.wikimedia.org/wiki/File:Vettii.jpg.

31. Indian Prophet's Lodge by Henry Rowe Schoolcraft (1855). Wisconsin Historical Society, Image ID: 56234. Used by permission. Not for further reproduction.

32. Florence—Boboli Gardens—House of the Vettii—Atrium reconstruction (Pompeii). Photographer: Mattes, September 2010. Accessed at http://commons.wikimedia.org/wiki/File:Pompeii_atrium_reconstruction,_House_of_the_Vettii,_Boboli_Gardens,_Florence,_Italy_-_20100908.jpg. Public domain.

33. Photo courtesy of Janine Gasco.

34. Courtesy Christopher J. Rodning. Copyright American Antiquity.

35. Courtesy M. Chesson and Eric Carlson. Copyright Expedition to the Dead Sea Plain. Not for further reproduction.

36. Photo by author.

Index

Abbey of St. Gall, 133–34
Acoma Pueblo, 110
Adler, Margot, 83–84
agriculture, origins of, 49, 60, 62–63, 234n7
Ain Mallaha (Eynan), 61
Alaywaram 42–43, 47
Alcock, Susan, 146, 147
American Civil War, 15–16, 214–15
Ames, Kenneth, 156, 158, 159
Ancestral Puebloan (culture area), 108–11, 241n26
ancient Egypt, 202–205
animal architecture, 17–19, 229n7
Ansimov, A. F., 176–78
Antony, Saint, 124–26
ape nests, 17–19
archaeology: in media, 9; and natural disturbances, 26, 142; as nonexperimental science, 28–29; as recovering unwritten past, 9–10, 222–24
Arnold, Jeanne, 55–56
Aztec ruins, New Mexico (site), 109

Baegert, Jakob, 37, 168
Baja California, 6, 37–39, 87, 166–69
Barnes, Gina, 126
Beard, Mary, 170, 183–84
Beowulf, 153, 160
Binford, Lewis, 33–34, 35–36, 44
Bingham, Hiram, 146–47
Bilzingsleben, Germany (site), 28

Blombos Cave, South Africa (site), 73, 74
Blust, Robert, 171
Boas, Franz, 76, 158
Borges, Jorge Luis, 60
Bowser, Brenda, 152–53
Bourdieu, Pierre, 71
Bradley, Richard, 164–66
Brown, Linda, 187–88
Buddhism, 126

C. C. Witt site, Kansas (site), 87–89
Campbell, Stuart, 191
Cañon de los Embudos, México (site), 44
Carlin, George, 48
Casa Grande, Arizona (site), 105
Caskey, John, 148
Çatalhöyök, Turkey (site), 94–96, 114–15, 240n3
Cerén, El Salvador (site), 184–88
Chaco Canyon, New Mexico (site), 106–107, 111, 242n28
Chacoan Great Houses, 106–107
Chambers, William, 34–35
Champlain, Samuel de, 96
Chan Chan, Peru (site), 126–29, 245n21
Chesowanja, Kenya (site), 30
Chapman, John, 191
Cherokee, 196–200
Cherry, John, 146, 147, 150–51
Chesson, Marilyn, 208
Childe, V. Gordon, 49

TEXT
10/13 Sabon

DISPLAY
Sabon

COMPOSITOR
BookMatters, Berkeley

PRINTER AND BINDER
Maple-Vail Book Manufacturing Group